By Force or By Default?
The Revolution of 1688–1689

The Birth of the Prince of Wales, 10 June 1688

'It could not have been more public if he had been born in Charing Cross', Bishop Atterbury.

The first mention of the words 'Glorious Revolution', 18 Nov. 1689

'The foundation of this glorious revolution was laid in the council of six whereof he had the honour to be a member', John Hampden M.P. before the committee of the House of Lords investigating the trials of Lord William Russell and Algernon Sidney. The leaders of the Rye House Plot against Charles II in 1683 were known as the Council of Six and met at Hampden's house.

By Force or By Default?
The Revolution of 1688–1689

Edited by
EVELINE CRUICKSHANKS

JOHN DONALD PUBLISHERS LTD
EDINBURGH

To Desmond Wyeth

ISBN 0 85976 279 3

Phototypesetting by Quorn Selective Repro, Loughborough
Printed in Great Britain by Bell & Bain Ltd., Glasgow

PREFACE

The tercentenary of the Revolution of 1688 has been marked by multifarious events and publications ranging from the learned to the popular. At a time when the French are reassessing their own Revolution of 1789 and the Russians are becoming more honest about their own history, English historians, several of them non-specialists in late seventeenth-century history, have been content to follow the well-worn paths of Whig interpretation. There has been disappointingly little real debate. 1688 was the last successful invasion of England. It did not take place by popular demand, very few knew of it in advance and relatively few took part in the rebellion. There were widespread fears that James II's policy of toleration would undermine the position of the Church of England, but this did not mean that the majority of people wanted to breach the hereditary succession. Knowing this, the Prince of Orange pretended he had no designs on the crown. By December, when James had been driven into exile, William could afford to show his hand and be able to dictate terms. He was to be no Doge of Venice nor his wife's gentleman usher, but king in his own right, exercising the whole power which was vested in Mary as well as himself. The result was neither constitutional monarchy nor parliamentary control. The royal prerogative remained virtually intact. It was even extended in one respect, for whereas Charles II had very seldom exercised the royal veto over parliamentary bills, William III vetoed many important, popular bills. The only concession he was forced to make was to accept annual sessions of Parliament, since he was not granted the revenue for life as James II had been. Official celebrations have ignored the bloodbath in Ireland and its aftermath, the civil war which took place in Scotland, the deep divisions the Revolution created in England, or the persecution of Roman Catholics and Nonjurors after 1689. A discreet veil of silence has been drawn over the 70,000 Jacobites driven into exile in France alone in William's reign and the major contribution they made to the French economy, as great as that of their Huguenot counterparts in England.*

As a commemoration and in an attempt to redress the balance somewhat, a Colloquium on the Tory perception of the Revolution of 1688 took place on 15 October 1988 in the Institute of Historical

Research in the University of London. It is a pleasure to thank the staff of the Institute for their help and the council and members of the Royal Stuart Society, under whose auspices the Colloquium was held, for their generous financial assistance. John Miller showed that James II's religious toleration was wider than that accorded by the Toleration Act of 1689, while Ian Cowan examined the political and religious circumstances of Scotland before and in 1688. Eveline Cruickshanks shows that the magistrates and clergy of Exeter were appalled at the Dutch invasion, while many other places either disapproved of it or resisted it. William III was interested in Britain only from the point of view of dragging her into a war against Louis XIV. Jeremy Black argues here that the Nine Years' War was unnecessary as well as unpopular and that the Tory view of foreign policy, reliance on trade and sea power, was the right one for these isles. To these papers have been added essays by David Davies on the role of the Navy in 1688, by Tim Harris on the Tory crowd in the Revolution, by Paul Monod on Tory/Jacobite representation of the Revolution in the theatre, and by Steven Zwicker on the lack of celebration of the Revolution in the English literature of the 1690s, concentrating on Dryden's perception of it. It is much regretted that an essay covering events in Ireland was not produced in time to be included in this volume. Gratitude is due to J. P. Kenyon for offering to write the introduction and thanks must go to John Donald for encouraging and publishing new and sometimes controversial work and to Alasdair Hawkyard for compiling the index.

* Much work on the economic and cultural contribution made by Jacobites in France has been done by G. Chaussinand-Nogaret and his pupils. Nathalie Rouffiac is preparing a thesis for the Ecole des Chartres in Paris on Jacobite exiles in France, extending and developing this theme.

CONTRIBUTORS

Jeremy Black graduated from Queens' College, Cambridge with a starred first, before doing research work at St John's College, Oxford and holding a Harmsworth Senior Scholarship at Merton College, Oxford. Since 1980 he has been a lecturer at the University of Durham. His publications include *British Foreign Policy in the Age of Walpole* (1985), *The British and the Grand Tour* (1985), *Natural and Necessary Enemies, Anglo-French Relations in the Eighteenth Century* (1986), *The British Press in the Eighteenth Century* (1987), *The Collapse of the Anglo-French Alliance 1727–31* (1987), *Sir Robert Walpole and the Structure of Politics in Early-Eighteenth Century Britain* (forthcoming) and *Europe in the Eighteenth Century 1700–89* (forthcoming). He has edited *Britain in the Age of Walpole* (1984), *The Origins of War in Early-Modern Europe* (1987) and *Knights Errant and True Englishmen, British Foreign Policy 1660–1800* (1989) and co-edited *Essays in European History in Honour of Ragnhild Hatton* (1985), *The Jacobite Challenge* (1988), *The British Navy and the Use of Naval Power in the Eighteenth Century* (1988) and *Politics and the Press in Hanoverian Britain* (1988).

Ian B. Cowan is Professor of Scottish History at Glasgow University. He has written several books on sixteenth- and seventeenth-century Scottish history, including *The Scottish Covenanters 1660–1688*.

Eveline Cruickshanks edits The House of Commons 1690–1715 volumes for the History of Parliament Trust. She published *Political Untouchables: the Tories and the '45* in 1979, edited *Ideology and Conspiracy: Aspects of Jacobitism 1689–1759* in 1982 and co-edited *The Jabobite Challenge* in 1988.

David Davies, who teaches history at Bedford Modern School, wrote an Oxford D. Phil. thesis on the personnel of the Restoration Navy, which he is preparing for publication. He has published several articles, including an essay on 'Pepys and the Admiralty Commission of 1679–84', for which he was awarded the Julian Corbett Prize for Naval Military History in 1986. At the moment, he is engaged on a new edition of Pepys's Admiralty letterbooks.

Tim Harris was a student and Research Fellow at Emmanuel College, Cambridge, and is now Assistant Professor of History at Brown University, Providence, Rhode Island. His book, *London Crowds in the Reign of Charles II*, was published by Cambridge University Press in 1987. He is currently co-editing a collection of essays on religion and politics in Restoration England, which is to be published shortly by Basil Blackwell, and he is also working on a book for Longman on Britain in the first age of party, 1660–1714.

John Kenyon is the Joyce and Elizabeth Hall Distinguished Professor of Early Modern British Legal and Constitutional History in the University of Kansas.

John Miller took his first degree and was a research student at Jesus College, Cambridge and was a research Fellow at Gonville and Caius College, Cambridge. He is now a Reader in History at Queen Mary College, London. His books include *Popery and Politics in England 1660–88* (1973), *James II: A Study in Kingship* (1978), and *Bourbon and Stuart: Kings and Kingship in France and England in the 17th Century* (1987). He published 'Seeds of Liberty: 1688 and the Making of Modern Britain' in 1988. He is currently working on a biography of Charles II.

Paul Monod is Assistant Professor of History at Middlebury College, Vermont. He completed a Ph.D. at Yale University in 1985. He has published articles on Jacobitism in *The Historical Journal* and *The Jacobite Challenge*, edited by Eveline Cruickshanks and Jeremy Black. His book *Jacobitism and the English People* will be published by Cambridge University Press in the summer of 1989. At present, he is working on a general study of kingship in Western Europe from 1660 to 1789.

Steven Zwicker is Professor of English at Washington University, St. Louis. He has published *Dryden's Political Poetry* (1972), *Politics and Language in Dryden's Poetry* (1984) and co-edited *Politics and Discourse: The Literature and History of Seventeenth-Century England* (1987). His *Lines of Authority: Politics and Literary Culture in the later Seventeenth Century* and his edition of *John Dryden: Selected Poems* are forthcoming.

ABBREVIATIONS

Note All books are published in London except where otherwise stated.

Add.   Additional manuscripts in the British Library
AECP   Archives étrangères, correspondance politique at the Quai d'Orsay
AEM&D   Archives étrangères, mémoires et documents at the Quai d'Orsay
Ang.   Angleterre
BIHR   Bulletin of the Institute of Historical Research
Bodl.   Bodleian, e.g. Bodl. Carte mss 181
BL   British Library, e.g. BL loan 29/10/3
CJ   Journals of the House of Commons
CSP Dom   Calendar of State Papers Domestic
CTB   Calendar of Treasury Books
CUL   Cambridge University Library
DNB   Dictionary of National Biography
EHR   English Historical Review
HC   *The House of Commons, 1660–1690*, ed. B.D. Henning or 1715–1754, ed. Romney Sedgwick
HMC   Historical Manuscripts Commission, e.g. *HMC 10th Rep.* I or *HMC Townshend* (if one report occupies a whole volume)
Howell, *A Complete Collection of State Trials*, ed. T. B. Howell, 33 vols. 1816–26
LJ   Journals of the House of Lords
NLS   National Library of Scotland
NLW   National Library of Wales
NSA   Niedersächsisches Staatsarchiv, Hannover
NUL, Portland,   Nottingham University Library, Portland mss.
RA   Royal Archives, Windsor Castle, e.g. RA (Stuart) 62/70
PRO   Public Record Office
RO   Record Office, e.g. Northants. RO
SHR   Scottish Historical Review
SP   State Papers, e.g. SP Dom. 35/33/40

CONTENTS

1
INTRODUCTION

J. P. Kenyon

The historiography of the Revolution of 1688 could best be described as being in a state of luxuriant confusion.

For nearly a century after his death Macaulay's great construct dominated the field, and the most that could be attempted was a cosy little summary by Trevelyan in 1938. Not that I mean to depreciate Macaulay in the least; his account of James II's reign is not only the most detailed but the most meaningful of any reign in English history, as well as a triumph of the historian's art. The late Dom David Knowles once said that all medieval historians would profit by re-reading volume II of Stubbs's *Constitutional History*, and some of his prefaces to the Rolls Series every five years or so, and I would say the same, *mutatis mutandis*, of chapters IV–XI of Macaulay's *History of England*. Quite apart from his magnificent technique, and his command of fact, his acuity of thought is astonishing, and often chastening.

However, history began to emancipate itself from the shackles of Macaulay in 1948, when F. C. Turner published his revisionist biography of James II. (Subsequent biographies of James by Maurice Ashley in 1977 and John Miller in 1978 have not added significantly to our understanding.) In 1954 came Lucille Pinkham's *William III and the Respectable Revolution*, which while disfigured by a kind of tiresome neo-Jacobitism, was the first serious attempt to deal with the European politics of the Revolution, and it was followed in 1955 by David Ogg's more conventional account of *England in the Reigns of James II and William III*. After a short gap came Stephen Baxter's *William III*, in 1966, and in 1969 John Carswell's *The Descent on England*. 1972 was a bumper year, with *The Revolution of 1688*, by J. R. Jones, and J. R. Western's *Monarchy and Revolution; the English State in the 1680s*, (this last one of the best books on the Revolution, and strangely neglected). These were closely followed in 1973 by John Miller's *Popery and Politics in England 1660–1688*. A brief lull, then came John Childs in 1980, with *The Army, James II and the Glorious Revolution*, and Lois G. Schwoerer

1

in 1981 with *The Declaration of Rights*, and finally, in 1988, we have
Reluctant Revolutionaries by W. A. Speck and *A Kingdom without a
King* by Robert Beddard.[1]

I apologise for this bibliographical drenching, but I think it is
important that we realise just how much has been published on
the Revolution in the past thirty years, leaving aside the occasional
learned article. Nevertheless, though each of these books, founded
on diligent research, has its own contribution to make to the history
of the Revolution, whether in domestic or foreign policy, war or the
establishment of law, none of them offer a complete picture of an event
which, though apparently simple enough in outline, now seems more
complex with every book which is published purporting to explain it.
And the book-to-end-all-books on the Revolution, the grand synthesis,
still awaits its historian.

For one thing James II still retains his mystery. Why did a man who
had had the longest apprenticeship to kingship of any English monarch,
at the very centre of power and policy making from 1660 to 1685, go
so badly adrift? He has been called stupid more often than any other
English monarch, but it is a grave mistake to suppose that stupidity is
easily penetrated or analysed. Here there is a distinct contrast between
him and his highly intelligent, rather dingily charismatic brother Charles
II — the kind of contrast an American reporter recently made between
Presidents Kennedy and Reagan:

> 'Kennedy was a president of action, and intellectuals thought he was
> brilliant. But they could watch his mind work. With Reagan, they could
> only watch his face work. He had an opacity to him that translated as
> thick-headedness'.[2]

This is why attempts to pin down James's views on abstract
questions like religious toleration, like John Miller's in this new
volume before us, run down into a kind of Mississippi delta of winding
possibilities and counter-probabilities.[3] James's policy of toleration was
so disastrous, politically so counter-productive, that we just have to
assume a quite strong element of moral sincerity behind it. In 1687 and
1688 he committed his political fortunes to the Dissenters, though he
had been around in 1676, when the Compton Census demonstrated that
the Nonconformists were at most 15% of the population, with perhaps
half of that percentage wielding political power where it counted, at the
hustings. In July 1687 James's most acute political adviser, the Earl of
Sunderland, gave the Papal Nuncio a long run-down on the situation
as he saw it, in which he pointed out that even if James obtained a

Dissenting House of Commons (and the stress lay on the word 'even'), they would be unwilling to betray the Protestant Interest by allying wholeheartedly with a Catholic king.[4]

Of course, as I have pointed out elsewhere,[5] James's policy was, in the twentieth-century liberal sense, the only 'right' policy, and if William and Mary had agreed in June 1687 to endorse it, then opposition amongst the ruling classes would have collapsed, and James could have recalled the 'loyal' parliament of 1685 without a qualm. England would then have moved into the forefront of 'enlightened' European nations.

This was not to be; but Ian Cowan's brief paper on Scotland reminds us of an area of the British Isles in which his policy of toleration had every chance of success, simply because of the preponderance of Presbyterianism. Indeed, if he had taken the trouble to espouse, or even understand, the Presbyterian interest there, the outcome might have been very different. Instead, he allowed himself to be led astray by intriguers who represented minority interests, like Melfort and Hamilton. As Paul Hopkins says, and this applies to more than Scotland:

'Except over a few basic matters, adroit advisers could manoeuvre him into accepting serieses of *fait accomplis* which left him pursuing the opposite policy but eerily unaware that it had changed'.[6]

It is particularly strange that he never returned to Scotland as king. Though his exile was involuntary it does seem that his service as the King's High Commissioner in Scotland from 1680 to 1683 was one of the most contented and fulfilled periods of his life. When his brother died in February 1685 he was on the point of returning to Edinburgh to hold another parliament, and the old myth that this was a move to get him out of the country so that Monmouth and Halifax — a bizarre combination! — could effect some sort of palace revolution can safely be discounted, though it was espoused by historians as hard-headed as Andrew Browning and David Ogg. Thereafter there were occasional rumours, some as late as the winter of 1687-8, that he would shortly re-visit Scotland and be crowned King James VII at Scone, but they came to nothing, though he betrayed his continuing interest in things Scottish when he established the Order of the Thistle in 1687. Perhaps, though I agree that it is a big 'perhaps', if he had gone to Scotland and cultivated his undeniable Scottishness the Jacobite movement there in 1689 might have been much more robust that it was.

With Eveline Cruickshank's entertaining and erudite paper we move on to the physical aspects of the Revolution. (I particularly relish her mention of that old fox, Nathaniel Crewe, Bishop of Durham, lurking off the coast in a boat until the 'trouble' was over.) She also reminds us of the *suddenness* of the Revolution. James himself did not believe in William's intention to invade until September 18th, 1688, nor did he announce the news by proclamation until the 28th. Even then, news of the sudden storm which dispersed William's fleet on October 27th must have led many to think that the danger was over until the following spring. Indeed, Dr Davies reminds us of the enormous gamble which William was undertaking, and his paper is the first substantial contribution to the naval side of the Revolution since E. B. Powley's monograph sixty years ago,[7] and he does much to moderate Powley's assumption of a serious conspiracy in the English fleet — just as John Childs has cast doubt on the importance of the Army 'conspiracy'.[8] Davies and Childs, taken together, underline James's total military failure in 1688, a failure scarcely to be expected in a man who in the 1650s, 1660s and 1670s had proved himself a bold and decisive (if not very successful) commander on land and sea.

Gradually a picture of the physical aspects of the Revolution is forming, supplementing and enlarging Macaulay's account. Cruick-shanks deals here with Devon and Durham, two key counties; Andrew Browning has dealt with Yorkshire, David Hosford with the Midlands.[9] Perhaps there is something to be said about the Duke of Norfolk in East Anglia, the Duke of Beaufort in Bristol, and Lovelace's reckless buccaneering ride down the West Country, but the picture is beginning to jell.

London's place in that picture is surprisingly unimportant. The issue was decided by armies and navies deployed afar, and by noblemen and gentlemen meeting together in provincial cities a tenth the size of the capital. All we hear from London is an account of mindless mob violence against Catholic chapels and the houses of Catholic nobleman; and even this, I might add, is replicated across the nation. So thorough was the iconoclasm that the progress of the Catholic Church under James II has now to be reconstructed from occasional scanty references in the *Victoria County History*. Tim Harris shows us that most of the London rioters of 1688 could be described as Tories; but need this surprise us? James's ruthless purge of the City government and the Livery Companies in the second half of 1687 had left the establishment predominantly Whig, and men rioting against the establishment will always, naturally, adopt the opposite political stance. We are left wondering what had happened to the London trained bands, which had proved so effective in keeping order during the Exclusion Crisis. It seems that James was using the regular army to keep order, a dubious luxury which Charles II only allowed himself at Oxford in 1681.[10]

In one of the most interesting papers presented here Jeremy Black tries to fill what has always been a yawning gap in the historiography of James's reign, beginning with Macaulay, and he applies to the seventeenth century the immense erudition and command of archive material which is the hallmark of his work on the eighteenth century. (It could be argued that he is over-reliant on the French archives, but then, James II's relations with Louis XIV, whichever way you look at it, are clearly crucial.)

The fact that James was not a servile crony of Louis XIV's — a caricature re-inforced by Macaulay — scarcely needs demonstrating now; indeed, the two men were at loggerheads for most of James's reign. Black reminds us that way back in 1677 James had been all for an anti-French alliance between England, Spain, the Empire and the Netherlands — the pattern, in fact, which emerged after 1689. Subsequently, after a brief period of destabilisation in 1685, James tried to avoid foreign entanglements altogether while he was pursuing a controversial and hazardous domestic policy, but the result was that he found himself without allies at all in 1688, though he was generally credited, not least in England, with being an ally of France. Unfortunately, Louis XIV enjoyed nowhere near the commanding position in the 1680s with which he has been credited, and as Black remarks, 'rather than supporting a dangerous threat to the balance of power, James was loosely aligned to a ruler who was increasingly isolated' [t/s, p. 14]. He would have done much better to align himself with the anti-French Catholic powers, the Empire and Spain; if he did not I attribute this to the fact that Louis maintained a permanent ambassador in London, who from 1677 onwards built up a cosy, intimate, man-to-man relationship with Charles and James. It is customary, following Macaulay, to play down Barrillon's diplomatic skill, but at least he had the virtue of always being on the place.

But as for Black's thesis that the reversal in foreign policy inaugurated by William in 1689 was deleterious to England's long-term interests, and that the alliance with France in 1716 marked a return to a more 'natural' policy, I think this is over-stated. Certainly the French Wars of 1689 to 1713 imposed a severe strain on the English economy and people — even a sunny, applausive historian like Trevelyan admitted this — but can a policy which established a great military tradition, which made London the world's finance and trade centre, which elevated her to great power status, really be dismissed as some kind of perversion? The reversal of alliances in 1716 was an attempt to police the Utrecht settlement, to give

England and France a much-needed period of rest and recuperation, and above all to prevent the re-establishment of a Jacobite base in France, Walpole's main pre-occupation.

Finally comes Stephen Zwicker's exploration of the 'high culture' of the Revolution. This is a stimulating paper, but rather tantalising. For instance Zwicker raises a very interesting point when he talks of the 'neutralising' language employed in the Convention debates of 1689, but I would like to see chapter and verse for this. There were many words spoken in heat and anger, certainly in the crucial debate of 28 January 1689, and my confidence in his conclusions are not bolstered by the fact that he is not apparently using the best record now available.[11] However, he is more specific on the poetry with which the Revolution was saluted, which he dismisses as bloodless and uninspired as the Revolution itself was bloodless and uninspired. (In fact, he is very hard on the Revolution, though no more so than Macaulay and Acton.)[12] In the sphere of drama, however, he is heavily committed to Dryden's *Don Sebastian*, which he describes as 'the literary masterpiece of the Revolution'. Yet if this was a piece of lightly disguised Jacobite propaganda on the theme of deposition and familial ingratitude, as he says, we have to ask why it did not arouse more controversy; like Addison's *Cato*, for instance, in 1713, with audiences loudly displaying their partisanship. Zwicker assures us (twice) that it met with 'popular success', and that 'it played very well to London audiences', but he adduces no hard evidence for this. The point is, would the subtle discussions of 'title' in this play have aroused political passions, or even been noticed? Was this play on a fairly conventional dramatic theme of usurpation taken as a Jacobite statement? (*King Lear*, on the same theme, would have been much more apposite, given James's relationship with his two daughters.) I suspect that this mish-mash of Portuguese and Moorish history, crossed with fiction, was received as light entertainment. Zwicker himself admits that 'if we take 1688 to be the centre of *Don Sebastian*', this is a proposition 'that Dryden himself and some of his explicators would I think vigorously contest'.

Nevertheless, this is an interesting attempt to marry literature and politics, too often divorced in the past, and like the other essays in this volume it enlarges and deepens our knowledge of the Revolution.

NOTES

1. I have omitted summaries of received fact, like Maurice Ashley's *The Glorious Revolution of 1688* (1966) and Stuart Prall's *The Bloodless Revolution* (1972).

2. Henry Allen, *Washington Post Weekly*, November 14–20, 1988.

3. See Maurice Ashley's pioneering discussion in *Historical Essays presented to David Ogg*, ed. H. E. Bell and Richard Ollard (1963), 185–202.

4. J. P. Kenyon, *Robert Spencer Earl of Sunderland* (1958), 160.

5. *Stuart England* (Harmondsworth 1985), 252.

6. *Glencoe and the End of the Highland War* (Edinburgh 1986), 84.

7. *The English Navy in the Revolution of 1688* (Cambridge 1928).

8. *The Army, James II and the Glorious Revolution* (Manchester 1980), ch. vi.

9. *Thomas Osborne Earl of Danby* (Glasgow 1944–51), i, ch. 17; *Nottingham, Nobles and the North* (Hamden, Connecticut 1976).

10. D. F. Allen, 'The Political Role of the London Trained Bands in the Exclusion Crisis', *EHR*, lxxxvii. (1971), 287–303; John Childs, 'The Army and the Oxford Parliament of 1681', ibid, 94 (1978), 580–87.

11. 'A Jornall of the Convention', ed. Lois G. Schwoerer, *BIHR*, lix. (1976), 242–63.

12. John Kenyon, *The History Men* (1983), 79, 138.

2
JAMES II AND TOLERATION[1]

John Miller

James II's grant of a general toleration in 1687 provoked a variety of responses, then and later. Some saw in it evidence of a sincere aversion to the coercion of conscience: not only later Catholic apologists for James, but also a number of Nonconformists, not all of them hack pamphleteers living down their Whig past. William Penn, for one, seems to have had no doubts about James's sincerity; nor has one of the most recent historians of the Revolution.[2] The prevailing Protestant view, however, has been that the toleration was a cynical ploy to divide English Protestants and so to facilitate the imposition of Catholicism. One of the earliest, and most forceful expressions of this view came in Halifax's *Letter to a Dissenter*. He warned the Dissenters:

> This alliance between Liberty and Infallibility is bringing together the two most contrary things that are in the world. The Church of Rome doth not only dislike the allowing liberty, but by its principles it cannot do it . . . The continuance of their kindness would be a habit of sin, of which they are to repent and their absolution is to be had upon no other terms than their promise to destroy you. You are therefore to be hugged now only that you may be the better squeezed at another time.[3]

Halifax's argument rested on a view of Catholicism, as authoritarian, morally dishonest and cruel, which found far wider acceptance in his day than in ours. But others, not obviously influenced by anti-Catholic prejudice, have also expressed scepticism about his motives. They see his grant of toleration as means to a political end, the subjugation of Parliament and the creation of a more absolute monarchy.[4] This emphasis on the political may reflect the reluctance of many late twentieth-century historians to take religion seriously as a stimulus to action; but to say that past writers have been prejudiced in various ways does not, in itself, invalidate their arguments. We need to go back to the evidence, to look at what James did and to place his actions in their contemporary context. To this end, I shall first look at the religious scene in late seventeenth-century England. I shall then discuss James's religious views and attitude towards toleration and conclude by considering the consequences of his Declaration of Indulgence.

The fragmentation of English Protestantism, upon which continentals so often remarked, was a product of the 1640s and 1650s. Before the civil wars there had often been bitter disagreements about the Church of England's worship and theology, but few openly challenged the need for a single established church. With the collapse of episcopal authority and the upsurge of millenarian enthusiasm, a new and very different type of 'church' appeared. The adherents of 'gathered churches' argued that a true church consisted only of true believers, 'visible saints', who had a duty to separate from the sinful majority, in eager anticipation of the (supposedly imminent) Second Coming and Day of Judgment. Once the process of separation had begun, it could not easily be contained. Freed from the constraints of the Thirty-nine Articles, the 'gathered churches' developed diverging theological views; the Quakers subordinated even the authority of Scripture to that of the 'inner light'. Thus the emergent sects were at odds not only with traditional Protestantism, but with each other.

When Charles II returned to England in 1660, the religious scene was far more complicated than it had been in 1640. It was to become apparent with hindsight that religious pluralism was now an established fact and that the existence of this pluralism was to contribute to the development of religious toleration. Many at the time, however, did not see this pluralism as permanent, still less as constituting a valid argument for toleration. The logic of separatism was, perhaps, that each congregation, each individual should be free to seek after truth and salvation: indeed, this was a logical extension of the basic Protestant tenet that any believer could discover God's purposes through prayer and the Bible. In practice, however, as Protestantism became established, church and denominational leaders limited the range of permissible opinions and harassed those who overstepped those limits. Moreover, the strong Protestant consciousness of sin led to attempts to regulate behaviour as rigorous as those of the Catholic Church. Thus while some gathered churches asked only to be left alone, others bickered about theology and competed for converts. Convinced that they were God's elect, the Fifth Monarchists claimed a divine mandate to rule over the unregenerate mass of mankind; the Quakers' inner light bred an assurance of rectitude, expressed in the disruption of church services and the harassment of those whose views differed from theirs. Even Cromwell's much vaunted tolerance was limited primarily to 'the godly': others, like Anglicans and Catholics, enjoyed a far more restricted liberty.[5]

Pluralism, then, did not necessarily breed tolerance. Not only did the sects often hate one another — everyone hated the early Quakers — but the largest Dissenting denomination, the Presbyterians, did not wish to be a sect at all and was, in 1660, firmly committed to the principle of a single national church. Presbyterians had seen the sects as a cancer eating away at the church; many (not least William Prynne) believed that Quakerism was a cunning device of the Jesuits to divide Protestantism from within.[6] Such arguments as there were for toleration in the 1660s, therefore, were based not on a belief that differing views were equally tenable, but on pragmatic considerations. Some claimed that the Dissenters were so numerous that it would be politically dangerous to try to force them into conformity. Others argued that their role in trade and industry meant that persecution would harm the economy, whereas the Dutch example showed that toleration encouraged immigrants with economically valuable skills.

The case for toleration was thus political and economic rather than religious, couched in terms of pragmatism rather than inherent natural rights. Indeed, people talked of 'indulgence' — allowing views and practices that might seem to be wrong, with the implication that toleration was at best a regrettable necessity, rather than something good of itself. By contrast, later 'Whig' historians have seen the growth of toleration as a 'good thing'. Many see Puritans and Dissenters as dynamic and progressive — economically productive, committed to 'liberty' — whereas the Church of England appears backward and reactionary, the lapdog of authoritarian monarchy. Such a view slides easily into a caricature, in which Puritanism and Dissent represent a 'popular' challenge to a Church that was little more than an instrument of aristocratic rule and social control. Such a caricature has severe flaws. On one hand, early seventeenth-century Puritanism was often morally authoritarian and (literally) elitist: the essence of predestination was that only a few should be saved and those who saw themselves as the chosen had little tolerance for the liberty (or licence) of the unregenerate.[7] On the other hand, the strength of popular support for the Church of England can be seen in the dogged resistance to the attempts to suppress the Prayer Book services in the 1640s and the spontaneous readoption of those services at the Restoration.[8] Dissenters made up no more than ten per cent of the population of Restoration England and many were prepared to attend Anglican services for some of the time.[9] This was especially true of the Presbyterians, who were forced into nonconformity only because of the failure to agree terms upon which they could be comprehended within the Church of England. To stress the relatively small number of Dissenters is not to suggest that the remainder of the population consisted of enthusiastic Anglicans: clearly there were many whose knowledge of, and enthusiasm for, any sort of organized religion were exiguous. It does, however, indicate that attempts to re-establish a single uniform church were not utterly impractical.

Arguments against toleration, however, were based less on practicality than on principle. The 1662 Act of Uniformity has not had a good press from historians. Nonconformists have naturally denounced the ensuing 'persecution', while Anglicans, writing in a more ecumenical age, have been reluctant to defend it. Nevertheless, strange as it may now seem, the later Stuart Church was in many respects militant and efforts to reimpose uniformity rested on a clearly perceived vision of the role of a Christian church in a Christian society. Many believed that religious truth was indivisible and that the Church's theology and worship rested on the dual authority of God's Word and the English state. To allow separation, or diversity of opinions, would open the way to abominations like the Ranters[10] or the Anabaptists of Münster. Moreover, the Church not only preached but enforced Christian morality. Its courts punished sexual misconduct, drunkenness, defamation, etc. (The Presbyterians, indeed, wished to strengthen the church's role in moral discipline, notably by more rigorous use of excommunication). For this discipline to be effective, however, it had to extend to all: it could not operate if people could opt out. Finally, the Church was an expression of the unity of the community. Puritans and separatists clearly distinguished the godly few from the unregenerate many. The Church, with its stress on collective acts of worship, sought to bring parishioners together. This unity had a political dimension. Sad experience — not least the English civil wars — showed that a nation divided in religion was also likely to be divided politically. For this reason, since the Reformation the Church had stressed subjects' duty to obey established authority. 'From all sedition, privy conspiracy and rebellion . . .' ran the Litany 'Good Lord deliver us.'

The re-establishment of the old Church of England should not necessarily, then, be dismissed as a return to outmoded bigotry. Many saw it as an essential first step towards restoring orthodox theology, Christian morality, social unity and political obedience after two decades of confusion and sin. Moreover, it was followed by a

serious attempt, notably under Archbishop Sancroft, to improve the
pastoral standards of the clergy. In fact the laws against Dissent were
not vigorously enforced all of the time. (Much the same was true of
those against Catholicism).[11] Some magistrates were more zealous than
others, some denominations (notably the Quakers) were more disliked
than others. Above all, the intensity of persecution varied with political
circumstances. In the early 1660s old Royalists were eager to exact
revenge for their sufferings and rumours of plots made Dissent seem
politically dangerous. Similarly, when the Exclusion Crisis revived fears
of civil war, the Dissenters' identification with Whiggism encouraged
Tories to persecute them. Anglican polemicists claimed that Dissenters
had started the civil war and killed Charles I. Their pleas of tenderness
of conscience were hypocritical: pride and arrogance alone led them to
defy lawful authority in church and state. They met, 'on pretence of
religion', to plot sedition: in other words, they were not persecuted for
religion at all.[12] To allow them toleration was not only unnecessary but
positively dangerous: any sign of weakness would only make them more
insolent. There was no room for half measures: unless Dissenters were
repressed, they would turn the world upside down again and repress the
Anglican majority; it was a simple matter of self-preservation. Thus one
widespread response to religious pluralism was a call, not for toleration,
but for the reassertion of authority in church and state.

The commitment to persecution was, however, far from universal. In
many places (especially towns) religious pluralism was a fact of life: the
need to live, work and do business with those of other denominations was
bound to foster a measure of *de facto* tolerance. Even among the clergy,
a more eirenic, 'latitudinarian'[13] element stressed the common ground,
rather than the differences, between denominations. The decades after
1660 saw a reaction against the zeal of the civil wars, a waning of the
intensity of religious belief and of the habit of seeing earthly events as
marks of divine intervention. For some, a preference for a more private
personal religion blended with traditional anti-clericalism in a denunciation of 'priestcraft': indeed, the party divisions of the Exclusion Crisis
soon took religious forms. By their vigorous defence of royal authority
and of the Duke of York's right to succeed, Anglican clerics laid themselves open to charges of favouring Popery (and absolute monarchy).
Conversely, the Whigs' attacks on the bishops and other clergy and
calls for 'Protestant unity' against the Popish menace enabled the Tories
to depict them as hostile to the Church. Thus the toleration of Dissent
became a party issue. In the early 1680s the Whigs were defeated and
persecuting Anglicanism triumphed. But the previous twenty years had

shown that, for whatever reasons, there was considerable public support for some measure of toleration.

James II was raised as an Anglican. His mentors were High Churchmen, in many ways more hostile to Dissent than to Catholicism, not least because, during the civil war, many Catholics had actively supported Charles I.[14] For much of the 1660s James was politically identified with his father-in-law, Clarendon, and his strongly Anglican following. Until the late 1660s, James does not seem to have thought deeply about religion, but, when he considered the matter, he became convinced that the Catholic Church was the one true church. He was blessed with a straightforward mind. He saw life in terms of polar opposites: right and wrong, good and bad. To find out what was right, he needed (he thought) to find out where authority lay. In an army, it lay with the commander in chief. (James was a military man). In a state, it lay with the king. In religion it lay with the only church that could trace its foundation back to Christ Himself. Without such authority, there could be only confusion. He talked to Gilbert Burnet 'of the necessity of having but one church, otherwise we saw what swarms of sects did rise up on our revolt from Rome'. Having found where authority lay, his doubts were stilled and he ignored awkward questions. As he told Burnet: 'I might be too hard for him at any point of learning, but I could never convince him.'[15]

Thus far the story of James's conversion is of a simple man finding what he saw as a simple key to the mysteries of life, death and salvation. The consequences of his conversion were far from simple. It subjected him to conflicting pressures and raised dilemmas which were not easily resolved. When considering historical figures, many historians like to find clearly defined motives and are especially concerned to demonstrate consistency (as if inconsistency were a mortal sin). Yet human behaviour and motivation can be highly complex. People can behave in ways which seem reasonable to them at the time, but which to others seem bizarre and inconsistent. Life, especially for kings, is full of difficult choices, which may be transformed by changing circumstances. To expect 'consistency' (or to impose it retrospectively) may be misleading and simplistic. James II was in many ways a straightforward and honourable man; yet the problems he faced led him into actions which many saw as devious and dishonest. Such perceptions of his conduct may, in part, be explained by anti-Catholic prejudice, which led his Protestant subjects to place the worst possible construction on his actions. But there can be no doubt that his own perception of the options open to him changed over time, which led him into actions which were at variance with his avowed — and no doubt sincerely held — principles.

His central problem was that his conversion identified him with a small, unpopular religious minority.[16] This raised the problem of his attitude to other religious groups, the Anglicans and the Dissenters. Emotionally and politically he had more in common with the former. Raised as a High Churchman, taught to believe in a 'real but inconceivable' presence in the eucharist, he found the transition to Catholicism easy, even natural. Everything that he had found reassuring in the Church of England — its claims to authority, the regularity and order of its worship — he found in greater measure in the Roman Church. His mind was not attuned to subtlety and he believed (in the words of French ambassador Barrillon) that 'the Anglican Church is so little removed from the Catholic that it should not be difficult to bring the majority of them to declare themselves openly . . . they are Roman Catholics without knowing it'.[17] Socially and politically, too, James found the Church more attractive than Dissent. It was a hierarchical institution and taught obedience to authority and acceptance of the status quo. The ruling elite was (at least nominally) overwhelmingly Anglican: the sects soon lost their patrons among the nobility and gentry and became identified with the middle and lower orders. Moreover, James was well aware that the Church, with its stress on obedience, was the natural supporter of monarchy, whereas Dissenters were inclined to insubordination and even rebellion.[18]

Thus socially, politically and aesthetically James had much in common with the Anglican majority; but, at bottom, that majority was anti-Catholic. The Cavalier House of Commons passed severe laws against Dissent, but also passed the Test Acts and called repeatedly for the enforcement of older laws against 'Popery'. Admittedly, at times when the threat from Dissent seemed greater than that from Catholicism, the Churchmen showed relatively little animus against Papists; but, as James found to his cost, when provoked Anglican anti-Popery was as strong as ever in the 1680s. In such circumstances, James had to face up to the logic of having joined one of the smaller separatist sects. Throughout his life he expressed what seems to have been a genuine aversion to persecution for conscience' sake. He told Burnet 'he desired nothing but to follow his own conscience, which he imposed on nobody else, and that he would never attempt to alter the established religion.'[19] Even before his conversion gave him reason to sympathize with religious minorities, he proved tolerant of the religious beliefs of individuals, provided they behaved themselves well in other ways.[20] Talking of Louis XIV's persecution of his Protestant subjects, James said he disliked the Huguenots 'for he thought they were of anti-monarchical principles', yet 'he thought the persecution of them was unchristian . . . that they might be no good men, yet might be used worse than they deserved'.[21]

Thus we find James, at different times, taking diametrically opposite positions. At times he supported the Church, which sought to impose uniformity, using legal penalties and coercion. At other times, he denounced persecution as an affront to conscience. This apparent inconsistency can be resolved in part by reference to political considerations.

For James, the greatest attraction of the Church was its inculcation of obedience. As he declared at his accession.

> I know the principles of the Church of England are for monarchy and the members of it have shown themselves good and loyal subjects: *therefore* I shall always take care to defend and support it.[22]

At that time, James did not stress the conditional nature of his assurances: he doubtless felt no need to do so. The Anglicans had vigorously supported his claim to the throne over the past five years, while many Dissenters had actively opposed it. Hence he assured two of the bishops that 'he would never give any sort of countenance to Dissenters, knowing it must needs be faction and not religion if men could not be content to meet five besides their own family, which the law dispenses with.'[23] Thus in 1685 James's tolerance of Dissent extended only to those who worshipped quietly at home (as, by law, they were entitled to do); but he saw any public meetings as a threat to the state. Thus, for James, 'liberty of conscience' could not be used to justify any activity which carried even a hint of sedition.

Thus, although James's social and aesthetic preferences inclined him towards the Church, whether he leaned towards Church or Dissent depended ultimately on political considerations. As circumstances changed, so might his policies, but that should not necessarily be seen as evidence of unprincipled opportunism. If his preference was for co-operation with the Church, in return he expected the Churchmen to live up to what he saw as their principles. Throughout Charles II's reign, but especially in the early 1680s, Anglican clerics stressed the impiety of resistance to royal authority, in an effort to counter the spirit of sedition and rebellion which they saw manifested in the civil wars and Exclusion Crisis. Some also implied that subjects should always obey their king, but most said that if he made unacceptable demands subjects should follow the example of the primitive Christians, who refused to obey the unjust commands of the pagan Emperors and suffered the consequences. Non-resistance did not necessarily imply a commitment to obey the king in all things; James seems to have assumed that it did. Burnet had warned him in 1673 that 'he could not expect to enjoy a peaceable reign if he outlived our king. He objected to me the doctrine of the Church of England on the point of submission to princes.' Burnet warned him not to trust too much to that: self-preservation was a powerful instinct.[24] James neither grasped this distinction, nor heeded this warning, which explains his sense of anger and betrayal when the Churchmen defied him. Just a month after his accession, he reprimanded some of the bishops for failing to prevent anti-Catholic sermons by their clergy:

> I will keep my word and undertake nothing against the religion which is established by law, unless you first break your word to me. But if you do not do your duty towards me, do not expect that I shall protect you. You may be sure that I shall find means to do my business without you.[25]

As these remarks made clear, James knew he always had the option of seeking Dissenting rather than Anglican support, an option he had taken in 1675–6, when Danby sought to enforce the laws against both Dissenters and Catholics. But to what end? Under Charles, his concerns were essentially negative: to defend the monarchy against Whiggism and 'republicanism', to defend the Catholics against renewed persecution. As king, he was free to pursue more ambitious policies: to 'establish' his religion, so that 'those who professed it could live as Catholics in complete security'.[26] Convinced of the obvious rightness of Catholicism, he believed that people were inhibited from turning Catholic only by fear of punishment under the penal laws (against every aspect of Catholic practice) and Test Acts (which debarred Catholics from Parliament and public office). 'Did others enquire into the religion as I have done,' he wrote 'without prejudice or prepossession or partial affection, they would be of the same mind in point of religion as I am.'[27] James thus wished to remove these laws, believing that, in free competition, the truth of Catholicism would become apparent to all; converts would come in so fast that Catholicism would become the dominant religion and the question of toleration would lose all meaning. Without diversity of religion, what need would there be of toleration?

In the first year of his reign, James suspended proceedings against Catholics and tried in vain to persuade a strongly Anglican Parliament to repeal the laws affecting Catholics; those against Dissenters continued to be rigorously enforced, the rebellions of Monmouth and Argyll having underscored the link between Dissent and rebellion. In November 1685, however, both Houses protested at James's commissioning Catholic army officers. He regarded these protests as utterly unreasonable. The commissions were technically legal: the officers had to take the test within three months, which time was not yet up. James also thought it contrary to natural justice that he should be deprived of the services of these loyal and experienced men. As with the clergy's anti-Catholic sermons, James could not reconcile Parliament's behaviour with the Tories' much vaunted loyalism. As his feelings of reciprocal obligation towards the Anglicans melted away, he began to rethink his attitude towards the Dissenters. Perhaps, as Penn claimed, they were not inherently anti-monarchical; perhaps they did have genuine scruples of conscience and had been driven to defy authority only by harsh and unreasoning persecution by the Church. As in 1675–6, James came to see Dissenters as fellow-sufferers, with the Catholics, under the Anglican lash. The persecution of Dissenters was scaled down and James began to move towards a general toleration.

It is easy to be cynical about this 'U-turn'. Barrillon, who knew James well, thought he would much have preferred to continue to work with the Churchmen, 'as 'the Dissenters' principles are very much opposed to monarchy'.[28] A year later, when James issued his Declaration of Indulgence, Barrillon stated that his aim was to sow dissension between Anglicans and Nonconformists, so that the latter would join with the Catholics against the former; he added that he thought James would be far happier if only the Anglican and Catholic religions were established by law.[29] I think, however, that Barrillon underestimated the complexity of the problems that James was wrestling with and, perhaps, his capacity for self-delusion: if he was seeking to fool his subjects about the purity of his intentions, he may also have been fooling himself. Charles had really enjoyed misleading people; James lacked his fondness for duplicity. He liked to think of himself as honest and straightforward, but unfortunately his conceptions of justice and fair dealing did not always coincide with those of his subjects. James could not see why he should discriminate against loyal (Catholic) subjects on the grounds of their religion — and proceeded to discriminate in their favour, employing them simply because they were Catholics.[30] Conversely he did not see why he should employ self-styled 'loyal' Tories who, in his eyes, behaved disloyally; but to those who had supported his cause through thick and thin since the Exclusion Crisis and had taken at face value his assurances to the

Church, the 'disloyalty' was all on the other side.

A similar disparity of views can be seen in relation to the law. If James wished to repeal the penal laws and Tests Acts, he would need a compliant Parliament, if not of Anglicans, then of Dissenters. But Dissenters were relatively few, of limited political weight and were forbidden by law to worship freely or to hold public office. The Tories, meanwhile, dominated local government and the municipal corporations that returned four-fifths of the Commons. To compensate for the Dissenters' weaknesses, James used his prerogative to enhance their influence. First, after the judges' ruling in *Godden vs Hales*, he dispensed many individuals from the penalties of the penal laws and Test Acts and then, in the Declaration of Indulgence, suspended the former altogether. He also purged Tories from local and municipal offices and put Dissenters in their places. Now kings had often, in the past, dispensed individuals from the penalties of law and, in the early 1680s, Charles had issued many new borough charters which gave the king the power to remove members of the corporation (but not, as James did, to appoint others to replace them). It could be argued, therefore, that James's actions differed only in degree from those of his predecessors, but a difference of degree can be so large as to constitute a difference in kind; and so it seemed in this case. Besides, the intention behind James's actions differed markedly from Charles's occasional dispensations to clergymen or Oxbridge dons, while the charters of 1682–5 had been intended mainly to instal loyal Tories in municipal offices, where they could be relied upon to enforce the laws against Dissent.[31] James, by contrast, was aiming to promote Dissent and, above all, Popery. English law was full of inconsistencies, contradictions and grey areas, leaving considerable scope for the ingenuity of lawyers. For this reason, conceptions of 'legality' were to a considerable extent subjective.[32] In other words, what people thought was fair, reasonable or in their interest was, to them, 'legal'. The measures of the Tory reaction had won wide support. By contrast, although one might make a technical legal case for James's suspending power and campaign to pack Parliament, they were widely regarded as 'illegal'.

James's decisive move towards toleration came in his Declaration of Indulgence of April 1687, which suspended a wide range of laws, pending their repeal by a Parliament. When Charles had tried to do this in 1672, the Commons had told him that it was illegal and he had backed down; now James tried again. He said, bluntly, that he wished all his people were Catholics, but that he had long believed that 'conscience ought not to be constrained, nor people forced in matters of mere religion'. Persecution was bad for trade, discouraged immigration and never succeeded. He promised to protect the clergy and laity of the Church in the exercise of their religion and extended the same liberty to all, provided nothing was taught that could alienate the people from the government.[33] Whereas in 1672 Dissenters were allowed to worship only in buildings specifically licensed for that purpose, and Catholics only in their own homes, there were now no such restrictions. In a little over a year, England had passed from a vigorous persecution (of Dissenters) to the most complete toleration it had ever known.

The suddenness of James's conversion from persecution to toleration is, I think, a sufficient argument against claims that he consistently favoured toleration. He did declare consistently against persecution for conscience' sake — but he often equated religious nonconformity with political sedition, in which case claims of freedom of conscience did not apply. (Indeed, one might ask what was the value of freedom of conscience if it did not bring with it a measure of freedom of action). On the other hand, I have suggested that those who saw James's advocacy of toleration as an example of Popish duplicity were also wide of the mark. Here as in other policy areas — towards Ireland or the persecution of the Huguenots — James was torn between conflicting principles.[34] He was not a tolerant man in the sense of being able to see others' points of view — just the reverse. A combination of arrogance and a lack of mental subtlety made him dismiss views which differed from his as wrongheaded or malicious. It was perhaps in character that this authoritarian person should embrace an authoritarian religion; the irony was that this was the religion of a small, largely quiescent and intermittently persecuted minority. To improve that minority's condition, the temperamentally intolerant James was driven to argue for toleration — either for Catholics alone (as in 1685) or for all denominations (in 1687–8). James's advocacy of complete toleration, then, was born of an odd mixture of motives and circumstances and it is unlikely that James saw any great inconsistency in his conduct: most of us are able to convince ourselves at times that what we desperately want is eminently fair and reasonable. In the last analysis, however, James's convoluted mental processes must remain the subject of conjecture. The consequences of his actions are easier to describe.

James's Declaration stimulated a widespread debate on toleration, but one which differed in character from debates in the 1660s and 1670s. Then Anglicans had argued the case for authority and uniformity in religion. Most people, they claimed, were weak and sinful and needed careful guidance: dissent from the established church was motivated by spiritual pride and wilful disobedience. Their aim was to show (in Stillingfleet's phrase) 'the unreasonableness of separation'.[35] Faced with James's bid for the Dissenters' support, the Churchmen changed their tune. Few now questioned the merit of indulgence (for Protestants), but in sermons and pamphlets they argued (like Halifax) that James was merely using the Dissenters in a cunning scheme to impose Popery. James's propagandists countered by pouring scorn on the Churchmen's sudden change of heart and stressed the sufferings to which they had subjected Dissenters in recent years. James's reign, then, saw a vigorous paper debate on both religion and toleration. Given his public commitment to toleration and his belief in the innate truth of Catholicism, James might have been expected to allow this debate free rein; he did not. He tried, through the ecclesiastical commission, to force the bishops to suppress anti-Catholic preaching. He used the machinery of press censorship (re-established in 1685) to deny licences to anti-Catholic works and tried hard to suppress the many unlicensed publications that appeared, many of them printed in Holland. He also ordered the suppression of the pedlars and petty chapmen who distributed much of this literature. But the resources of the seventeenth-century state were insufficient to control the press effectively and works hostile to James found an appreciative readership and played a significant part in his downfall.[36]

By the summer of 1687 James and the Churchmen were locked in a battle for the hearts and minds of the Dissenters. The latter's response was mixed. Most were happy enough to worship freely, but proved less willing to pay the price James demanded — not so much freedom of worship for Catholics, but opening the way (by repealing the Test Acts) for Catholics to hold office. Given traditional presuppositions about the behaviour of Papists in power, it seemed to many suicidal to put them into a position where they could persecute Protestants. In an effort to dispel such mistrust, James approached his presumptive successor, Mary and her husband, William, urging them to support the repeal of the Test Acts. William replied that he favoured liberty of worship for both Dissenters and Catholics, but not the repeal of the Test Acts: 'he could never agree or consent to allow [Catholics] to become dominant'.[37] The views of William and Mary were given widespread publicity in *A Letter Written by Mijn Heer Fagel* (1688) which assured Dissenters that they would continue to enjoy liberty of worship after James's death, without the risks involved in putting Catholics in power. No longer need they fear (as James's agents claimed) that William and Mary would reintroduce persecution, so that their future security would depend on confirming the Indulgence by Act of Parliament. As a result, few Dissenters would give James formal thanks for his Declaration or co-operate in his electoral preparations. Most, especially the Presbyterians, watched him with suspicion: generations of anti-Catholic prejudice could not be dissipated overnight.[38]

As we have seen, James's treatment of the Church was far from tolerant: indeed, it became increasingly authoritarian and vindictive. He set up the ecclesiastical commission 'to regulate the licence of the Protestant ministers and to curb the audacity of the bishops'.[39] The commission forced the universities — most notably Magdalen College, Oxford — to admit Catholics. James doubtless saw such conduct as morally justified: he now regarded the Church (and not Protestants in general) as responsible for the persecution of Catholics and argued that Oxbridge colleges were mostly Catholic foundations. To his subjects his conduct appeared dubiously legal — the deprivation of the fellows of Magdalen was seen as a gross infringement of property rights — and as unjust. It was yet another example of what an assize sermon called 'torturing the laws to make them speak contrary to the intention of the makers'.[40] It also seemed a poor reward for the clergy's staunch support for James's claim to the throne. The last straw came in May 1688: James ordered the clergy to read his Declaration in their churches. It seemed a clever ploy. If they obeyed, they would (in effect) endorse the destruction of the Church's established status, for the Indulgence made it just one denomination among many. If they refused, they would seem hostile to toleration for Dissenters. In fact, encouraged by their bishops, the overwhelming majority did refuse, in the largest demonstration of civil disobedience in the reign. Moreover, when seven bishops petitioned against their being made to read it, the petition was published and the bishops were prosecuted for seditious libel.

For James, the petition was final proof of the Churchmen's moral turpitude. 'This is a standard of rebellion' he cried, and asked 'Is this what I have deserved, who have supported the Church of England and will support it?' (The bishops might well have responded that James's view of 'support' differed from theirs.) 'I will be obeyed' he thundered.[41] But most of the clergy failed to obey him. The bishops' petition (itself the product of careful discussions with the leading London clergy) showed that the Church could be pushed only so far. It also showed how far the clergy had moved from their earlier implacable hostility to Dissent. Their refusal to read the Declaration, they said, was not due to 'any want of due tenderness to Dissenters, in relation to whom they are willing to come to such a temper as shall be thought fit, when that matter shall be considered and settled in Parliament and Convocation.'[42] James's order to read the Declaration had been intended to drive a wedge between Churchmen and Dissenters. Instead, Dissenting leaders and London Churchmen discussed terms for the possible comprehension of moderate Dissenters within the Church; the tone, if not the wording, of the petition, also implied a measure of indulgence of those Dissenters who wished only for toleration. Meanwhile, Dissenting ministers visited the bishops in the Tower. James had, it seemed, far from dividing his Protestant subjects, united them in support of a comprehension and toleration in which only his fellow-Catholics were to find no place.[43]

It soon became clear that the bishops' conversion to comprehension and toleration was less than whole-hearted, and their reservations were increased by events. The prospect and then the reality of William's invasion seemed to offer a heaven-sent opportunity to extort concessions from the beleaguered James. Their aim was to 'set all things back upon the foot they were at his coming to the crown'. On 3 October the bishops called on James to call a free Parliament that could secure the Church, on the basis of the Act of Uniformity, while also providing for liberty of conscience — demands which seem inherently contradictory unless 'liberty of conscience' was understood as meaning something much less than toleration and which apparently left no room for comprehension at all.[44] Their calculation that James would be forced to make substantial concessions was upset by his loss of nerve and flight. The clergy were profoundly embarrassed. It they had not openly transgressed their principles of non-resistance they had, by refusing to help James, aided and abetted his expulsion. Moreover, they soon came to see William as hostile to the Church and biased in favour of Dissent. While outwardly continuing to favour 'a due liberty to Protestant Dissenters', both Sancroft and Thomas Tenison remarked privately that 'the Dissenters would never agree among themselves with what concessions they would be satisfied' and that it would be better to settle the matter in Convocation or in Parliament without consulting them.[45] Sir Edward Seymour was more blunt. William, he said, had duped them: having claimed his only aim was to secure a free Parliament, he now sought the crown. Moreover, 'the countenance he gave to the Dissenters gave too much jealousy to the Church of England, who . . . were the most considerable and substantial body of the nation.'[46]

In political terms, the Tories' growing disillusionment with the turn of events found expression in their stubborn efforts to deny William the crown.[47] Meanwhile, both the High Church clergy and their lay allies did the least they could to make good their assurances to the Dissenters. They were not helped by a collapse of leadership: Sancroft was noted to be 'politically sick' and expressed doubts as to whether the bishops could legally do anything in James's absence.[48] The initiative passed to the Church's supporters in Parliament, whose dislike of Dissent was intensified by moves to repeal the Corporation Act and to exempt Dissenters from the Test Act, and thus give them free access to public office. Two bills were drafted, one for comprehension, one for indulgence. The former had a rough passage through the Lords; the Commons were so displeased with it (in its amended form) that they drew up their own bill, which was more radical and aroused the ire of the Churchmen. After an ill-tempered debate on 8 April 1689, it was clear that agreement would not be easy: one MP moved that the debate should be adjourned till doomsday. Next day, a large meeting of MPs at the Devil Tavern agreed that both comprehension bills should be dropped and that the issue should be referred to Convocation, from which (given the mood of the clergy) little was likely to emerge. In return, the Tories agreed to let the indulgence bill go through.[49]

The first statutory grant of toleration in English history was thus the product of an unedifying mixture of ecclesiastical backtracking and political horse-trading. Appropriately, the official title of the 'Toleration Act' made no mention of toleration. It laid down that those who made a very general profession of Christian belief and subscribed thirty-six of the Thirty-nine articles were to be allowed to worship in meeting houses licensed for that purpose; Baptists were also exempted from subscribing the endorsement of infant baptism. In order to prevent religious meetings being used as a cover for sedition, the doors were to be unlocked during service time. Attendance at some form of religious worship was to remain compulsory (although this proved unenforceable). The benefits of the Act were to apply neither to non-Trinitarians (at this time, very few in number) nor to Catholics.[50]

The aim of the Act was to allow Dissenters freedom of worship, while denying them access to municipal and other offices; these, in theory, would remain an Anglican monopoly, as officeholders were still required to take communion according to the Anglican rite. In this respect, and in the insistence that meeting houses should be licensed, the liberty granted was narrower than that allowed by James. It represented the least that the Churchmen could, in honour and decency, concede to make good their assurances, the least that the Dissenters deserved for resisting James's blandishments. Without his Indulgence, it is inconceivable that toleration would have been granted so soon. It is also one of the many ironies of this story that the most notable group excluded from the benefits of the Act — the Catholics — was the one whose liberty James had most at heart. Indeed, the Catholics were soon subjected to new penal laws. Even the few who argued for toleration as a matter of principle — like Locke — mostly excluded Catholics as subjects of a foreign power — and probably Jacobites to boot.

For all but a few small minorities — Catholics, Unitarians, Jews — 1689 marked the beginning of true religious liberty. People could choose whether to attend church, meeting house or (in practice) neither. The exclusion of Dissenters from office proved less than effective, thanks to the practice of occasional conformity and then to a series of indemnity acts. Their exclusion from Oxford and Cambridge proved only a limited disability, as they established their own schools and academies. From 1689, then, *de facto* toleration of Protestants was a fact of life. For many it was unwelcome. High Churchmen blamed the Toleration Act for the growth of atheism and heterodoxy, the collapse of public morals and the lewdness of the stage. 'Church and king' mobs rabbled Dissenting, and later Methodist, preachers and smashed their meeting houses. Yet gradually, the fact of toleration bred a greater degree of tolerance. Religion became accepted as a private matter, bigotry and 'enthusiasm' came to be seen as marks of bad taste and bad manners. The large windows of late eighteenth-century meeting houses showed that there was no longer any need to fear sticks and stones. The animus against Catholics and Jews lasted longer, but in general foreign visitors regarded England as unusually tolerant. In seeking the roots of this tolerance, one is left (I think) with two paradoxes. First, the bitter religious conflict of the civil wars left England with a religious pluralism unmatched in Europe — except, perhaps, in the Dutch Republic. Second, the conversion of the most dogmatic — even bigoted — of the Stuarts to one of the smaller denominations gave him a vested interest in promoting toleration. Without the civil wars, without James II's conversion, toleration would not have become established in England as early as it did.

NOTES

1. Early in 1988 I had the pleasure and privilege of spending three months at the Center for the History of Freedom at Washington University, St Louis, working on a collaborative volume on 1688 and the making of modern freedom. During that time I learned a great deal from the authors of the two chapters on religion, Gordon Schochet and Bob Webb, whose work helped to clarify the

thinking behind this chapter. Any confusions, errors and misconceptions that remain are, of course, my responsibility.

2. V. Buranelli, *The King and the Quaker* (Philadelphia, 1962); W. A. Speck, *Reluctant Revolutionaries: Englishmen and the Revolution of 1688* (Oxford, 1988), ch. 8.

3. G. Savile, Marquis of Halifax, *Complete Works*, ed. J. P. Kenyon (Harmondsworth, 1969), 106.

4. J. R. Jones, *The Revolution of 1688 in England* (London, 1972), 11–12, 109–10; both Professor Speck, *op. cit.*, and J. R. Western, *Monarchy and Revolution: The English State in the 1680s* (London, 1972), 185–93 seem to see James as seeking both the establishment of absolutism and a measure of toleration (although on p. 191 Western suggested that the original motive for James's conversion may have been 'largely political').

5. B. Worden, 'Toleration and the Cromwellian Protectorate', in W. J. Sheils (ed.), *Persecution and Toleration* (Studies in Church History, xxi Oxford, 1984), 199–233. The term 'Anglican' is anachronistic, but I think the meaning is clear.

6. The classic Presbyterian denunciation of the sects was T. Edwards, *Gangraena* (1646); on the Quakers, see W. Prynne, *A New Discovery of Some Romish Emissaries* (1656).

7. See especially K. Wrightson, *English Society 1580–1680* (London, 1982), 206–221; C. Haigh, 'The Church of England, the Catholics and the People' in Haigh (ed.), *The Reign of Elizabeth I* (London, 1984), ch. 8.

8. J. S. Morrill, 'The Church in England, 1642–9', in Morrill (ed.), *Reactions to the English Civil War, 1642–9* (London, 1982), ch. 4.

9. See A. Whiteman, *The Comton Census of 1676* (The British Academy, London, 1986).

10. Whether or not the Ranters actually existed as a sect, they were certainly believed to be one.

11. A. Fletcher, 'The Enforcement of the Conventicle Acts, 1664–79', in Sheils (ed.), *Persecution and Toleration*, pp. 235–46; J. Miller, *Popery and Politics in England, 1660–88* (Cambridge, 1973), 57–66, 189–91, 265–8.

12. A similar argument was used to justify the persecution of Catholics under Elizabeth: Miller, *Popery*, 76–80.

13. J. Spurr, '"Latitudinarianism" and the Restoration Church', *Historical Journal* xxxi (1988), 61–82 questions whether there was a 'Latitudinarian' party in the Church, but whether or not one uses the name, some of the clergy were clearly tolerant towards Dissent: see G. Burnet, *History of my Own Time* (6 vols., Oxford, 1823), i.323–30, ii.210–12.

14. For his religious upbringing and conversion, see J. Miller, *James II: A Study in Kingship* (Hove, 1978), 49–50, 57–9.

15. Burnet, *History*, ii.23; Add. 63057B, f. 22.

16. As J. P. Kenyon astutely pointed out: *Robert Spencer, Earl of Sunderland* (London, 1958), 112.

17. J. Lingard, *History of England* (6th edn., 10 vols., London, 1855), x.203.

18. PRO, Baschet transcripts, PRO 31/3 (hereafter Baschet) bundle 121, Colbert to Louis XIV, 15/25 April 1669; Baschet 164, Barrillon to Louis 28 Jan./7 Feb. 1686; PRO, PC 2/71, p. 1.

19. Burnet, *History*, ii.26–7. See also J. S. Clarke, *Life of James II* (2 vols., London, 1816), I.656.

20. S. Pepys, *Diary*, ed. R. C. Latham and W. Matthews (11 vols., London, 1971–83), IV.135.

21. Add. 52279, f. 10. For conflicting views of James and the Huguenots, see R. D. Gwynn, 'James II in the light of his treatment of Huguenot Refugees in England', *English Historical Review*, XCII (1977), 820–33; J. Miller, 'The Immediate Impact of the Revocation in England' in C. E. J. Caldicott, H. Gough and J-P. Pittion (eds.), *The Huguenots in Ireland* (Dublin 1987), 161–74.

22. PRO, PC 2/71, p. 1. My italics.

23. Sir H. Ellis (ed.), *Original Letters Illustrative of English History* (2nd edn., 3 vols., London, 1825), iii.339.

24. MS 63057B, f. 22. This is a draft of Burnet, written in 1683. In the printed edition of the *History*, after 'submission to princes' he added 'and passive obedience' (ii.27). See also Burnet, ii.428n.

25. Lingard, x.203.L. von Ranke, *History of England* (6 vols., Oxford, 1875), iv. 228–9 also quoted part of this dispatch of Barrillon's, dated 2/12 March 1685. It has since been torn out of its volume: AAE, Correspondance Politique Angleterre (hereafter AECP Ang.) 154.

26. AECP Ang. 165, Barrillon to Louis, 18/28 June 1688. I have argued elsewhere that the establishment of 'absolutism' was not James's main concern: *Popery and Politics*, 196–202; *James II*, 124–8, 176.

27. *HMC Dartmouth*, I.36.

28. Baschet 164, Barrillon to Louis, 28 Jan./7 Feb. 1686.

29. Baschet 168, Barrillon to Louis, 24 Mar./3 April 1687.

30. Miller, *Popery and Politics*, 218–222.

31. J. Miller, 'The Crown and the Borough Charters in the Reign of Charles II', *EHR*, c (1985), 70–84.

32. I owe this point to Howard Nenner.

33. A. Browning, *English Historical Documents, 1660–1714* (London, 1953), 395–7.

34. See J. Miller, 'The Earl of Tyrconnell and James II's Irish Policy, 1685–8' *Historical Journal*, XX (1977), 803–23; Miller, 'Impact of the Revocation'.

35. See R. Ashcraft, *Revolutionary Politics and Locke's 'Two Treatises of Government'* (Princeton, 1986), ch. 2.

36. Speck, 174–8; Miller, *Popery and Politics*, 252–7.

37. PRO,FO 95/573, Albeville to d'Avaux, c. 7/17 May 1687.

38. R. Thomas, 'Comprehension and Indulgence' in G. F. Nuttall and W. O. Chadwick (eds.), *From Uniformity to Unity 1662–1962* (London, 1962), 235–8; Miller, *James II*, 171–3. For James's electoral prospects, see Speck, 130–5.

39. Add. 15396, ff. 26–7.

40. A. Coleby, *Central Government and the Localities: Hampshire 1649–89* (Cambridge, 1987), 220.

41. J. Gutch (ed.), *Collectanea Curiosa* (2 vols., London, 1781), I.339–40.

42. J. P. Kenyon, *The Stuart Constitution* (2nd edn., Cambridge, 1986), 407.

43. Thomas, pp. 238–41; see also G. V. Bennett, 'The Seven Bishops: A Reconsideration' in D. Baker (ed.), *Religious Motivation: Biographical and*

Sociological Problems for the Church Historian (Studies in Church History, xv, Oxford, 1978), 267–87.

44. *Clarendon Correspondence*, ed. S. W. Singer (2 vols., London 1828), ii.189; Gutch i.412. See also J. Miller, "'Proto-Jacobitism?'": The Tories and the Revolution of 1688' in E. Cruickshanks and J. Black (eds.), *The Jacobite Challenge* (Edinburgh, 1988), ch. 1.

45. E. Bohun, *History of the Desertion* (1689), 94–6; *Clarendon Correspondence*, ii.240.

46. *Clarendon Correspondence*, ii.238.

47. See J. Evelyn, *Diary*, ed. E. S. De Beer (6 vols., Oxford, 1955), iv.614.

48. Dr Williams's Library, MS 31Q, p. 382; *Clarendon Correspondence*, ii.240; Bennet, 'Seven Bishops', 287.

49. Thomas, 244–51; G. V. Bennett, 'The Revolution and the Church' in G. Holmes (ed.), *Britain after the Glorious Revolution* (London, 1969), 160–2.

50. Browning, 400–3. At first the Quakers too were excluded from the Act's benefits because they were unwilling to swear oaths, but this problem was alleviated by an Act of 1696, *ibid.*, 404.

3
THE REVOLUTION AND THE LOCALITIES: EXAMPLES OF LOYALTY TO JAMES II

Eveline Cruickshanks

A great deal has been written about the Revolution of 1688 before and in the course of this Tercentenary year, mainly on the political, intellectual and diplomatic aspects of this event. Little, however, has been done on local reaction to the Dutch invasion in various parts of England and what has been done has been from the standpoint of the insurgents. This essay is an attempt to examine the complexities of Tory reaction to the Revolution in the localities.

The Prince of Orange's landing at Torbay and Brixham came as a complete surprise, as he had been expected to land in the North East where his principal allies were. Having done so, it was expected, rightly as it turned out, that his first objective would be Exeter, the capital of the West. The corporation had been divided in 1687, when James II's agents purged the Church of England aldermen and replaced them with Dissenters and one Roman Catholic. The new mayor, Thomas Jefford, a wealthy dyer and a Nonconformist, was regarded as 'a little inconsiderable fellow' with little interest in the town.[1] It is not surprising, therefore, that the dean ordered the cathedral bells to be rung in joy at the arrival of Lord Bath, the lord lieutenant of Devon and Cornwall, on 31 Oct.[2] As elsewhere, Lord Bath removed men of 'mean quality and small estates' and placed power once more into 'loyal hands'.[3] The town charter was restored on 1 Nov., whereupon the town sword was 'rescued from a conventicle and carried once more after the ancient manner to the Cathedral Church', where the bishop, Thomas Lamplugh, the dean, Francis Annesley, the chapter, and the restored magistrates welcomed it with expressions of 'joy and perfect satisfaction'. That this happened only a few days before the Dutch descent makes the opposition of the Exeter clergy and corporation to William all the more remarkable. In great alarm, members of the corporation sent scouts to find out the size of the invading army.[4] It was about 15,000, but it was gradually inflated, partly by the invaders themselves, to 48,000.[5] Local people were amazed by the polyglot character of the Dutch army, which included many mercenaries: Brandenburgers, Greeks, Swiss, Poles, Swedes, Hessians, Finlanders in bearskins, and Black slaves from the Dutch plantations.[6] They carried banners with the motto 'For the defence of the Protestant Religion and the Liberty and Property of the subjects of England'. Their leaders proclaimed everywhere that the Prince of Orange claimed not the crown and drank the health of the King, the Church of England and the Bishop of London.[7] Some of the Exeter magistrates wondered what religion, if any, many of the soldiers belonged to. According to Robert Ferguson, who was with them, there were twice as many Roman Catholics in William's army as in James's, though others put the numbers in each as equal.[8]

The Prince of Orange had tried to build up support in the west in advance, for as early as January 1688 Sir William Waller, the son of the parliamentarian general, had written to his brother-in-law, Sir William Courtenay of Powderham, with a message from the prince. Waller, who had been an Exclusionist in Parliament and a patron of Titus Oates, had fled from his creditors to Holland. In this letter were assurances that the prince's only concern were 'the Protestant interest and the welfare of poor England' and a claim that James II was trying to force his daughter, Mary, to divorce her husband in order to get her to 'marry elsewhere'. This was one of several lies in William's propaganda campaign of that year. Courtenay was urged to enhance the favour in which he was held in Holland by writing a suitable letter to the prince, but there was no reply.[9] Courtenay had been an Exclusionist, but when he heard that the prince was coming to stay at his house at Ford Abbey on the way to Exeter, he promptly left for Powderham, leaving instructions to his tenants not to join the invaders.[10]

As the Dutch army advanced, the aldermen of Exeter reported to the secretary of state that though Exeter was 'in a good posture to defend itself, or make a defence against a small party', there was little they could do against a force of this size, but that they would endeavour to prove themselves 'his Majesty's dutiful and loyal subjects'. The mayor, Christopher Brodridge, began by arresting on a charge of high treason one John Jenckes, an officer in the prince's army, who had been enlisting men for the rebels in the town and confiscating a treasonable paper he was dispersing, presumably the prince's Declaration. All the aldermen of Exeter, with the possible exception of one, stood by James II, particularly Christopher Bale, Tory Member for the city from 1689 to 1695.[11] They were further alarmed when the prince's supporters captured and held prisoner the collector of the excise for Exeter and Devon, seizing

£4,400 of the excise money.[12] Since James II having collected the excise after his accession, before being granted it by Parliament, was one of the grievances in the Declaration of Rights, one could ask by what right William was collecting it? As the prince drew nearer, Bishop Lamplugh, one of the bishops who had made no opposition to the second Declaration of Indulgence, left, but not before exhorting his clergy 'to remain steadfast in their sworn allegiance to their crowned and legitimate king, James II'. The dean also departed.[13] On Friday 9 Nov. the prince and his army entered Exeter. The magistrates had been urged in advance to receive him in state at the entrance, but they refused and ordered all the gates to be shut against him. According to a local tradition, however, Alderman George Tuthill secretly opened the West Gate to save the prince from having to break an entrance.[14] Exeter was a city normally full of gentry, but they and the substantial citizens had all left. Many of the common people, though, who came to attend one of the larger annual fairs held there at the time, welcomed them. It was reported that 'some of the scruff and meaner part run into them as they would to see a shrewe, but generally retreat the next day'.[15] William took up residence in the empty deanery, cold-shouldered by the corporation and local clergy. Dr. Burnet, the prince's chaplain, informed the prebendaries that a solemn service would be held in the cathedral in honour of the prince, but that the prayer for the Prince of Wales must be omitted. None of the canons were in their stalls when the service began and when Burnet started to read the prince's Declaration, the choristers walked out. Burnet then sent the prince's Declaration and a form of prayer for his good success to all the local clergy, but they 'unanimously refused' to read them in their church.[16] 'The doctrines of passive obedience and non-resistance had been carried so far and preached so much' Burnet commented, 'that clergymen . . . could not all on a sudden get out of that entanglement'.[17] Dissenters were not very forward either for when Robert Ferguson wished to preach and read the prince's Declaration in the great Presbyterian meeting house, he had to fight his way in with armed men, breaking down the door with a hammer and declaring that he would take the kingdom of Heaven by force.[18] The mayor and corporation were still refusing to recognise William's authority so that the prince asked his council to look at their charter (his first public act being to try and remodel a charter!). In the end, he suspended the corporation from acting for the time being.[19] No person of any social standing or influence had joined him and, according to some contemporaries, the Prince of Orange began to entertain thoughts of returning to Holland.[20]

In mid-November, circumstances began to change. The first people of note to join the prince at Exeter were all Whigs and not from the West Country: Thomas Wharton, Lord Colchester and Col. Godfrey. Then came Sir Edward Seymour, a Tory and the greatest electoral magnate in the west, followed by many local gentlemen, Whigs and Tories. At Seymour's suggestion, they entered into an Association to defend the prince and to protect themselves.[21] This is not to say, of course, that Seymour and other Tories who joined William wanted to make him king, for they believed the terms of his Declaration stating he had no designs on the crown. Seymour said that 'all the west went into the Prince of Orange upon his declaration, thinking in a free Parliament to redress all that was amiss; but that men now began to think that the Prince aimed at something else'. Seymour, who thought we could not have a Dutch king because England and Holland 'followed the same mistress, trade', later complained that the pattern of English trade had been changed to the benefit the Dutch and to the detriment of England.[22] He and other west country Tories who had joined William at Exeter, voted against the transfer of the crown in 1689. Of worse significance, militarily and psychologically, was the defection of the Earl of Bath to the prince, for ever since the heroic conduct of his father Sir Bevill Granville fighting for the king at the battle of Lansdowne in 1643, the name of Granville had stood for loyalty to the Stuarts. Sent by James to Plymouth to hold it against the Dutch, Bath handed it over, giving them safe anchorage. Unlike Seymour, he voted for the transfer of the crown in 1689.[23] Thomas Lamplugh was made archbishop of York by James, voted against the offer of the crown to William, but took the oaths and kept his see. The long-time losers were the corporation of Exeter, on whom the resentful prince quartered his sick soldiers. Year in year out, the aldermen, Christopher Bale especially, tried to get repayment for this considerable debt on the town chamber. Others too had been at some expense in nursing, feeding and housing sick foreign soldiers. Their pleas were in vain, William never paid.[24]

However successful the high-ranking officers, John Churchill particularly, involved in the Army Plot in favour of the Prince of Orange, there were many examples of loyalty to the king in the army. The Dutch had landed without enough horses for their needs, so that when they encountered Major Norton and some of his troops of horse near Honiton, they enjoined him and his fellow officers to come over to them for the sake of their religion. Norton and the others replied that the Church of England had not taught them to serve against their king, whereupon their horses were seized without compensation.[25] In what has been called a bloodless Revolution, officers and men fought bravely for James in the bloody skirmishes at Wincanton and Reading. Most of the common soldiers remained faithful to James, even though they were offered a month's pay in advance for deserting to the prince.[26] Lord Cornbury, the never-do-well son of the Earl of Clarendon, took his regiment over to William in the west, but most of his troops refused to follow him when they discovered where they were being taken. This was true of other regiments too.[27] After the prince's advance on London and the king's first flight, Lord Feversham gave out orders to disband the army, when eye-witnesses reported 'many of the soldiers weeping and others trembling with anger whilst they heard the order read'. When William re-formed the regiments, massive desertions among the soldiers ensued.[28] In March 1689 there was a mutiny of the army at Ipswich, where the Scots Guards under Lord Dumbarton, refused to serve under the German Duke of Schomberg or to embark for Holland, were joined by others, proclaimed James as the rightful king and marched north. This led to the passing of the first Mutiny Act of 1689, imposing the death penalty for mutiny and desertion in the British army.[29]

In the north, the conspirators were led by Thomas Osborne, Earl of Danby, who had been lord treasurer under Charles II but had been out of office for the last ten years. He was one of the Seven who had issued the Invitation to William of Orange. Their advice had been for William to come with a large fleet but with a small army, so that it would not look like a conquest and for the descent to be made in Bridlington Bay in Yorkshire, or near Hull, at the heart of the Danby country. The Prince of Orange, however, wanted no power broker and he chose to come with a large professional army, as well as with a large fleet, though his first intention, when the Dutch fleet sallied forth before being beaten back by storms, seems to have been to land in the north east. Having landed in the west, the prince made no attempt to get into touch with Danby or his fellow conspirators and Danby was astounded by William's failure even to reply to letters asking for orders.[30]

Most of the Yorkshire gentry were unaware of the conspiracy. The lord lieutenant of the three Ridings was the Duke of Newcastle, a High Church Tory, who resolved to remain 'very loyal and firm to his master the King', but who was indecisive and tormented with the gout.[31] The governor of York, Sir John Reresby, who had sat as a Tory M.P. in 1685, wrote to Newcastle on 14 Nov. informing him that a meeting of the militia for the three Ridings had been called at York 'for the safety and defence of these parts for his Majesty's service, that we might assure the King of our intention to adhere to him faithfully in this conjuncture'.[32]

As a garrison town, York was strategically important. Neither Newcastle nor Reresby had any suspicion of Danby's real intentions, nor of those of his chief henchman, Sir Henry Goodricke, a prominent Member of Parliament, who had just been put back in the militia commission. Goodricke proposed 'to draw some instrument or declaration of our loyalty to the King at this time of danger and to consult on such things as might be to the honour of God and our own safeties'. He did own, however, that 'he did intend to petition for a free Parliament'. James II had called a Parliament for the 27 Nov. but had recalled the writs because of the Dutch invasion, in the belief that Parliament could not sit while foreign troops were on English soil. Like Reresby, the Duke of Newcastle, was absolutely opposed to appending a petition for a free Parliament to a loyal address. When Goodricke persisted, the duke 'then said he would not stay to be affronted or overruled by his deputies' and left before the 22nd Nov. that 'fatal day' as Reresby called it, intending to return the next day. On his way to the meeting, Reresby had an accident when his horse fell over him, so that there was no one loyal to the King to give a lead. On the 22nd, before about a hundred gentlemen assembled at York, Goodricke made a speech saying that the only remedy for attempts to introduce Popery was a free Parliament and produced a petition on the model of that already presented by the Lords in London. This met with opposition, some arguing that the terms of the petition should be altered, others that a loyal address must come first. Only two had signed when, on a prearranged signal, Christopher Tancred (an associate of Danby and Goodricke) ran into the hall crying out that 'the Papists had risen and had fired at the militia troops'. This was untrue as well as absurd, but it ended the meeting in total disarray. Outside, Danby's son Lord Dunblane, Lord Lumley (one of the Seven) and others rode at the head of about a hundred horsemen to the cry of 'A Free Parliament, the Protestant religion, and no Popery'. Within a short time they captured York Castle and declared for the Prince of Orange. Danby asked Reresby to join them, but he refused, declaring he was for 'the Protestant religion as well as they' but he was for the King so that he was placed under arrest.[33] The Dean of York, Thomas Comber, and most of the city declared for the insurgents.[34] Reresby found it difficult to believe 'that men of such quality and estates (however dissatisfied) would engage in a design so desperate and so contrary to the laws of the land and the religion they professed'.[35] Sir John Lowther of Lowther, a prominent Member of Parliament before and after the Revolution and a friend of Danby's, proposed a general meeting of the Cumberland militia at Carlisle.[36] This was opposed by Sir Christopher Musgrave, a High

Tory politician. Musgrave had resisted any repeal of the Test Act and penal laws, but asured James II that 'his Majesty might strip him of his shirt, if he pleased, but that he would sell his shirt, if he had nothing else, for a sword to fight for his Majesty'.[37] Musgrave prevented Carlisle being surprised as York had been surprised, by disarming Roman Catholics in the garrison, but holding the city for James II.[38]

Danby sought the support of Lord Chesterfield, a great landed magnate in the Midlands, writing it would be preferable to lose life itself rather 'than live under an arbitrary power and see our laws and religion changed, which is now visibly the King's intention'. To this Chesterfield replied:

> My Lord, though my obligations to the Court are far from being great, yet I confess there are things in this business which I cannot approve, especially since I have yet the honour (against my will) to be of his Majesty's council, but besides that consideration I have ever had a natural aversion to the taking arms against my King, which the law justly terms designing the King's death . . . I am confident that a continual remorse and disquiet would attend my thoughts after such an action. And therefore my Lord if you are not already too far ingaged, consider once more with yourself any other motive now prevails and persuades you, yet neither you nor any man foresee till the tragedy is past, whether you will not often wish that you had not been an action in it.[39]

This was prophetic for Danby and his son Lord Dunblane repeatedly asserted subsequently that had they known that the Prince of Orange, whom they had heard so often say he had no designs of the throne, would insist on taking the crown, they would have had nothing to do with him.[40] At this stage, Danby would not have been averse to entering into negotiations with James, but he found himself unable to dictate the terms of the Revolution settlement and he had the mortification to get orders from the Prince of Orange, sent on 11 Dec., the day after the King's departure, to disband his forces.[41] Lord Chesterfield, who had joined Princess Anne at Nottingham in order to protect her, was disgusted at William's pretence 'to come only to secure the laws and religion of this kingdom'. He refused to join the Earl of Devonshire's Association 'to destroy all Papists in England in case the Prince of Orange should be killed or murdered', as did Lord Scarsdale, Lord Ferrers and about another hundred of the gentlemen at Nottingham. In the Convention of 1689 Lord Chesterfield declared that 'there was no abdication, nor no vacancy in the throne, for the Crown being hereditary, the Prince of Orange could not legally be elected', and he voted against the transfer of the Crown. Ironically enough William, who always believed that the men who had plotted with him against James might plot with James against him, an assumption frequently justified, made persistent endeavours to win over Chesterfield, even offering him the post of lord privy seal in preference to Danby (now Marquess of Carmarthen) in June 1689. Lord Chesterfield rebuffed the King's advances. He 'absolutely refused' to sign the Association in 1696, which declared William to be the 'rightful and lawful' king and would not take the oath to abjure 'the pretended Prince of Wales', James III, in 1701. He lived the rest of his life in retirement.[42]

The turn of events at Chester, a garrison town like York and more vital because of the passage of troops to and from Ireland, was quite different. In mid-October 1688 James II dismissed Caryll, Lord Molyneux as lord lieutenant of Lancashire and Cheshire. A Roman Catholic, Molyneux was the largest landowner in and around Liverpool and he had been the royalist hero of the siege of Liverpool during the Civil War. He was replaced by the Earl of Derby, in whose family these two lord lieutenancies had been quasi-hereditary. Taking up his commission from the King's hands, Lord Derby gave assurances that 'he was a Stanley' and 'his ancestors were ever loyal'. On 1 Nov. Derby had a meeting with Lord Delamere, a professional conspirator who had been arrested for complicity in Monmouth's rising in 1685, 'a clapped out bankrupt nobleman on the make'. Delamere was not one of the Seven and he was planning a rising of his own. Several deputy lieutenants, including Thomas Preston (M.P. Lancaster 1689–1697) and Col. Rigby, pressed Lord Derby for action expressing themselves 'ready and willing to serve his Majesty'. On 14 Nov. Lord Delamere raised his standard for the Prince of Orange and caused a sensation by announcing that Lord Derby would follow his example. The same day two of the Cheshire deputy lieutenants, Peter Egerton and William Hulme, wrote to Roger Kenyon (M.P. Wigan 1690–1695), then clerk of the peace for Lancashire and Lord Derby's man of affairs:

> you are very sensible, we know, what a consternation the country is upon the late potent invasion and what a clatter the red-letter men [clergy] make and in what a readiness they unanimously shew themselves to serve the King upon that occasion . . . It is now some weeks since . . . the Earl of Derby had received again his commission and was restored to his full power, as before, and we have been in expectation of his calling the militia together every day.

Thomas Preston and other leading militia officers urged the 'fatal' consequences of 'sitting still' and repeatedly sent for Lord Derby at Knowsley, who pleaded illness. In actual fact, Derby did absolutely nothing to support or oppose the rising, he just sat on the fence.[43] His attitude also enraged some of Delamere's supporters, who threatened to kill him. They, like their Devon counterparts, were collecting the excise in the Prince of Orange's name by force.[44]

The governor of Chester was Peter Shakerley (M.P. Wigan 1690–1698, Chester 1698–1700) who, hearing that Lord Delamere was planning to attack Chester, pledged to be 'loyal and faithful to the King', despite the inadequate forces at his disposal. There was said to be an 'understanding' between Shakerley and Lord Derby, but this did not mean any complicity with Delamere, Shakerley's personal enemy against whom Shakerley had given evidence of high treason. Reporting to William Blathwayt, the secretary-at-war, Shakerley pledged his fidelity to James II.

> from which I shall never swerve nor be deterred by any higher principle (as some are pleased to phrase their excuses for their revolts) to the best diminution of my duty and allegiance to the King whom God bless and preserve.

Lord Derby took no action when Col. Henry Gage, who commanded a newly-raised regiment which contained many Roman Catholics, took up their quarters in Chester Castle, indeed he entertained Col. Gage and some of his officers at Knowsley. They were reinforced on 27 Nov. by a militia regiment raised by Lord Molyneux, mostly of Roman Catholics, an event which was said to have created as great a sensation in England as any battle in the Civil War! With all this additional help, Chester town and castle were secured, and Shakerley declared himself ready to see off any enemy assault.[45] Bishop Cartwright of Chester, who had accepted the 2nd Declaration of Indulgence, stayed and stood firm for the King. The fate of the kingdoms, however, was not to be decided by happened in this or that major city or garrison, but by professional armies. After James's first flight on 10 Dec., Col. Gage and Lord Molyneux's forces laid down their arms in obedience to Lord Feversham's orders to disband the Army. The Bishop of Chester was then arrested, Col. Gage escaped in disguise, while Lord Molyneux, who was exempted from the Act of Indemnity, had to pay a huge fine to regain possession of his estate. After the garrison had laid down their arms, Shakerley professed himself ready to obey the orders of the Prince of Orange, adding 'the loyalty and fidelity I showed to my King will not, I hope be imputed to me a crime by the victorious Prince'.[46] The situation in Chester, as elsewhere, was brought to fever pitch by the

Irish fright of mid-December. Evidence in Shakerley's papers shows that this was deliberately orchestrated and that false reports that 10,000 Irish were on the march, that they had burnt down Birmingham and Wolverhampton and were preparing to burn down Sheffield, killing all Protestants, were deliberately circulated.[47] In the wake of these, the mayor of Chester, Alderman Streete a supporter of Delamere, read the Prince of Orange's Declaration, asking Shakerley to fire a 21-gun salute in celebration. Shakerley refused, writing to Blathwayt 'though I was well pleased with the preservation of the Protestant religion yet the sorrow I had (and which every Englishman ought to have) for the banishment, distress and misery of my King would not permit me to make such tokens of joy'. Obtaining the keys to the castle by stealth, the mayor imprisoned Shakerley in his own castle.[48] Dismissed by William as governor of Chester, Shakerley was in the Tower of London by May 1689, accused of dispersing commissions in James II's name, remaining a Jacobite for the rest of William's reign.[49] Lord Derby had the mortification of being replaced by Delamere as lord lieutenant of Cheshire. Even more ironic was the choice of his successor as lord lieutenant of Lancashire: Charles Gerard, Lord Brandon, a Whig who had been in arms for King James even after the transfer of the Crown, faithful as he said to a King to whom he owed his life (James II had pardoned him for involvement in the Rye House Plot and Monmouth rebellion), but whose father, the Earl of Macclesfield, had come over with William from Holland.[50]

Durham presents another type of loyalty and resistance to usurpation. The three principal manors in Durham were held by the bishop, the dean and by William Tempest of Old Durham (M.P. Durham 1679–81 and 1690–1695). The Bishop was Nathaniel, Lord Crewe, a time-server, who had collaborated heartily with James II's policies of religious toleration, ordering the 2nd Declaration of Indulgence to be read in his chapel at Auckland and throughout the diocese, when 20 out of 65 parishes complied.[51] The Dean of Durham was Dennis Granville, who had married a daughter of Bishop Cosin of Durham, obtained through the influence of his brother, Lord Bath, the rectories of Easington and Sedgefield, two rich livings in the diocese, becoming Archdeacon of Durham and retaining all these posts when he was appointed dean in 1684. His appointment had been in the face of opposition from Bishop Crewe, who had wanted his own nephew, Dr. Montagu to be dean. This amounted to very high preferment indeed with a very large income. Dean Granville was not a careerist, however, but a saintly, devout man, who reintroduced weekly communion in the cathedral and revived the ancient practice of twice-weekly sermons in Advent and Lent.[52] Unlike so many other Anglican clergymen, Granville thought that obedience and non-resistance were the appropriate responses to James II's policy of religious toleration and that the Church of England would still be *primus inter pares*. Of the 2nd Declaration of Indulgence he said:

> if the King goes beyond his commission, he must answer for it to God, but I'll not deface one line thereof. Let my liege and dread sovereign intend to do what he pleases to me or mine. Yet my hand shall never be upon him, so much as to cut off the skirt of his garment . . . In this Magna Charta aimed at by the King for establishing his Declaration, our religion will be established in the first place, and others incapacitated to hurt us as much as we to hurt them. And if we can't be put into better circumstances without resisting the King in lawful commands, there is no remedy but Christian patience.[53]

Dean Granville's reaction to the Dutch invasion was one of horror. In his Visitation sermon of 15 Nov., he condemned this 'vile rebellion', which was 'hatched in Hell' and 'harboured in Holland'. The 'barbarous Dutch' he went on, had had the impudence to fight with us for supremacy of the seas under Charles II, and now had the insolence 'to fight for the imperial crown of this Kingdom' under the pretence of defending our liberty and religion. (For someone who was an idealist, Granville was shrewder about the Prince of Orange's real intentions than many contemporaries.) When the Stadholder's pretences to the Crown had been postponed by the birth of 'a hopeful young prince', more cruel than Herod, he endeavoured to prove his illegitimacy and so disinherit him. The Church of England, he believed, could no more be saved from Amsterdam than it could be saved from Salamanca.[54]

After the Prince of Orange had landed, Dean Granville summoned the Durham chapter, urging the prebendaries to assist the King with their purses as well as with their prayers and they agreed to collect £700 for the royal service: £100 from the dean and £50 each from the others, all of whom but one complied. He was unable, however, to get them to sign a loyal address to the King.[55] Bishop Crewe was in London at first and then went into hiding, lurking in a ship off the coast. In his absence Dean Granville was unable to call the Durham militia together. William Tempest, a friend of the dean, rejoined the colours and served in the garrison of Tynemouth which, like Newcastle, was held for James until his departure.[56]

On 5 Dec. Lord Lumley entered Durham at the head of about 50 insurgents. Meeting with no opposition, he read the Prince's Declaration the next day at the castle and the market cross in the presence of many of the country gentry. With quite extraordinary courage, Dean Granville mounted the pulpit of Durham Cathedral and gave what he called his Farewell sermons of 5 and 9 Dec., preaching the doctrines of divine hereditary right and non-resistance. He argued that

> our ancient laws and government (so much dependant upon monarchy) cannot be preserved by the destruction of the Prince; and true liberty and property cannot be secured by the destruction of ancient government; noe more can the right protestant religion.

Rebellion, he thought was 'the foulest of all sins', destructive to monarchy and episcopacy and in this case it was being fostered by 'the darling of Presbytery and a Commonwealth', tempting subjects to fight against their lawful sovereign. He went on to extol

> the gracious goodness of the present King, in not only continuing but protecting our religion: whereby he did in an unexpectedly blessed manner, defeat the bitter calumnies of his malicious enemies, who, for seven years before, had most seditiously hammered into the spirit of the vulgar most dismal and dreadful apprehensions of a popish successor: he thereby proving all those (God be thanked) false prophets, who had insinuated into the people's minds, (to the scaring them almost out of their senses) that, as soon as the Duke of York came to the Crown, we should have mass said in all the cathedrals in England.

He added that the Roman Catholics deserved 'some respite' in the reign of a prince of their own religion because of their great services during the Great Rebellion. Urging his parishioners 'to stand firm in their allegiance in that day of temptation and never to join in the least ways in that horrid rebellion which was . . . set foot in the nation' by remaining true to their King. 'Contend and fight', he told his clergy, 'as well as pray, as heartily as you please, against our insolent neighbours the Dutch: but cease to dispute with your Prince'.[57] After his first sermon, Dean Granville was summoned by Lord Lumley to deliver up his horses and his arms. When he refused, he was placed under house arrest. Lord Lumley's march to Newcastle, which he failed to capture, freed the dean and enabled him to give his second sermon, returning to the same themes. Dean Granville left his deanery on 11 Dec., the day after his King had left Whitehall. He said he went into exile because he would not 'bow down to Baal, or in plain English, submit to an usurper, who would have to maintain himself by the sword'. The King, he concluded, had been deposed 'by fraud and by force' by his unnatural nephew and son-in-law.[58] After 15 Dec. he was harrassed in the Irish fright, which he called 'the false and malicious reports of the landing of Irish papists, burning of towns and massacring of people', but he made his way to Carlisle where Sir Christopher Musgrave helped him to get to Edinburgh and hence to France.[59]

Dean Granville landed at Honfleur in Normandy on 19 Mar. 1689, not all that far from the town after which his own family took its name. His ancestors had come with one Conqueror and he was driven out by another. Making his way to St. Germain, he became chaplain in ordinary to the Stuart court. According to John Macky, the British government spy, Anglicans were slighted and prevented from worshipping at St. Germain. Modern research, however, shows that though James II was at times under pressure from Louis XIV who disapproved of Church of England services on French soil, the exiled king never gave way, insisting that his subjects must be allowed to worship according to the dictates of their conscience.[61] With secret help from his brother Lord Bath, Dean Granville was able to receive some of his income in France.[62] In April 1695 he made a secret visit to Durham, presumably in connection with the Fenwick plot, when he may have met William Tempest, who was arrested as a Jacobite suspect shortly afterwards.[63] In later years, he retired to a house in Corbeil, a town he had traced as the place of origin of his ancestors and he spent happy days fishing in the Seine. He died 18 Apr. o.s. 1704 and was buried in Paris, entirely at the expense of Queen Mary of Modena. On his last journey he was attended by his nephews, Sir Thomas Higgons the Queen's secretary, (who had been appointed Fellow of Magdalen, Oxford by James II), by Bevill Higgons, the poet and other Nonjuring friends.[64] Another nephew, George Granville, Lord Lansdowne, the Tory politician, revered the memory of Dean Granville as a model of sanctity and for redeeming his family's reputation for loyalty to the Stuarts.[65]

Durham offered another type of loyalty in the person of Thomas Baker, the celebrated antiquary. The grandson of Sir George Baker of Crook Hall, a prominent Royalist in the Civil War, Baker was a friend of Dean Granville. Baker had been collated to the rectory of Long Newton by Bishop Crewe, but fell under the bishop's displeasure for refusing to read the 2nd Declaration of Indulgence. A believer in divine hereditary right, however, Baker could not accept William of Orange as king. As a Nonjuror, he was ejected from his living in 1690. He then resumed his Fellowship at St. John's, Cambridge. On the death of James II, he contemplated taking the oaths, but his conscience would not let him abjure the 'pretended Prince of Wales', James III. After the Hanoverian succession, he was deprived of his Cambridge Fellowship. Living in reduced material circumstances until his death in 1740, he was held in high esteem in Cambridge because of his piety, learning and meticulous scholarship, so much so that Bishop Warburton wrote that the Fellows and students of St. John's 'almost adore the man'.[66] Dean Granville and Thomas Baker were friends whose paths had diverged, but in point of loyalty they were equals.

NOTES

1. *HMC Exeter*, 181, 188; G. Oliver, *The History of the City of Exeter* (Exeter 1861), 219; Add. 41805 f. 63.

2. Exeter cathedral and chapter archives, 'Solutiones Extraordinariae', 31 Oct. 1688. I am obliged to the Dean and Chapter for permission to use their manuscripts.

3. Bucks RO D. 175, papers of George Jeffreys (I owe this reference to the kindness of Peter Le Fevre); Add. 41805 f. 122.

4. Add. 41805 ff. 118, 122.

5. Add. 41805 f. 161.

6. N. Japiske, *Correspondentie*, xxiii (1927), 45–6; T. B. Macaulay, *The History of England from the Accession of James II*, Firth ed. (1913–15), 1137. The cross-section of the nationalities involved is given in the lists of sick soldiers left by William at Exeter, Devon RO, Exeter corporation archives, Misc. Papers, Box 6.

7. Add. 41805 ff. 54, 154. The Bishop of London was, of course, Compton one of the 'Immortal Seven'.

8. Robert Ferguson, *The History of the Revolution* (1706 ed.), 2; *The Memoirs of Sir John Reresby*, ed. A. Browning (Glasgow, 1936) compute the number of Roman Catholics in the Dutch army as about equal to that in James II's (p. 553).

9. Devon RO, Courtenay of Powderham mss, W.W. to Sir William Courtenay, Utrecht 8 Jan. 1687/8, Add. 3510/1.

10. *HC 1660–1690*, ii. 144–6. Sir William's sons, Francis and George, who were later Tory M.P.s are reported to have joined the Prince at Exeter, but this is in an inaccurate list which states that the dean had joined the insurgents (*HMC 7th Rep.*, 416).

11. Add. 41805, ff. 129, 160.

12. Add. 63780 f. 79; Add. 41805 ff. 168, 207; Add. 4194 ff. 404, 412.

13. G. Oliver, *The Lives of the Bishops of Exeter* (Exeter 1861), 156–7; *Hist. Exeter*, 144.

14. Oliver, *Hist. Exeter*, 144–5; *HMC Exeter*, 184–5; Add. 41805 f. 407.

15. Add. 4194 f. 404; Japiske, *Correspondentie*, xxviii (1937), 55.

16. Oliver, *Hist. Exeter*, 145; Add. 4194 ff. 408, 426.

17. Gilbert Burnet, *History of his Own Time* (6 vols. Oxford 1833), iii. 330.

18. Sir John Dalrymple, *Memoirs of Great Britain and Ireland* (3 vols. 1790), ii. Bk vi. Pt. 1, 195–6; Macaulay, 1140.

19. Add. 25347 f. 114; Add. 4194 f. 417; Add. 41805 ff. 201, 207; Add. 63780 f. 79.

20. Dalrymple, ii. Bk. vi. Pt. 1, 196; T. Bruce, *Earl of Ailesbury Memoirs*, ed. W. E. Buckley (2 vols. Roxburgh Club, 1890), ii. 186.

21. Burnet, iii. 337; *Correspondentie* xxviii. 65, 57–8.

22. *Reresby Mems*, 547, 553; *The Correspondence of Henry Hyde, Earl of Clarendon . . . with the Diary*, ed. S. W. Singer (2 vols. 1828) ii. 238. For Seymour's views on the Dutch getting the better of English woollen trade see E. Cruickshanks, 'Religion and Royal Succession', in *Britain in the First Age of Party 1680–1750*, ed. C. Jones (1987), 29.

23. Ironically enough, Lord Bath and his son John Granville were dismissed from all their offices after accusations of being involved in the Fenwick Plot. In Parliament, John Granville denied his or his father's involvement, but he attended Fenwick on the scaffold and helped him to die.

24. *HMC Exeter*, 219–21, 227; Devon RO, Exeter corporation archives, Misc. Papers, Box 6.

25. Add. 63780 f. 81.

26. Japiske, *Correspondentie* xxviii, 73.

27. John Childs, *The Army, James II and the Glorious Revolution* (Manchester, 1980), ch. 8.

28. Dalrymple ii. Bk vi. Pt. 1, 214, *Reresby Mems.*, 547.

29. *CJ*. x. 49.

30. Burnet, iii. 302–3; A. Browning, *Thomas Osborne, Earl of Danby* (3 vols., Glasgow 1944–51), i. ch. 17; J. P. Kenyon, *The Nobility in the Revolution of 1688* (Hull, 1963), 13.

31. D. Hosford, *Nottingham, Nobles and the North* (Hamden, Connecticut, 1976), 67, 83.

32. Add. 28053 f. 353.

33. *Reresby Mems.*, 525–31; Browning, *Danby* i. 400–1; Add. 63780 f. 96; *HMC 7th Rep.*, 417, 420; Add. 41850 f. 241; Add. 28053 f. 362.

34. *Autobiography and Letters of Thomas Comber* (Surtees Soc. clvi., 1946) pp. l–lvii.

35. *Reresby Mems.*, 532.

36. BL Egerton 3336 ff. 18–19.

37. *Memoirs of Nathaniel, Lord Crewe*, ed. A. Clarke (Camden Miscellany ix, 1893), 30.

38. *HMC 5th Rep.*, 198; *HC 1660–1690* i. 387.

39. Add. 19253 ff. 167–8; *Letters of Philip, Second Earl of Chesterfield* (1832), 338–9.

40. Cruickshanks, in *Britain in the First Age of Party* ed. C. Jones, 24.

41. Hosford, 114; Add. 28053 f. 275.

42. Add. 15953 ff. 161, 162, 169 and unfoliated notes by Lord Chesterfield at end of letterbook.

43. *HMC Kenyon*, 199, 201, 208, 210; Add. 41805 f. 136; W. A. Speck, *Reluctant Revolutionaries. Englishmen and the Revolution of 1688*, (1988), 7.

44. *HMC Kenyon*, 202; Add. 41805 f. 234.

45. Add. 38695 ff. 86, 92, 100; *HMC Kenyon*, 202, 205, 207; Hosford, 87; G. Ormerod, *The History of the County Palatine of Chester* (3 vols. 1882),

i. 248; W. Denton to Sir R. Verney, 4 Dec. 1688, quoted in G. Molineux, *Memoir of the Molineux Family* (1882), 22; *HMC 7th Rep.* 502.

46. Add. 38695 ff. 100, 103; Add. 33589 f. 300; *HMC Kenyon*, 211.

47. Cheshire RO, Shakerley mss. Sir Richard Middleton of Chirck to Peter Shakerley, 14–15 Dec. 1688; Thomas Fairfax to John Darcy, York 15 Dec. 1688.

48. Add. 38695 ff. 106, 112, 134.

49. Dr. Williams Lib. Morrice enter'ing bk. Q, 556. *HMC Kenyon*, 222; N. Luttrell, *Brief Historical Relation of State Affairs* (6 vols. Oxford, 1857) i. 532.

50. *HC 1660–1690*, ii. 386–7.

51. *The Remains of Dennis Granville*, Surtees Soc. xlvii (1865), 147.

52. *The Remains of Dennis Granville*, Surtees Soc. xxxvii (1860), pp. xxxiv–xxxv.

53. Surtees Soc. xxxvii., p. xxxvi.

54. Surtees Soc. xxxvii., 45–47.

55. Surtees Soc. xxxvii., pp. xxxvii–xxxviii.

56. Surtees Soc. xxxvii., p. 70; *DNB* v., 79–81. *HC 1660–1690*, iii. 535.

57. Surtees Soc. xxxvii., 34, 45, 59, 70.

58. Surtees Soc. xxxvii., 96, 108, 122.

59. Surtees Soc. xxxvii., 76.

60. *A View from the Court of St. Germain, from the year 1690 to 95, with an account of the entertainment Protestants meet with them. Directed to the Malcontent Protestants of England* [by John Macky], 1696.

61. I have benefited from discussing this matter with Professor Bruno Neveu.

62. Surtees Soc. xxxvii., p. xxxix, 208; xlvii, pp. 208–10.

63. Manuscript letters bound in BL copy of Dennis Granville, *The Resigned and the Resolved Christian* (1701).

64. Surtees Soc. xlvii., 207, 210–1.

65. R. Granville, *The History of the Granville Family* (Exeter, 1895) 381.

66. Robert Masters, *Memoirs of the Life and Writings of Rev. Thomas Baker of St. John's College, Cambridge* (1784), 1–2, 5, 7, 94, 99, 136. I am obliged to Dr. J. C. D. Clark for information on Baker's career in Cambridge.

4

LONDON CROWDS AND THE REVOLUTION OF 1688*

Tim Harris

As is well known, there was extensive crowd unrest in London in the later part of 1688 as Londoners took to the streets to demonstrate their hostility towards the pro-Catholic policies of James II. Normally these disturbances have been seen in a Whig context. William Sachse, in his famous article on the mob and the Revolution, although in general sceptical about how politically-minded the crowds were, saw a continuity between the anti-Catholic incidents of 1688 and the activities of the Exclusionist crowds at the time of the Popish Plot, and what little evidence he found of mob incitement at the time of the Revolution came from Whig leaders, such as Lord Lovelace and Hugh Speke. Most others would agree that ordinary Londoners were overwhelmingly Whig in sympathy at this time. Throughout the 1680s it was the Whigs who were the party of the people, advocating reforms which would enhance the populist element in government, whether at the local or national level. Since by the early eighteenth century the London crowd appears to have been predominantly Tory in sympathy, it is thought that a fundamental transformation in popular political attitudes took place in the years after William's accession.[1]

Such a view, I believe, is unsatisfactory in a number respects. In fact, there was no Whig consensus in London during the Exclusion Crisis, since Londoners were bitterly divided along Whig-Tory lines. If anything public opinion was turning against the Whigs in the early 1680s, and by the time of James's accession the Whig threat had been largely contained in London. Collective unrest only began to break out again in the capital, which it did from 1686, because James had alienated those types who had been loyal to the Crown in the last years of his brother's reign. In this respect, it is better to see much of the crowd agitation of James's reign in a Tory, rather than a Whig, context; indeed, as will be seen, many of the crowds seem to have been encouraged, at least indirectly, by members of the Tory-Anglican establishment. In stressing the Tory dimension,

44

I do not wish to downplay the significance of Whig disaffection at the time of the Revolution; by the end of 1688 most Londoners, Whig and Tory, had come to unite in rejection of James's catholicizing policies. I shall, however, argue that no genuine consensus emerged at the level of crowd politics, and that once James was gone, the old divisions between Tory-Anglicans and Whig-Nonconformists soon reappeared.

In order to understand the crowd agitation that broke out in James II's reign, it is necessary to appreciate certain features of the dimensions of street politics in the capital during the Exclusion Crisis.[2] Much of the activity of the Whig crowds, of course, reflected a deep-seated hostility towards Popery (witness the famous Pope-burnings of 5 and 17 November) and explicit opposition to the Duke of York's succession. Yet it is important to recognize the close associations of the Whig platform with the cause of Dissent. Many of the Whig leaders were committed supporters of religious toleration for Protestant Non-conformists and fierce critics of the High-Church establishment, whilst their propaganda campaign was run predominantly by Dissenters. Some of their propaganda revealed a distinctive pro-Nonconformist bias and was often critical of the High-Anglican clergy, especially the bishops.[3] Dissenters were particularly active in promoting the Whig cause in the streets, and sometimes Whig crowd activity took on a definite anti-episcopalian flavour, as on Gunpowder Treason Day, 1682, when a pro-Monmouth crowd, amongst other things, ritualistically destroyed the sign of the Mitre at Stock's Market.[4] Indeed, to a large degree, popular Whiggism grew out of a deeply rooted tradition of anti-episcopalianism in the capital, the roots of which can be traced back to the 1660s and before.

These close associations of the Whigs with the cause of Dissent were exploited by Tory propagandists and the High-Church clergy. In their view, Nonconformists and Papists were equally as bad, since both threatened to undermine the Church and State as established by law. There were a number of anti-Exclusionist demonstrations in London during the early 1680s, as crowds gathered to demonstrate their support not only for the Duke of York but also for the Established Church, and their hostility towards Nonconformists. What must be stressed is that the Tories were as anti-Catholic as the Whigs. For example, one group of Tory apprentices from the Strand, who planned to celebrate Charles II's birthday in 1680 by burning the Rump, believed there were two plots against the 'King and his Government, and Protestant Religion, as it is now established by Law', one 'by the Papists, and the other by the Presbyterians', and they sought 'the confusion of both Papists and

Presbyterians'.[5] Tories even appropriated the anti-Catholic calendar, burning effigies of Jack Presbyter on 5 November 1681.[6] Support for the Established Church also entailed support for the bishops. Tory propaganda was often explicitly pro-episcopalian. In one of the rare cases of Tory seditious words, which was prosecuted whilst the Whigs dominated the London courts, we find a Westminster man expressing his concern that, if the Whigs were successful, 'ere long, noe bishopps should weare lawne sleeves, nor the King's armes stand in any churches'.[7]

The Crown eventually assured itself control of the capital through its attack on London's political autonomy — the *quo warranto* proceedings against the City's charter of 1683 and the subsequent purges of the livery companies — which destroyed the Whig power base and firmly established Tory-Anglican predominance. Nevertheless, public opinion genuinely seems to have been turning against the Whigs and Nonconformists in the later years of Charles II's reign.[8] The Tories gained a majority on the Common Council after the elections of December 1681, elections at which London's numerous body of freemen could vote, and that majority increased the following year after Nonconformists had been excluded from voting.[9] More and more Londoners came to accept the need for a strict enforcement of the penal laws in the 1680s to eradicate the Whig and Nonconformist threat, especially after the revelations of the Rye House Plot in 1683. Some of the more moderate clergy thought the anti-Nonconformist reaction was going too far, and began to express concern about the excessive hostility their parishioners showed towards the Dissenters.[10] The Whig and Nonconformist challenge was successfully contained by the local, amateur peace-keeping forces, and never once did Charles II need to have recourse to the army to maintain order in the streets. The trained bands, who in the past had often shown themselves reluctant to act against public opinion, were used successfully to police the Whig crowds during the Exclusion period. It is true that efforts were made to ensure the steadfast loyalty of the officer corps, but there is very little evidence of any disaffection amongst the rank and file, who were less easy to control.[11] Even the local constables, who were notoriously reluctant to inform upon the faults of their neighbours, seemed increasingly willing to aid in the suppression of Nonconformist conventicles after 1683.[12]

Thanks to the efforts of the local peace-keeping agencies, London was kept virtually free from disorder in the years 1683–5, and James's accession in 1685 went rather smoothly in London. Although the new king was faced with a rebellion in the West Country, the capital remained quiet, and the opportunity for a popular rising based on London seems to have passed.[13] What needs to be emphasized, however, is that the strength of James's position in the capital in 1685 rested on the Crown's alliance with High-Anglican, anti-Nonconformist and anti-Catholic forces of opinion. Tories supported the Crown because they believed that the Church of England would be safer under the legitimate successor — and James had issued repeated assurances that he would protect the Church — than it would be from an alliance of Whigs and Nonconformists. They were soon to be disillusioned.

Disorder broke out again in the streets of London in April 1686, provoked by the opening of a Catholic chapel in Lime Street. The property nominally belonged to James Stamford, who as the Elector Palatine's envoy had a right to establish such a chapel for his own private use, but James was using Stamford as a way of establishing Catholic worship in the heart of the City under the cloak of legality.[14] Some youths created a disturbance when mass was held for the first time in the chapel on Sunday 18 April, one of the Catholics being dragged through the gutter. There was further trouble the following Sunday, when a crowd 'got away a cross and set it up by a pump, paying a very disorderly adoration to it with hollowing, and then going back and taking a crucifix, and saying they would have no wooden gods worshiped there'.[15]

Hostility towards Catholic worship in the City had, of course, been revealed by Whig crowds during the Exclusion Crisis.[16] Yet there are reasons to doubt whether we should see the disturbances of April 1686 in a Whig context, for if anything the cue for opposition to the chapel in Lime Street came from the leaders of the Tory-Anglican establishment in London. In late March, the Tory Lord Mayor, Sir Robert Geffery, convinced that the chapel was illegal, had ordered work on its construction to stop. He told the king that it was unprecedented for a foreign minister residing in the City to exercise the Catholic religion, and that besides, Stamford was English by birth, but James rebuked him and ordered the work to continue.[17] When the disturbances broke out, James blamed the Lord Mayor for not taking proper measures to secure the peace, and again reprimanded him before the Privy Council. The trained bands, who had been efficient in suppressing Whig and Nonconformist activity during the later years of Charles II's reign, were reluctant to act against the rioters. On the 18th, a militia man, in connivance with a local constable, allowed one of the ringleaders to escape. On the 25th, the trained bands asked the crowd what they were doing, and receiving the reply 'Only pulling down

Popery', apparently said 'if that be all, we cannot in conscience hinder'.[18] The trained bands were not completely negligent, since some arrests were made. After the 25th some of the regiments were even used to protect the Catholics on their way to mass, which led to further conflicts in the streets, the Lord Mayor having been stung into action by James's threats to use his own troops to protect the chapel. Yet significantly a number of those whom they arrested were Catholics, presumably more victims than instigators of the riots, and they were subsequently discharged by special warrant.[19]

The riots occurred at a time when there was a heightened public awareness about the issue of Popery. But unlike the Exclusion Crisis, when public concern had been stimulated by Whig, and especially Non-conformist, polemicists, now the lead was being given by the Anglican clergy. The London clergy met frequently to co-ordinate what amounted to a deliberate anti-Catholic propaganda campaign, 'managed with that concert', Burnet tells us, 'that for the most part once a week some new book, or sermon, came out, which both instructed, and animated, those who read them'. In early January, 1686, one Londoner reported that 'The Bishop of London's fame runs high in the vogue of the people. London pulpits ring strong peals against Popery'.[20] The Court seems to have held the bishop, Henry Compton, partly responsible for the disturbances of April, because of his role in encouraging opposition to James's policies, and in fact it was probably he who had prompted the Lord Mayor to take action against the chapel in Lime Street.[21] In contrast the Dissenters, virtually all sources agree, did not participate in this campaign against Popery. Not only Anglican historians such as Burnet and Echard, but also the Independent divine and radical Whig, Robert Ferguson, pointed to the Dissenters' failure to preach and write against the doctrines of the Church of Rome; indeed, it appears to have been a deliberate policy on the Dissenters' behalf 'to leave the Province of defending our Religion, and of detecting the falsehood of Papal Tenets, to the Pastors and Gentlemen of the Church of England'.[22]

There were further anti-Catholic demonstrations in London on 5 November that year, when Gunpowder Treason Day was commemorated with bonfires and illuminations in many parts of the capital. Hundreds of lighted candles were set up around the Monument on Fish Street Hill and along parts of London Wall, whilst elsewhere they were fixed on ropes and hung across the streets from the tops of houses. One group marched down Fleet Street in charivaresque fashion, carrying a man on their shoulders 'with hornes on his head stuck with candles'. Since the horns were the symbol of the cuckold, this ritual was presumably designed to satirize the way people worshipped 'the Whore of Babylon', as the Pope was known. It was also reported that in Warwick Lane an effigy of a Pope was carried in procession out of the Oxford Arms, although the neighbours later claimed that in reality it was the corpse of a dead maid servant, 'attended by the company and lincks'.[23]

This appears to have been the first significant commemoration of 5 November since the disturbances on Gunpowder Treason Day in 1682 and, without wishing to deny the possible involvement of Whig elements, we must again point to the defection of the Tory-Anglican interest in explaining these incidents. During the intervening period the Tory magistrates and local peace-keeping forces had effectively prevented the celebration of 5 November, and James, certainly, thought that it was the failure of the Tory magistrates to restrain 'the liberty of the populace' which accounted for the revival of demonstrations in 1686.[24] The role of the Anglican clergy in heightening the public awareness about Popery was clearly an important factor. It is significant that the previous year, when, according to Luttrell, there had been 'hardly any bonefires at night', there had also been 'little or no ringing of bells', whereas in 1686 the church bells were rung on 5 November.[25] Some of the demonstrations were centred around the parish church. One group managed to get into Lothbury Church and place a great number of candles on the church wall, locking the doors to frustrate the efforts of the constable and the watch who came to extinguish the candles, a deed presumably accomplished with the connivance of the parish officials. There were also candlelight illuminations near the church of St John Zachary in Aldersgate within. One of the largest gatherings was in the precinct of Ludgate within, which had been the location for a number of Tory demonstrations during the Exclusion Crisis.[26]

There were no more large-scale demonstrations in London until the summer of 1688, when again it was the opposition from the Church establishment to James's policies which provoked renewed crowd activity. The occasion was provided by the arrest, and subsequent trial, of the Seven Bishops for petitioning against James's second Declaration of Indulgence. Thousands gathered to express their support for the bishops as they were dispatched to the Tower on 8 June, and even the soldiers at the Tower drank the bishops' health. There were great celebrations when the bishops were released on bail the following week, the night spent making bonfires and drinking their healths. Huge crowds assembled at Westminster Hall for the trial on 29 June, and the eventual return of a not guilty verdict the next morning was greeted with 'wild huzzas and acclamations', followed by multitudes of bonfires in the evening, and in several places effigies of the Pope were burnt.[27]

Such enthusiasm for the bishops seems to be more in tune with the popular Toryism of the Exclusion period rather than popular Whiggery. Moreover, most of the Seven Bishops had in the past shown themselves to be inveterate enemies of the Nonconformists, and the keenest opposition to the Indulgence in London came from clergymen who were more troubled by the toleration it allowed Dissenters than by the use of the suspending power[28] Nevertheless, these demonstrations cannot be seen purely in Tory-Anglican terms, since the trial of the Seven Bishops marked the beginning of a temporary rapprochement between two sides which had previously been mutually antagonistic. Whereas James's first Declaration of Indulgence of 1687 had achieved a certain amount of success in winning over the support of the Dissenters, a year later, after careful courting from the Anglicans, the Nonconformists were persuaded to rally behind the bishops. For their part the bishops took their stance on the illegality of the suspending power, and their petition stressed that they did not act 'from any want of due tenderness to Dissenters, in relation to whom they are willing to come to such a temper as shall be thought fit, when that matter shall be considered and settled in Parliament and Convocation'.[29] On 23 May the London Dissenters met and decided they would not issue an address of thanks for the Indulgence, claiming that they wanted 'liberty by law'.[30] James did not lose all the Nonconformists. The Quakers did present an address of thanks. Moreover, it was the Independent divine, Stephen Lobb, who advised the King to send the bishops to the Tower.[31] But most had clearly decided to throw in in their lot with the bishops.[32] On 10 June a delegation of ten Nonconformist ministers visited the bishops in the Tower, saying 'they could not but adhear to them as men constant to the Protestant faith'.[33] Nonconformists probably did join in the demonstrations, since we are told that the Dissenters were not backward 'in showing themselves well pleased' with the acquittal of the bishops on 30 June.[34]

Nevertheless some of the crowds of June showed a degree of adulation for the bishops — kneeling down and praying out loud for them, and begging their benedictions — which it is difficult to imagine could have been shared by Dissenters and many others who had supported the Whigs during Exclusion Crisis. On 15 June the Earl of Clarendon had to rescue William Lloyd, Bishop of St Asaph, from the midst of a crowd near the house of Lords, 'the people thinking it a blessing to kiss any of these bishops' hand or garments'.[35] There was a certain amount of hostility shown to Dissenters who had collaborated with James II. According to a government source, on 15 June a crowd attacked the house of 'a Loyal Dissenter' in Watlin Street who refused to make a contribution to their bonfire, throwing a fire-ball through an upstairs window and setting the bedroom on fire.[36] It seems likely that some championed the bishops as much for their opposition to religious toleration as for their stand against the suspending power. On 1 September a correspondent to John Ellis reported that it was said that a medal had been produced, showing the Seven Bishops on one side, and on the other 'a church undermined by a Jesuit and a fanatic, with these words; "The gates of Hell shall not prevail against her!" '[37] In reality the obverse showed not a Jesuit and a Nonconformist but Jesuit and a monk seeking to destroy the church.[38] Communications research has demonstrated that people typically interpret propaganda in a way which conforms to their existing prejudices, even to the point of subconsciously misreading the message contained in the propaganda,[39] and so the way in which the imagery of the medal had become distorted through rumour suggests that some people probably did see the bishops as trying to protect the Church against Protestant Nonconformists as well as Catholics.

In the months following the release of the Seven Bishops there was a consolidation of the new alignment in politics, as Tories and Whigs, Anglicans and Nonconformists, came closer together in opposition to James's policies. The anti-Catholic agitation of the last months of 1688, I would suggest, did reflect a degree of consensus which had emerged at the level of the crowd. Yet it should be clear that no simple continuity can be assumed between the activities of the anti-Catholic crowds of late 1688 and the activities of the Whig crowds of the Exclusion period. A new unity had emerged only because James had lost the support of the very types who were loyal to the Crown during the last years of Charles II's reign, and those who had done most to bring about this transformation of public opinion were not the Whigs or the Dissenters, but the Anglican establishment. Moreover, the consensus that had emerged was in rejection of James's catholicicizing policies and the ministers responsible for them. It is far from clear whether a consensus had emerged in rejection of James as king.

A careful scrutiny of the unrest which resumed in the autumn of 1688 suggests that the crowds had fairly prescribed aims, the chief one being the suppression of Catholic worship. Usually, there was a specific incident which provoked crowd action. There was a disturbance at the Catholic chapel in Lime Street on 30 September, when a Jesuit priest, Charles Petre, was pulled from the pulpit by an angry crowd for 'scurrilously reflecting on the translation of our

Bible'.[40] A crowd returned when Petre preached the following Sunday, this time 'pulling down the Pulpit' and 'breaking the Altar'' and that day there were also attacks on the Carmelite chapel in Bucklersbury and a friary in Lincolns Inn Fields.[41] The evening of 29 October, the day of the Lord Mayor's show, often a holiday of misrule, saw a further attack on the chapel in Bucklersbury, the youths removing the altar furnishings and burning them in the streets, and another attempt on the chapel in Lime Street, which the trained bands eventually managed to repulse.[42] There were attacks on mass-houses throughout London on 11 November, prompted by rumours that 'Gridirons, Long Knives and Caldrons', were being kept for the torture of Protestants in a monastery in St John's Clerkenwell. The next day the monks at Clerkenwell started removing their effects for safe-keeping, but in the evening the two last cartloads were seized by a crowd in Holborn and burnt publicly in the streets.[43]

Following these disturbances, James ordered all Catholic chapels to be shut up, apart from those used by the royal family and foreign ambassadors, which were given the protection of a strong guard of horse and foot.[44] However, the attacks on Catholic chapels resumed in early December, provoked by the publication of William's spurious third declaration (probably penned by the Whig Hugh Speke), which warned that 'great numbers of Armed Papists' were preparing 'to make some desperate Attempts' upon the inhabitants of London and Westminster 'by Fire, or a sudden Massacre, or both'.[45] The greatest disturbances happened on the evening of 11 December, the day that James fled the capital, when huge crowds attacked all the houses where they suspected mass was said or Catholic priests were lodged, including not only the chapels which had recently been closed, but also the chapels in the private residences of some foreign ambassadors.[46] In particular, the Spanish ambassador's residency in Wild House was 'plundered of all its rich furniture, plate, money', and even its library was destroyed.[47] Not only were all kinds of furnishings removed from the various houses and burnt in the streets, but a number of buildings appear to have been almost totally demolished, down to the 'Summers, Girders and Joystes'.[48]

Some contemporary observers stressed the lawless nature of the crowds. Concerning the attack on Catholic chapels on 11 December, Sir John Bramston thought that 'some of the offenders were common theeues, and those set the boys to work first'.[49] Sachse tended to this interpretation in his study of the riots, arguing that 'it is obvious that mob demonstrations and attacks cloaked and abetted many a crime and misdemeanour on the part of the London underworld', describing the disturbances on 11 December as amounting to a night of 'near anarchy'.[50] Most recently, Robert Beddard has written of 'the indiscriminate orgy of looting and destruction' unleashed by James's flight.[51]

It is true that there was extensive destruction to property committed. The damage done to the altar furnishings of the chapel in Bucklersbury on 29 October amounted to some £400.[52] It was estimated that between £15,000 and £20,000 worth of damage was done during the attack on the Spanish ambassador's house on 11 December.[53] But this violence to property was typically carried out in a ritualistic manner, and conformed to a tradition of collective action deeply rooted in the political culture of Londoners. The furnishings were always removed from the building, and destroyed publicly, by burning, in a large street.[54] One observer recorded how on 11 December crowds 'carried all the trumpery in mock procession and triumph' before they 'bequeathed these trinkets to the flames'.[55] Oldmixon, who knew one of those involved in the riots of 11 November, thought that the 'justice' shown by the crowds on that night was 'remarkable',

> for having decreed the Furniture and Implements to the Fire, there was nothing of it plunder'd, and when some Rascals endeavour'd to purloin some part, they were immediately taken hold of, and us'd in a worse manner than the Law uses Pilferers.[56]

Burnet commented on the discipline of the crowds which attacked the Catholic chapels in early December, and even with regard to the events of 11 December he thought that 'Never was so much fury seen under so much management', since 'none were killed, no houses burnt, nor were any robberies committed'.[57] The Austrian ambassador was amazed that worse was not done on 11 December, and that no lives were lost.[58]

The pulling down of houses was a common form of collective action in London, typically directed against places where activity was carried on which was either illegal or at least offensive to the populace. It had long been a tradition for apprentices to pull down brothels on Shrove Tuesdays, and occasionally during other holidays too. In the fierce anti-sectarian reaction that accompanied the Restoration, some separatist meeting-houses were attacked in this way.[59] The pulling-down of houses was also a legal sanction which had been used by Charles II's government against illicit religious assemblies. Thus after the passing of the 1670 Conventicle Act, the Privy Council actually ordered the demolition of a number of Nonconformist meeting-houses, even sending in carpenters to do the job.[60] In late 1688, then, we find crowds invoking a legal sanction against religious assemblies which, following the failure of James's second Declaration of Indulgence, were widely regarded as being in violation of the law. When a King's Bench jury drew up a presentment concerning the riots of 11 November, it concluded that the priests and Jesuits who resided at the monastery in St John's 'then were there contrary to the lawes of the land'.[61] The crowds of early December probably believed they were afforded special licence by William's third declaration, since this not only instructed the local magistrates to disarm all Papists — an order which the Lord Mayor did execute, thus appearing to confirm its legitimacy — but further asserted that all Papists found in the possession of arms should be treated 'as Robbers, Free-booters, and Banditti', and that 'all Persons . . . found any ways aiding and assisting to them' were to 'be looked upon as Partakers of their Crimes, Enemies to the Laws, and to their Countrey'.[62]

At first glance this quasi-legal rationale does not seem to work for the attacks on the foreign ambassadors, since they were allowed to establish chapels for their own private worship. Most contemporaries regarded these attacks as a violation of the law of nations and an outrage to humanity.[63] It may have been that the crowds felt that the king's sudden flight had occasioned an interregnum, during which time the laws were temporarily in abeyance until the new government was established.[64] Yet it was clear that the ambassadors' chapels were also being used for public worship, which was of questionable legality, whilst the ambassadors had further provoked the hostility of the crowds by allowing a number of Court Catholics to store their valuable goods in their houses. Thus the crowds focused their attention first and foremost on the Spanish ambassador's residence at Wild House, the Dutch ambassador heard, because 'this was the principal House where the people went mostly to Mass, and that the said Embassador had taken considerable quantities of Property belonging to the principal Catholics under his care'.[65]

There is evidence to suggest, then, that the crowds showed a certain discrimination in their targets, and that the violence was often constrained. There was admittedly some physical violence offered to Catholic priests and worshippers. At the chapel in Bucklersbury on 11 November, Oldmixon recalled that 'a Priest sneaking off with one of the Silver Candlesticks, had his Hand, Candlestick and all, cut off, by a Goldsmith's Apprentice whom I knew'.[66] But some of the worst violence seems to have been suffered by the crowds. On 21 October two Irish soldiers, who were being teased by some youths who had seen them come to Lime Street chapel only to find it shut up that day, 'ran upon the boys with their naked swords'.[67] Soldiers who were sent to suppress the disturbance of 11 November, were so provoked by the crowds that they opened fire, killing at least four, and wounding several others.[68]

Those who had served James in his attempt to promote the interests of Catholics were singled out for attention by the populace. On the night of the acquittal of the Seven Bishops, crowds made bonfires outside the houses of all the Catholic peers in London, soliciting contributions for them from their victims. The house of the Earl of Salisbury was attacked when, instead of paying up, he ordered his servants to fire on the crowd, thereby killing a beadle who had come to put out the fire.[69] In October, Sir William Williams, the prosecutor at the trial of the Seven Bishops, had his chamber windows in Grays Inn 'broken very much one night, and reflecting inscriptions fixt over his door'.[70] Henry Hills, the King's printer, had his printing-house attacked three times in November, and again on the night of 11 December.[71] All three were recent Catholic converts. Lord Chancellor Jeffreys, taken in disguise at Wapping on 12 December, received severely intimidating treatment by crowds who threatened to 'pull him to peces', before he was eventually conveyed to safe custody in the Tower.[72] Yet there is no evidence of any hostility to James in London. During the Exclusion Crisis Whig crowds had been quite explicit in their opposition to James's title to the throne, their typical chant being 'No York, No Popish Successor', and he had even suffered harassment by hostile crowds in the streets.[73] James did receive some intimidating treatment when, along with Sir Edward Hales, he fell into the hands of a crowd at Faversham in Kent, after his attempted first flight on 11 December. But the crowd had mistaken the King, who was in disguise, for Hales's chaplain; once he was recognized, he appears to have been treated with due respect. The inhabitants of Faversham were still determined that James should not be able to make good his escape, and James himself was certainly frightened by what he described as the great insolence of the crowds which gathered outside the inn where he was being kept; yet even he realized that their anger was directed predominantly against Hales.[74]

There was, of course, the world of difference between opposing a man as king and opposing him as heir to the throne, and it is difficult to imagine that any crowds would have dared show explicit hostility to the legitimate occupant of the regal office, even if that hostility was deeply felt. Nevertheless, there is evidence which forces us to question whether those who took part in the crowd agitation of the second half of 1688 necessarily conceived of their action as being a rejection of James as king. On the day of the bishops' acquittal, several noblemen who had attended the trial provided money for the celebrating crowds, and bid them 'drink the Health of the King, the Prelates, and the Jury'.[75] When James was brought back to the capital on 16 December, after his flight and after the widescale disturbances of the past few weeks, he was given an extremely enthusiastic reception by multitudes who gathered in the streets to cheer him on his way.[76] The Whig historian, John Oldmixon, thought that the accounts of James's reception were exaggerated: 'I remember it well, that there was some shouting, by Boys, and that some of the Guards bid them hollow'.[77] According to the Williamite Tory, Edmund Bohun, in a work written as a defence of the Revolution, 'a Set of Boys' followed James through the City, 'making some Huzza's, whilst the rest of the People silently looked on', whilst in his autobiography he wrote that 'there was much gaping but no rejoicing'.[78] But others remembered the event differently. The Earl of Ailesbury, an eye-witness, recalled how the streets from Southwark to Whitehall were so crowded, 'there was scarce room for the coaches to pass through, and the balconies and windows besides were thronged, with loud acclamations beyond whatever was heard of'.[79] Most other accounts reinforce this view, adding that in the evening there were illuminations, bonfires, the ringing of bells, and other public demonstrations of joy, which, as James himself wrote, made his return seem 'liker a day of tryumph than humiliation'.[80] Bramston thought that 'the people huzzainge as he came, put hopes into his Majestie that the anger was not at his person, but at his religion'.[81]

This is not to deny that there was extensive public support for William. Some of the crowds on 11 December marched brandishing oranges on the tops of their staves.[82] When William came to St James's on 18 December, he too was greeted with large acclamations from crowds which, despite the wet weather, gathered in the streets, and likewise there were bonfires and ringing of bells in the evening.[83] It is not necessary to conclude that the mob was fickle in its sympathies; support for William as the saviour of the Protestant religion was quite compatible with support for a James who had abandoned his Catholic policies and ministers (although it was perhaps true that James's decision to surround himself with some of his former Catholic advisers on his return to Whitehall helped 'extinguish the remaining Pity of his Protestant Subjects').[84] Indeed, William's first Declaration, his invasion manifesto, blamed all the problems on James's evil counsellors; James himself was not charged with anything, and William did not demand the throne but merely a free Parliament to settle things.[85]

Attitudes towards William as a claimant to the throne, however, appear to have been somewhat ambiguous. Clearly, many did want the throne settled on William and Mary. In the City elections for the Convention Parliament on 9 January 1689, London's liverymen chose four Williamite Whigs: Robert Clayton, Patience Ward, William Love, and Thomas Pilkington.[86] The Whig peer, Lord Lovelace, was able to get 15,000 signatures to a petition urging that the throne be settled on William and Mary which he presented to the Convention on 2 February 1689.[87] Yet other commentators noted a more lukewarm attitude towards William. On 31 January, which had been declared a day of thanksgiving for the Prince of Orange and the delivery of the nation from Popery and slavery, 'it was observed', Sir John Reresby informs us, 'that the rejoiceing was not soe great either by ringing of bels or makeing of bonefires as was expected in the citty of London, soe mutable are the minds of Englishmen that they are never long very fond of anything'. When William and Mary were proclaimed King and Queen on 13 February, there were 'bonfires at night, and other expressions of joy', but, Reresby informs us, 'a great many looked very sadly upon it'.[88]

The views of a Tory such as Reresby must, of course, be treated with caution. Nevertheless, there does seem to be a discernible decline in William's popularity from mid-December 1688.[89] Certainly there are signs that tensions were beginning to re-emerge in the weeks following James's final departure, a chief cause of division being religion. A number of Tory-Anglicans grew suspicious of William, because he seemed to give too much countenance to the Dissenters.[90] Tensions between Anglicans and Nonconformists are apparent during the elections to the Convention in January. The Tory divine, William Sherlock, noted that in London 'all old Animosities are revived', with 'no Contentions so fierce as those about Religion', and he blamed the Dissenters whom he thought were seeking to undermine the Church.[91] One Anglican tract noted that broadsides and other papers had been 'dispers'd about, tending to the villifying of the Church of England', and after recalling the stance taken by the Church during James II's reign, asked whether having 'bravely resisted all the Bombs and Assaults of Rome' the Church was now to be blown up by 'a Geneva mine'?[92] A number of tracts and sermons argued against the transference of the crown to William, and indeed it was the bishops and the High-Anglican clergy who were pressing most keenly at this time for a solution which would keep James on the throne.[93] There are thus reasons for doubting whether a popular consensus in support of William did exist in early 1689. Indeed, there are hints that the petition in his favour of early February reflected more the views of religious partisans. It was promoted by Lord Lovelace and Luke Robinson, two former members of the Whig Green Ribbon Club, both of whom were probably Nonconformists, and seems to have been motivated by hostility to the bishops for supporting a regency.[94]

Pro-William propagandists denied that there were renewed animosities between Churchmen and Dissenters, although they did accuse the Papists of trying to stir up such divisions, which in itself is interesting, since they accused Anglicans such as Sherlock, who sought to maintain James's title to the throne, of Catholicism.[95] Yet if tensions between Anglicans and Nonconformists were still a little muted because of the crisis provoked by James's promotion of Popery, a year after the Revolution they had certainly re-emerged as the major theme in London politics. By now there was definite anxiety about the security of the Church of England under a Calvinist ruler, especially after the Toleration Act of 1689 which had broken the Anglican monopoly of worship. What is noticeable is the strength of the Tory-Anglican position at this time. Bishop Compton and the parochial clergy made religion a critical issue in the parliamentary elections of February 1690, and as a result the four Whig members who had represented the City in the Convention were defeated by four Churchmen.[96] In the Common Council elections which took place in June, the Tories were able to take advantage of a fierce anti-Nonconformist backlash amongst the freemen electorate and return three Common Councilmen to every two Whigs. Significantly, the Whigs at this time were still standing on a radical populist platform. Indeed, one of the reasons why the Whigs abandoned their programme for radical constitutional reform in the City was the shock realization they received in 1690 that enhancing the political voice of the London populace would actually work to the Tories' advantage.[97]

When we look at the pattern to popular politics which emerges in London during the years after the Revolution, then, it is clear that the basic tensions between Tory-Anglicans and Whig-Nonconformists, which had been there during the Exclusion Crisis, survived. This is not to deny that there was some realignment. Quakers had gained more from the toleration won under James than they were to under the Toleration Act of 1689, and some did become Jacobites, amongst them William Penn.[98] It is less easy to get at rank and file Quaker Jacobitism, but there are some examples of Quakers being charged with speaking seditious words against William's government in the early years of the new regime.[99] Some radical Whigs and Nonconformists, disillusioned with the conservatism of the Revolution, did turn to Jacobitism, a notable example here being Robert Ferguson.[100] Economic dislocation caused by William's war was another cause of alienation from the government which potentially could cut across the old party alignments. A Jacobite broadside of August 1689, addressed 'to the Brave Apprentices, Journey-men, and Honest Porters, Labourers, and others', rehearsed the typical argument that 'the Dutch have got all our Trade abroad, while an Army of them drain the Treasure, and devour our Goods at home'. It conceded that James II 'did too many hard things; but we had no such Taxes under him', and urged people to 'assist your Old Master' and 'kick these Damn'd Dutch Tubs out of the nation'.[101]

However, the degree of realignment should not, in my opinion, be exaggerated, although further research is still needed to establish fully the contours of street politics in London in the reigns of William and Anne. Most is known about the 1710s, when the Tory/Whig divide, centring around the issues of Dissent and the security of the Established Church, is particularly marked.[102] Given the state of present research, we must be wary of positing too simple a continuity in crowd politics between the Exclusion Crisis and the Hanoverian Succession. But the view of the Revolution as marking a major watershed in popular political sympathies in the capital, with Londoners being predominantly Whig in sympathy until then and increasingly Tory thereafter, must certainly be modified. Toryism had strong roots in London political culture in the 1680s. Recognizing this not only fundamentally alters our perspective on the crowd unrest in London during the reign of James II, to which there was, I believe, a crucial Tory dimension; it also, I would suggest, makes it easier to understand why grass-roots Toryism was so strong in London after the Revolution.

NOTES

*I should like to thank Eveline Cruickshanks and John Miller for their comments and criticisms on an earlier draft of this paper.

1. William L. Sachse, 'The Mob and the Revolution of 1688', *Journal of British Studies*, iv. (1964), 23–40; Gary S. De Krey, 'Political Radicalism in London after the Glorious Revolution', *Journal of Modern History*, lv. (1983), 585–617; Gary S. De Krey, *A Fractured Society: The Politics of London in the First Age of Party 1688–1715* (Oxford, 1985).

2. The themes addressed in this and the following paragraph are explored fully in Tim Harris, *London Crowds in the Reign of Charles II: Politics and Propaganda from the Restoration until the Exclusion Crisis* (Cambridge, 1987), chs. 5, 6, 7.

3. See, for example: *The Contents (Hats for Caps) Contented* (1680); *A Prospect of a Popish Successor, Displayed by Hell-Bred Cruelty* (1681).

4. *CSP Dom., 1682*, 528–9.

5. *Mercurius Civicus*, 24 Mar. 1680.

6. *Loyal Protestant Intelligence*, no. 74, 8 Nov. 1681.

7. Greater London Record Office, MJ/SBB/380, p. 52.

8. This question is explored in full in my 'Was the Tory Reaction Popular?', *London Journal*, xiii (1988), 106–20.

9. Arthur G. Smith, 'London and the Crown, 1681–1685', unpublished Wisconsin PhD thesis (1967), 24, 129, 211–12, 218–19, and appendix, tables 4, 5. It has been estimated that some 80% or more of the City's 20,000 householders were freemen who could vote in municipal elections. See De Krey, *Fractured Society*, 40–1.

10. Edward Fowler, *A Discourse of Offences* (1683), 26; Edward Fowler, *A Sermon Preached Before the Judges* (1681), 28–9; Benjamin Hoffman, *Some Considerations of the Present Use* (1683), 21–2.

11. David Allen, 'The Role of the London Trained Bands in the Exclusion Crisis, 1678–1681', *EHR*, lxxxvii. (1972), 287–303; Smith, 'London and the Crown', 228.

12. John Hilton, *The Conventicle Courant*, no. 29, 31 Jan.–7 Feb. 1682/3

13. Harris, 'Was the Tory Reaction Popular?'.

14. Gregory Macdonald, 'The Lime Street Chapel (1686–88), Part I', *Dublin Review*, clxxx. (1927), 253–65.

15. *The Ellis Correspondence, 1686–1688*, ed. G. A. Ellis (2 vols., 1829), i. 111–12, 118; Narcissus Luttrell, *A Brief Historical Relation of State Affairs from September, 1678, to April, 1714* (6 vols., Oxford, 1857), i. 375; Dr Williams's Library, Roger Morrice, Entring Book [hereafter Morrice], i. 531; T. B. Macaulay, *The History of England from the Accession of James the Second*, ed. Firth (6 vols., 1913–15), ii. 754; John Miller, 'The Militia and the Army in the Reign of James II', *Historical Journal*, xvi (1973), 666.

16. Library of Congress, MS 18,124, VIII, f. 98.

17. Add. 34,508, ff. 110–11; Add. 4182, f. 66; *Ellis Corr.*, i. 83–4.

18. *Ellis Corr.*, i. 111, 118–19; Luttrell, i. 375.

19. Add. 34,508, ff. 112–13; Morrice, 3 I, 531, 532.

20. Gilbert Burnet, *History of His Own Time* (1838), 430; Richard Kidder, *Life*, ed. A. E. Robinson (1924), 37; *Ellis Corr.*, i. 3; Laurence Echard, *The History of England* (3 vols., 1707–18), iii., 799–800; Henry Hyde, Earl of Clarendon, *Correspondence*, ed. S. W. Singer (2 vols., 1828), i. 258.

21. Gregory Macdonald, 'The Lime Street Chapel, Part II', *Dublin Review*, clxxxi. (1927), 1; J. R. Jones, *The Revolution of 1688 in England* (1972), 70.

22. [Robert Ferguson], *A Representation of the Threatening Dangers* (1689), 46. Cf. Edmund Calamy, *An Abridgment of Mr Baxter's History of His Life and Times* (2 vols., 1713), i. 373, note. According to Edward Gee, *The Catalogue of All Discourses Published against Popery* (1689), Nonconformists published 3 books against Popery in James II's reign, compared to 228 by members of the Church of England.

23. Corporation of London Record Office [hereafter CLRO], Shelf 552, MS Box 3, no. 5.

24. *Ellis Corr.*, i. 180–1; Add., 34,508, f. 135.

25. Luttrell, i. 362, 388.

26. CLRO, Shelf 552, MS Box 3, no. 5; Harris, *London Crowds*, 170–1, 219.

27. Add. 34,510, ff. 126, 129–30, 134, 138–9; Add. 34,515, ff. 82, 88; Burnet, 469–70; *HMC Portland*, iii, 410; Echard, iii, 861, 868; *Ellis Corr.*, ii, 11–12; Clarendon, ii, 177, 179; Sir John Bramston, *Autobiography*, ed. P. Braybrooke (1845), 309; Thomas Bruce, Earl of Ailesbury, *Memoirs*, (2 vols., 1890), i, 170; *Hatton Correspondence*, ed. E. M. Thompson (2 vols., 1878), ii, 81; John Evelyn, *Diary*, ed. E. S. De Beer (6 vols., Oxford, 1955), iv, 588; Macaulay, ii, 1006–7, 1016, 1032–4.

28. Roger Thomas, 'The Seven Bishops and their Petition, 18 May 1688', *Journal of Ecclesiatical History*, xii. (1961), 59, 61; G. V. Bennett, 'The Seven Bishops: A Reconsideration', in D. Baker, ed., *Religious Motivation: Biographical and Sociological Problems for the Church Historian* (Studies in Church History XV, Oxford, 1978), 267–87.

29. J. P. Kenyon, *The Stuart Constitution 1603–1688* (Cambridge, 1966), doc. 126, p. 442.

30. J. R. Western, *Monarchy and Revolution* (1972), 233.

31. *London Gazette*, no. 2354, 7–11 June 1688; Burnet, 468.

32. Add. 34,512, ff. 82–3.

33. Sir John Reresby, *Memoirs*, ed. A. Browning (Glasgow, 1936), 500; Thomas, 68–70.

34. A. C. Edwards (ed.), *English History from Essex Sources, 1550–1750* (Chelmsford, 1952), 107.

35. Clarendon, ii, 177. See references in footnote 27 above.

36. *Publick Occurrences*, no. 19, 26 June 1688.

37. *Ellis Corr.*, ii, 157.

38. J. R. S. Whiting, *Commemorative Medals. A Medallic History of Britain, from Tudor Times to the Present Day* (Newton Abbot, 1972), 74, 77.

39. Eunice Cooper and Marie Jahoda, 'The Evasion of Propaganda: How Prejudiced People Respond to Anti-Prejudice Propaganda', *Journal of Psychology*, xxxiii (1947), 15–25.

40. Luttrell, i, 465, Evelyn, iv, 599; Add. 34,512, ff. 108–9.

41. Add. 38,175, f. 140; Add. 34,510, f. 154; *HMC 12th Report*, VII, 214; Luttrell, i, 467; *Ellis Corr.*, ii, 240; *Hatton Corr.*, ii, 95.

42. Morrice, ii, 310; Add. 34,510, f. 161; Evelyn, iv, 602; Luttrell, i, 472; *HMC 14th Report*, IX, 448; *Ellis Corr.*, ii, 269.

43. Add. 34,487, f. 35; Add. 34,510, f. 173; *Ellis Corr.*, ii, 291–2; *Hatton Corr.*, ii, 99–100; Morrice, ii, 317; John Oldmixon, *The History of England during the Reign of the Royal House of Stuart* (1730), 757; Luttrell, i, 474; Bramston, 332; Miller, 673–4.

44. Luttrell, i, 475; Bramston, 332.

45. Edmund Bohun, *The History of the Desertion* (1689), 88; Burnet, 503; Morrice, ii, 348; *DNB*, sub. Hugh Speke.

46. Bramston, 339–40; Burnet, 505. Detailed accounts of these riots can be found in Macaulay, iii, 1206–8; Sachse, 28–31; Miller, 676.

47. *Ellis Corr.*, ii, 351; *Universal Intelligence*, no. 2, 11–15 Dec. 1688; Evelyn, iv, 610.

48. Morrice, ii, 351.

49. Bramston, 340.

50. Sachse, 26, 35.

51. Robert Beddard, 'Anti-Popery and the London Mob, 1688', *History Today*, xxxviii (July, 1988), 36.

52. Morrice, ii, 310.

53. *Ellis Corr.*, ii, 351; *Universal Intelligence*, no. 2, 11–15 Dec. 1688.

54. Cf. the actions of the London weavers in the riots against engine-looms in 1675: Harris, *London Crowds*, 196.

55. *Ellis Corr.*, ii, 350–1.

56. Oldmixon, 757. Oldmixon, then a youth of 15, appears to have been present in London in late 1688 — ibid., 762 — and it is conceivable that he was involved in some of the disturbances.

57. Burnet, 503, 505.

58. La Marquise Campana de Cavelli, *Les Derniers Stuarts a Saint-Germain-en-Laye* (2 vols., 1871), ii, 423.

59. Harris, *London Crowds*, 22–4, 52, 82–91; Keith Lindley, 'Riot Prevention and Control in Early Stuart London', *Transactions of the Royal Historical Society*, xxxiii. (1983), 109–10. Cf. The actions taken by the Sacheverell rioters in 1710: Geoffrey Holmes, *The Trial of Doctor Sacheverell* (1973), ch. 7.

60. W. C. Braithwaite, *The Second Period of Quakerism* (Cambridge, 1961), 75–6.

61. Morrice, ii, 323. Cf. Luttrell, i, 477, who reports that the inquest into the death of those who were killed on 11 November concluded that the rioters were 'loyal persons' who 'resorted to the mass house . . . in order to disturb traytors and enemies to the nation'.

62. Bohun, *History of the Desertion*, 87–8; Burnet, 503.

63. *Ellis Corr.*, ii, 351; *A Dialogue Between Dick and Tom* (1689), 8.

64. *Dialogue Between Dick and Tom*, 8.

65. Add. 34,510, f. 198; J. S. Clarke (ed.), *The Life of James II* (2 vols., 1816), ii, 257; Bramston, 339–40; Reresby, 537; Add. 34,487, f. 50; Campana de Cavelli, ii, 422; Echard, iii, 932. Cf. Sachse, 29–30; Miller, 676 and footnote 105.

66. Oldmixon, 757.

67. *HMC 12th Report*, VII, 216–7; *HMC 5th Report*, 379.

68. Morrice, ii, 317; Add. 34,487, f. 35; Bramston, 332; Miller, 674 and footnote 94.

69. Add. 34,515, f. 88; *HMC Portland*, iii, 414.

70. Luttrell, i, 468.

71. *CSP Dom., 1687–9*, 348; *English Currant*, no. 2, 12–14 Dec. 1688; *Ellis Corr.*, ii, 351.

72. *HMC 11th Report*, V, 232; *HMC, 12th Report*, VII, 228; Echard, iii, 932; *Universal Intelligence*, no. 2, 11–15 Dec. 1688; *English Currant*, no. 2, 12–14 Dec. 1688; *A Full Account of the Apprehending of the Lord Chancellor in Wapping* (1688).

73. Harris, *London Crowds*, 157–8, 181–2, 186.

74. 'Récit du Départ du Roi Jacques II D'Angleterre, Ecrit de sa Main', in Sir James Mackintosh, *History of the Revolution in England in 1688* (1834),

706; Echard, iii, 935; *Hatton Corr.*, ii, 123; Burnet, 505; Ailesbury, i, 208. Cf. Sachse, 34. At about the same time, Hales's house near Canterbury was attacked by a crowd.

75. Add. 34,510, f. 138.

76. Sachse relegated this important episode to a brief footnote: p. 34, footnote 57.

77. Oldmixon, 762.

78. Bohun, *History of the Desertion*, 100; Edmund Bohun, *Diary and Autobiography*, ed. S. Wilton Rix (Beccles, 1853), 82.

79. Ailesbury, i, 214.

80. *Life of James II*, ii, 262; 'Récit du Départ du Roi Jacques II', 707; Clarendon, ii, 230; *HMC 11th Report*, V, 236; *HMC 12th Report*, VII, 230; *Ellis Corr.*, ii, 362–3; *Universal Intelligence*, no. 3, 15–18 Dec. 1688; *London Courant*, no. 3, 15–18 Dec. 1688; *London Mercury or Moderate Intelligencer*, no. 2, 15–18 Dec. 1688; Burnet, 506; Reresby, 540.

81. Bramston, 340. Cf. Campana de Cavelli, ii, 436.

82. *Ellis Corr.*, ii, 350; Macaulay, iii, 1232.

83. Luttrell, i, 489; *English Currant*, no. 3, 14–19 Dec. 1688; Bohun, *History of the Desertion*, 105; Bohun, *Autobiography*, 82; Reresby, 541; Burnet, 508.

84. Echard, iii, 936.

85. *Declaration of His Highnes William Henry, Prince of Orange, of the Reasons Inducing Him to Appear in Armes in the Kingdome of England* (The Hague, 1688).

86. Clarendon, ii, 243.

87. Lois G. Schwoerer, *The Declaration of Rights, 1689* (Baltimore, 1981), 130, 210–11.

88. Reresby, 546–7, 554. Cf. Schwoerer, 252–3, 257, who sees the celebrations on 13 February more in a Nonconformist than an Anglican context.

89. Schwoerer, 142–4.

90. Clarendon, ii, 238; Reresby, 541.

91. William Sherlock, *A Letter to a Member of the Convention* (Edinburgh, 1689), 1, 3.

92. *Dialogue Between Dick and Tom*, 10–17.

93. Schwoerer, 146; Evelyn, iv, 614.

94. Schwoerer, 130, 211, 337 footnote 30, 355 footnote 66; Pepysian Library, Magdalene College, Cambridge, Pepys Miscellanies, vii, 489–91; *DNB*, sub. John Lovelace.

95. *London Courant*, no. 7, 29 Dec. 1688–1 Jan. 1689; *An Answer of a Letter to a Member of the Convention* (Edinburgh, 1689), printed with Sherlock, *Letter*, 5–6; *An Answer to the Author of the Letter to a Member of the Convention* (1689), 1, 3.

96. Henry Horwitz, 'The General Election of 1690', *Journal of British Studies*, xi. (1971), 84.

97. De Krey, *Fractured Society*, ch. 2.

98. Pierre Burger, 'Spymaster to Louis XIV: A Study of the Papers of the Abbé Eusèbe Renaudot', in Eveline Cruickshanks, ed., *Ideology and Conspiracy: Aspects of Jacobitism, 1689–1759* (Edinburgh, 1982), 114.

99. CLRO, Sessions File, December 1689, rec. 3, of Thomas Tysoe, Goldsmith, of All Hallows Lumbard Street; Ibid, April 1691, ind. of William Crouch, Merchant, of St Katherine Creechurch. For their identification as Quakers, see Gary S. De Krey, 'Trade, Religion, and Politics in London in the Reign of William III', unpub. Princeton University PhD thesis (1978), Appendix IV, 528–606.

100. Mark Goldie, 'The Roots of True Whiggism 1688–94', *History of Political Thought*, i. (1980), 228–9.

101. *A Copy of a Trayteros Libell which was Printed and Cast about the Streets, August 1689* (1689).

102. Geoffrey Holmes, 'The Sacheverell Riots: The Crowd and the Church in Early Eighteenth-Century London', *Past and Present*, 72 (1976), 55–85; Nicholas Rogers, 'Popular Protest in Early Hanoverian London', *Past and Present*, 79 (1978), 70–100. Cf. Paul Monod, '"For the King to Enjoy His Own Again": Jacobite Political Culture in England, 1688–1788', unpublished Yale Phd thesis (1985), p. 305, who argues, *pace* Rogers, that the Whigs still enjoyed a plebeian constituency of support at the time of the Hanoverian Succession, though mainly amongst Dissenting types.

5

THE RELUCTANT REVOLUTIONARIES: SCOTLAND IN 1688

Ian B. Cowan

The antecedents to the Glorious Revolution in England found few if any parallels in Scotland despite the similarity of the policies pursued by James VII in his northern kingdom. Even the birth of his son 'the Prince Royal and Stewart of Scotland' on 10 June 1688, which precipitated the succession crisis in England and led to the invitation to William of Orange to intervene by restraining, if not necessarily displacing, the king occasioned little interest north of the Border.[1] William's proclamation addressed to the Scots which echoed the corresponding English version issued on 10 October stressing the unconstitutional nature of James's rule and the threat of catholicism but silent on other ecclesiastical issues, fell on equally deaf ears.[2] Even the news of the outbreak of the revolution in England occasioned by William's landing at Torbay on 5 November brought little initial reaction among the Scots and if a number of anti-catholic riots characterised early December, only the flight of James on 23 December brought the Revolution in Scotland closer to fruition.[3]

The Scottish reluctance to rebel stemmed from a variety of reasons both political and ecclesiastical. In political terms James appeared to be impregnable and indeed enjoyed more widespread support than his brother before him. Much of this stemmed from James's inherent knowledge of the Scottish political situation which he had viewed at first-hand during his stay in Scotland as royal commissioner to parliament at the height of the Exclusion crisis which attempted to preclude his succession to the throne of England.[4] Even in this emergency, royal authority in Scotland was largely unquestioned for although there may have been mutterings in private, few, other than extreme presbyterians, publicly questioned the validity of the appointment of James duke of York as commissioner in a court in which, by an act of 1609, no catholic might be a member.[5] The passage of the Succession Act securing the right of hereditary succession and the Test Act requiring office holders to swear adherence to the protestant faith as expressed in the Scots Confession of 1560 meant various problems were soon to arise for the Confession (which contained statements totally at variance with the substance of the Test) uncompromisingly defined Christ Jesus as 'the only heid of his kirk' and further declared that the sovereign was only to be obeyed in matters 'not repugning to the worde of God'.[6] Not only was the recognition of the king's supremacy inconsistent with the Scots Confession, but the Test Act taken in conjunction with the earlier act of succession implied that James as a future catholic sovereign would become supreme governor of the protestant church. As Lord Belhaven astutely remarked, the Test Act was 'a very good act for securing our religion from one another . . . but not an act to secure our religion against a Popish or fanatical successor to the crown'.[7] Conveyed to Edinburgh castle for his pertinent remark and accused of treason, he was released only after a formal apology.[8]

The latent religious opposition to an otherwise obsequious parliament in 1681 should have alerted the duke that it was possible to put too great a strain on the obedience of the Scottish Estates. The loyalty of his Council, however, may have blinded him to this possibility for in May 1682, on his return to England after advising the Council to suppress rebellious persons and protect the orthodox clergy, the Council for its part praised the duke for 'the excellent patterns of government which wee have had from yow and for the great proffes of your kindnes to us upon all occasions'.[9] Moreover, James's first parliament after his accession to the throne, elected under the conditions prescribed and meeting during the excitement of Archibald Campbell, ninth earl of Argyll's anti-catholic rebellion in Scotland and of the duke of Monmouth's similarly motivated rising in England, was to prove exceedingly loyal despite fears to the contrary, when James warned his commissioner Queensberry 'to suffer nothing to pass to the prejudice of the Roman Catholics more than was already'.[10] Despite rumours of the king's intentions on religious issues, members of parliament evinced the most exemplary obedience, initially pledging their lives and fortunes to 'assist, support, defend and mentain king James the Seventh'.[11] In further token of their loyalty they ordered that 'all of this Nation, betuixt sixty and sixteen, armed and provyded according to their abilities, shall be in readiness for his Majesties service, where and oft as it shall be his royal pleasure to require them'.[12] As a more immediate sign of dutiful obedience parliament then proceeded to grant the excise duty to the crown for all time.[13]

Encouraged by this submissiveness and the ease with which the earl of Argyll's rebellion 'For God and Religion, against Poperie, Tyrannie, Arbitrary Government and Errestianisme' had been crushed, the king pressed on with his plans to promote catholicism by proceeding to announce the conversion of his subservient councillors, the pliant lord chancellor, James Drummond, fourth earl of Perth and of the two secretaries of state, the mischief-making John Drummond, first earl of Melfort (Perth's brother) and Alexander Stewart, fifth earl of Moray, who was rewarded by being chosen to replace the protestant William Douglas, first earl of Queensberry as commissioner in the new session of parliament in 1686.[14]

The state of euphoria which his previous successes had engendered led James to press on with his plans to benefit further his co-religionists with the recommendation to the Estates that 'others our innocent subjects, those of the Roman Catholick religion' might 'have the protections of our lawes and that security under our government which others of our subjects have, not suffering them to lye under obligations which their religion can not admitt of'.[15] Realising that some inducement might be required to achieve this goal, James also prudently announced that the opening of free trade with England would be 'oure particular care'. Even then parliament's reply was not enthusiastic, promising only to take the king's recommendations into 'serious and dutiful consideration' and with 'tendernes to their persones', it promised to 'go as great lengths therein as our conscience will allow'.[16]

Interpreting this answer in the spirit in which it had been given, the king's ministers tried to overawe this apparently intractable parliament into submission. Members of parliament who held commissions were ordered to attend to the duties of their posts, but they offered instead to tender their resignations.[17] Others who held offices under the crown were dismissed, while burgess members were threatened with an investigation into their qualifications as resident traders.[18] Attempts were made to persuade opponents to absent themselves and numerous pamphlets in favour of toleration were circulated.[19] All this was unavailing for, although the act narrowly survived its passage through the Committee of the Articles and parliament was kept in session until the middle of June 'to weary out the poorer sort, who had exhausted both their money and credit', parliament had eventually to be prorogued to prevent defeat.[20] 'The finger of God,' it was asserted by one contemporary, 'was much to be seen in the steadfastness of this Parliament, who had not one great man in publict place to oune them: and it behooved to be from some hyer principle that Noblemen, Gentlemen, Bishops and others cheerfully laid doune their places, rather than violat their consciences'.[21] The Tory parliament of James VII had shown for the first time since 1660 that there was a limit to the arbitrary power of the crown. Yet

in the overthrowal of James VII, parliament was to play no part and
the actions which it had taken in 1686 had no direct results. In the
eyes of James and his councillors parliament's action only confirmed
the view expressed in 1674 by John Maitland, second earl and duke
of Lauderdale, that 'Scots parliaments are . . . useless at the best'
and endorsed his conclusion of 1663 'that this kingdome returne to
the good old forme of government by his Majesties privie councell'.[22]
James after venting his spleen on Queensberry by removing him from
the presidency of the council, decided to follow Lauderdale's advice with
the added precaution of restructuring the Council's membership; a task
made somewhat easier by granting new members dispensation from the
Test and informing them that he had suspended the operation of the
penal laws against catholics.[23] The effectiveness of the purge was also
reinforced by a further edict which forbade municipal corporations to
elect new town councils and soon afterwards provosts were nominated
whom he authorised to choose magistrates and councillors.[24] This step
was accompanied by the dissolution of parliament, for the king intended
to summon another, in which he might rely upon support from the
burgesses.[25]

James's belief in his rectitude and in his own abilities was unshakeable.
His experience of Scottish affairs which might have proved an asset
remained unutilised and advice from others was unwelcome. His belief
in toleration appears to have been genuine, but this naive assumption
that others would share this feeling reveals how poor a politician he was.
These weaknesses were not lost, however, on other Scottish politicians
many of whom would have agreed with the judgement that James had
'nather great conduct, nor a deep reach in affairs, but was a silly man',
and in this belief they hoped to exploit these traits to their own advantage.[26] In consequence, James was open to manipulation by a series of
politicians whose advice to him was seldom disinterested. On a few basic
issues he could not be moved, but otherwise he could be manipulated and
this factor served not only to create an instability in Scottish politics,
but also to keep unscrupulous politicians loyal to his cause in the hope
that political influence could either be retained or hopefully obtained
at the expense of others. Thus, Melfort and Perth, two unprincipled
careerists who encouraged James in his most extreme policies, urging
him along on the claim that he was an absolute monarch, not only strove
to ingratiate themselves with the king, but also worked relentlessly to
undermine the influence of Queensberry whom James in deference to
their wishes dismissed in 1686 after an unremitting campaign against
him.[27]

John Campbell, first earl of Breadalbane, an intelligent but wary politician on the other hand, avoided this fate by supporting toleration in the 1686 parliament.[28] Success was, however, sometimes short-lived and the rise of George Gordon, first duke of Gordon was equally effectively blocked by the jealousy of Perth and Melfort. They too, like their royal master who suppressed his deep distrust of Scottish presbyterians when he imposed toleration in 1687, overlooked their hatred of presbyterianism to collaborate in James's policies. At least, they hoped by so doing to gain concessions for their co-religionists.[29] Others who served the king including Breadalbane, John Mackenzie, master of Tarbat and Sir John Dalrymple had no excuse other than rank opportunism.[30] Through such sycophants James ruled Scotland by means of an exceptionally unrepresentative government fittingly described as 'a strange mixture of rogues and converts to Roman Catholicism'.[31] If other politicians who were effectively barred from power by such a coalition might have been expected to resist the king's policies, it is clear that the hope of supplanting one or other of the councillors kept many equally unscrupulous rivals ostensible loyal to the crown, while others who may have contemplated rebellion may have remembered the fate of Argyll and those whose opposition had ended in exile in Holland. Even the knowledge that William of Orange had landed at Torbay brought no immediate reaction from politicians who wished to assure their own positions before committing themselves to a new master.

For the same reason established churchmen were equally unwilling to shed the status which they already enjoyed lest their privileged position be hazarded, and in the case of the presbyterians until further concessions were on offer. In this respect the catholic faction had much to lose and little to gain; certainly the Scottish catholics to whom James had shown singular favour were unlikely to assume the role of prospective revolutionaries and were instead committed to the support of a king who had steadfastly supported his co-religionists. Unfortunately for James, catholicism in Scotland was in a much weaker state than he had estimated. All in all there were perhaps only about two thousand catholics between the Moray Firth and the Solway, many of these concentrated in Dumfries-shire and in the highland areas of Aberdeen and Banff in north-east Scotland.[32] Many more, it was claimed, existed in the Highlands and Islands, but estimates sent in 1681 to the Congregation of Propaganda in Rome claiming some twelve thousand adherents in these parts are extremely unreliable, the correct figure being close to four thousand.[33] James VII's attempts to augment their numbers, however, were none too successful. Admittedly in many parts both catholics and protestants had only a superficial foothold but if the populace in some of these regions showed a greater proclivity for catholicism than protestantism it was an advantage which could not be readily exploited by the handful of priests who served the area.

The aftermath of the Popish Plot made this task even more difficult, the mission in the central and west Highlands and the Isles for a time being reduced to two priests.[34] However, with the encouragement of James and assisted with a royal grant of two hundred pounds the mission increased its strength to twelve.[35] In the new climate, some waverers who headed traditionally catholic clans — Alasdair Macdonald of Glengarry and Coll Macdonald of Keppoch — for example, were induced to embrace catholicism.[36] Clan influence possibly swayed these conversions which did not carry much personal conviction, but others were apparently prompted by a greater zeal for the faith. By 1685 Kenneth Mackenzie, fourth earl of Seaforth had not only converted, but also influenced his younger brothers John Mackenzie of Assynt and Alexander to do likewise.[37] Sir John Maclean, sent at the king's insistence for education in France in 1688 converted at the Scots College in Paris, and thereafter remained committed, as did most other converts, to the Catholic and Jacobite cause.[38] Other conversions, however, were motivated neither by clan interest nor by personal conviction but appear to have stemmed from purely self-interest. Archibald Campbell, Lord Lorne, for instance, embraced catholicism in the unrealistic hope that he would regain the Argyll estates.[39] The conversion of the master of Tarbat who hoped to gain Lewis from Mackenzie of Seaforth was not only in vain, but ill-timed, taking place in November 1688.[40] As has been observed, the cynical assumptions these conversions revealed was the belief 'that James would reverse his most important policies to please a convert or sacrifice the previous convert to the more recent'.[41]

Certainly in attempting to build up a power base on the strength of conversions, James proved singularly inconsistent. Some early converts obtained their anticipated rewards but even old established catholic families could not be certain of royal favour. The duke of Gordon obtained the governorship of Edinburgh castle in 1685, but had to wait another eight months before gaining a place in the Council and Treasury, and rose no further largely at the instigation of Perth and Melfort, who, despite their own conversions, bitterly opposed their fellow catholics.[42] Divisions of this kind did little to create a united catholic front which might have protected the king's interests north of the Border.

In other circumstances, such protection might have been more readily obtained from the established episcopal church, but here too while revolution was not on the agenda, criticism of the king's policies was at times very much to the fore. Nevertheless, the established church had become so dependent upon the state that although signs of opposition appeared over the Test act of 1681, the threat posed by the eventual succession of a catholic king was accepted by most members of the established church. Nevertheless ministers who had loyally supported the episcopal regime throughout all its previous difficulties found James's Catholicism a bitter pill to swallow. The ultra-conservative synod of Aberdeen was constrained to issue an explanation of the meaning of the Test Act after ministers had stated their objections to it. Among other features this apologia reserved for the establishment intrinsic spiritual power, permitted meetings for church discipline and for the protection of protestantism and admitted the possibility of the alteration of church government when not accomplished by arms or sedition.[43] A similar declaration was issued by the synod of Dunkeld and in the face of such protests the Council was constrained to issue their own interpretation of the Test on 3 November 1681.[44] It explained that ministers who took the Test need not swear to every proposition or clause contained in the Confession of Faith 'but only to the true protestant religion founded on the word of God . . . as it is opposit to poperie and phanatisisme'.[45] This concession which was in itself inconsistent with the declaration in the Test that it was to be taken 'in the plain genuine sense and meaning of the words, without any equivocation, mental reservation, or any manner of evasion whatsoever', had also been accompanied by the threat that those who deviated in the terminology of the oath should be 'esteemed persons disaffected to the protestant religion, and to his majesty's government'.[46]

No number of explanations and concessions could persuade some of the validity of the Test Act. Among the ministers who refused the Test, the most notable was Laurence Charteris, professor of Divinity at Edinburgh university, and his example was followed by a considerable number of ministers who were consequently deprived.[47] Just how many deprivations took place is questionable as estimates have varied between thirty and eighty.[48] Some clue to the actual number may be found, however, in the fact that many of these deprived were from the Lothians and that John Paterson, bishop of Edinburgh, stated in February 1683 that there were more recusants in the two contiguous presbyteries of Dalkeith and Haddington than in all the rest of Scotland.[49] At least seventeen ministers were ousted in these two presbyteries and, if accurate, this would favour the lesser of the two estimates, but a figure of thirty or so deprivations is probably a conservative assessment. The final count may have been nearer fifty, of whom about twenty followed the example of Gilbert Burnet, later bishop of Salisbury, and entered the Church of England, an action which has never been fully investigated.[50] Whatever the total number, the church once more had been purged of dissidents and emerged more strongly committed to the establishment and the dictates of the crown.

The church's unswerving loyalty was dutifully transferred to James VII in 1685 and thereafter continued unimpaired despite the king's overt catholicism. Indeed it appears that some episcopal ministers were even prepared to cast a blind eye at missionary activity by catholic priests in areas which had traditionally favoured that faith.[51] Catholic conversions among the magnates were met with an equally discreet silence and more positively by an injunction to the clergy not to preach on the subject of conversions, a reference in one sermon by an incumbent to 'fallen stars among us and yet they keipt their station' bringing swift retribution.[52] Even bishops were not immune from censure or even dismissal as was initially demonstrated when episcopal opposition arose during the crown's attempts to press for toleration in the 1686 parliament in which the bishop of Dunkeld imprudently stated 'old constitutions are, for their salubrity compared to old-lived men, and not rashly to be altered'; an allusion in the eyes of the chancellor to the antiquity of the laws against popery.[53] For his temerity the bishop was deprived of his see; a fate which the bishop of Ross narrowly escaped after preaching a sermon 'which scandalized the Papists extremely'.[54] To avoid further controversy, Robert Douglas the bishop of Dunblane was also forbidden to preach 'because he would not give assurance to forbear the preaching against Popery, nor show his papers'.[55] Even these salutary reminders of royal authority were insufficient to silence opposition: as in early 1687 Archbishop Alexander Cairncross of Glasgow was also deposed for allowing anti-catholic sermons to go unpunished.[56] This action far from provoking further opposition not only acted as a warning to other clergy that further criticism might prove unwise, but also as a salutary reminder that the security of the church lay with the crown, without whose protection, rival factions might triumph. The possibility of a meaningful catholic resurgence was, however, slight in comparison to that of a presbyterian revival.

For the presbyterians, revolution was not a new phenomenon as the struggle against royal authority had lasted for much of the seventeenth century. In the struggle against Charles I they had initially shared a common cause with the English parliamentarians, but had latterly fought for both Charles and his son against the Cromwellians, only to suffer conquest and military occupation. The Restoration brought independence to the Scots but little comfort to the presbyterians who found themselves yet again ranged against a state which had reimposed an episcopal establishment upon those who had favoured a presbyterian solution. In consequence, by 1663 almost one third of the ministry had either elected to leave the church or had been deprived for their failure to conform to an edict commanding ministers presented to their charges since 1649 to receive presentation from their former patrons and collation from their bishops.[57]

Some of the ousted ministers thereafter held meetings or conventicles while many of their parishioners followed their example and withdrew from their parish churches; an action which inevitably provoked government reprisals. This in turn culminated in two armed rebellions one in 1666 — the Pentland Rising, and another and more serious outbreak in 1679 which ended in the defeat of the conventicling army at Bothwell Bridge by a government army commanded by the Duke of Monmouth. Between these two incidents, a policy of offering Indulgence to non-conformists had met with only partial success and had created a rift between those able to accept some measure of state control and those who were not willing to accede to such a compromise. These differences came to a head before the battle of Bothwell Bridge in a series of declarations and counter-declarations which were to be crucial for both presbyterians and the covenanting cause.[58] One faction which was essentially clerical in its leadership, in a declaration affixed to the mercat cross of Hamilton re-affirmed the defensive nature of the rising which they averred had been occasioned by the woeful state of the land and church through the brutal execution of the laws and refusal of redress from the authorities.[59] In stressing the subjects' allegiance to the magistrates, their maintenance of the king's authority, and in their desire for a free parliament and a free General Assembly they accepted a degree of compromise and developed an appeal to presbyterianism at large which placed them nearer the Indulged than the extremists which they were destined to fight beside. Their opponents on the other hand railed against all the defectors and encroachments upon the perogatives of Jesus Christ and stressed in their declarations their abhorrence of the Indulgences and the Indulged. A king who had broken the covenant, altered the polity of the church and waged war against the godly was equally to be distrusted.[60]

Defeat at Bothwell Bridge brought these differences to a head with the extremists — the Cameronians, led by their minister Richard Cameron declaring war upon the king and the state in a series of declarations, while the moderate presbyterians, dispirited and powerless in defeat, faced continued persecution aimed at harrying their adherents back into the ranks of the established church. This policy, accompanied by the systematic withdrawal of licences granted under earlier Indulgences (including those given under a short-lived Indulgence of 1681 as a momentary attempt at conciliation following Bothwell Bridge) left the presbyterians seriously weakened, although in practice re-united with those who sought a measure of support from the state.[61] In the early 1680s concessions of this sort must have seemed a remote possibility and with the advent in 1683 of James Renwick as a preacher to the Cameronians; an event described by the moderate presbyterians as the 'great cause and occasion of all the troubles of the country', their cause declined further as persecution began to have its desired effect and dissidents reluctantly returned to the established church. The prospect of a united church at that point seemed attainable.[62]

That this in the end proved not to be so owed less to the Cameronians than to the folly of James VII who, in his desire to aid his co-religionists, was forced to include quakers and presbyterians in his concessions. If in the first Indulgence of February 1687, presbyterians were discriminated against, this was more than rectified in a second Indulgence issued in July in which all restrictions, with the exception of those against field conventicles, were lifted and leave was granted to all subjects 'to meet and serve God after their own way and manner, be it in private houses, chapels or places purposely hired or built for that use'.[63] The effect was immediate. Ministers and others released from prison were joined by exiled ministers from Holland. Many of them met in Edinburgh on 20 July and on the following day penned an address of thanks to the king. This gratitude influenced presbyterian attitudes to their catholic sovereign; further armed conflict was far from their mind; reliance on royal favour rather than revolution against royal authority was their immediate preoccupation.[64] Plans were drawn up for implementing the Indulgence and establishing of an embryonic presbyterian structure. The bitter infighting which had characterised the reception of the earlier Indulgences had all but disappeared and co-operation was henceforward to be the keynote. Presbyteries were to be established and meetings of these courts were to be convened at least once a month at which ministers were to seek advice and submit themselves to the discipline of their fellow ministers.[65] The setting up of meeting houses was also to be a co-operative venture since it was conceded that 'it cannot be expected, that there can be as many meeting houses as parishes'.[66] Provision was also made for encouraging students, licensing them and ordaining them to congregations.[67] In practice, the presbyterians set about re-erecting the body of their church in so far as this could be accomplished within the terms of the privileges conceded to them.

The gratitude shown to James by the presbyterians was not shared by the extreme Cameronians. Leaderless since the death of Richard Cameron in a skirmish and the subsequent execution of their sole remaining minister, Donald Cargill, in 1681, they had been led since 1683 by their minister James Renwick who viewed the Toleration Act as an erastian breach of Covenant and refused to accept its concessions or its terms. *A Testimony against Toleration* was transmitted to a meeting of ministers in January 1688 and the tradition of conventicling was commended by Renwick and his followers who even ventured to hold such gatherings in the vicinity of Edinburgh.[68] After one such meeting Renwick was apprehended on 1 February and after examination declared an irreconcilable opponent of the king. This position was maintained at his trail seven days later and made sentence of death inevitable. Thereafter, intensive efforts were made even by his prosecutors to gain some acknowledgement of the king's authority which might be used to mitigate the sentence. It was all to no avail, but if radical conventiclers could still expect such a fate, the ecclesiastical climate was already undergoing change. The shadow of religious rebellion had been dispelled by the Indulgences and the compromising attitude of the presbyterian ministers who were even willing to pray for a catholic king in order to retain their new-found privileges.[69] In isolation the Cameronians were revealed as a small insignificant sect who despite their spirited and sonorous declarations had no longer the ability or the resources for initiating, far less sustaining, war against the state, either to gain their objectives or to express their disapproval of James's catholicising policies. The open disapproval of the Cameronians coupled with the failure of the established church to accept their principles could not in themselves have been expected to initiate Revolution and even at this juncture decisive action by the Council might have contained the situation, but before the king's departure panic had replaced wise counsel.

On 10 December the chancellor, the earl of Perth, spurning the security of Edinburgh castle, fled to castle Drummond, leaving the Council who thereafter added several members to their secret committee, to their own devices.[70] That evening a mob sacked the abbey of Holyrood, the nave of which served as a catholic chapel royal, looted the Jesuits' quarters and schools and desecrated the tombs of Scottish kings.[71] Two days later the Council, meeting under Atholl's presidency, commissioned Breadalbane to explain the riot to James who, it was hoped, could be persuaded to abandon his pro-catholic policies and entrust the conduct of Scottish affairs, under the guidance of William of Orange, to traditional Scottish leaders.[72] The king's flight ended such hopes and revealed the venality and self-interest of many of the councillors who, as unrest swept the country, accepted a change of sovereign without any undue concern.

Mob rule, encouraged by the absence of standing forces which had been called south in anticipation of the expected invasion, rather than constitutional reform at first prevailed. Following the riot in Edinburgh, covenanting presbyterians seized the opportunity to rabble curates of the established church who before ejection from their manses and livings were forced to surrender their church keys and communion plate after being stripped of their clerical apparel; a process frequently accompanied by physical violence.[73] To much of this the Council was oblivious, its members intent only on protecting their own interests. Even the retention of Edinburgh castle by the catholic Duke of Gordon remained unchallenged on account of the bitter rivalry between Atholl and Queensberry who might have regained custody but for Atholl's intervention.[74] The departure of most of the councillors for London where office under the new regime could alone be secured, left Scotland in chaos with a privy council bereft of authority and largely ungoverned for almost three months.[75]

During this period, support for James wavered further. His ill-judged policies, his flight to France and the consequent declaration in the English Bill of Rights that he had thereby abdicated the throne allowed presbyterian politicians such as John Cunningham, tenth earl of Glencairn, William, eighteenth earl of Crawford and Sir James Montgomerie of Skelmorlie, an influence which they might have been otherwise denied.[76] A return to normality was not easily achieved for although the Council as early as 24 December had urged William to call a free parliament, this plea had to be re-iterated formally in early January 1689 when a meeting of Scots notables asked William to summon a convention, but it was not until 14 March that such a meeting took place.[77]

Although attempts had been made by the presbyterians to influence the composition of the convention, Jacobites were almost as numerous at its commencement as their opponents. However, whereas the opposition were single-minded in their resolve to dispose of James, his supporters through lack of direction and leadership were uncertain as to their best course of action. Waverers and place-seekers abounded, the narrowness of the gap between the contending parties being initially apparent in the close contest for the presidency of the assembly between William Douglas, third duke of Hamilton, representing the Williamites and John Murray, second earl of Atholl for the Jacobites, the former only narrowly winning the day.[78] Although important this result was not decisive, that moment being reserved for the reading on 16 March of letters from the rivals for the crown. That of William was a model of diplomacy, safeguarding the protestant faith, but making no firm pro-nouncement on the future form of church government. James's letter, on the other hand, threatened all who forsook their natural allegiance; a loyalty which many believed could encompass papal as well as royal authority. Even James's most loyal supporters were disheartened and many, including Atholl left the convention which was subsequently dominated by William's supporters.[79]

Thereafter events moved with an ever-quickening pace. On 4 April, it was resolved that James had not abdicated, but had rather forfeited the throne through his misdemeanours; A Claim of Right which laid down fundamental constitutional principles and condemned prelacy as 'a great and insupportable grievance and trouble to the nation' was accepted on 11 April and was followed by the proclamation of William and Mary as joint sovereigns.[80] Two days later the passage of the Articles of Grievances reinforced the ecclesiastical and constitutional ideals of the Revolution settlement in their reaffirmation of the rejection of episcopacy and their specific condemnation of the Committee of the Articles.[81] On 11 May, William and Mary accepted the crown of Scotland, apparently (though this was questioned) on the terms already outlined.[82] A basis of the Revolution settlement had been determined by this date. Only the Jacobite rising led by viscount Dundee which, despite victory at Killiecrankie on 27 July 1689, was halted by the death of its leader and the subsequent defence of Dunkeld on 17–18 August, delayed the final constitutional and ecclesiastical settlement until 1690.[83]

A revolution which had such inauspicious beginnings was to prove to be a major turning point in the political and ecclesiastical governance of Scotland. It is undeniable, however, that the Scots who so enthusiastically embraced such principles in the course of 1689–90 had at the onset been very reluctant revolutionaries.

NOTES

1. *The Register of the Privy Council of Scotland* [*Reg. Privy Council*] ed. J. H. Burton and others (Edinburgh, 1877 — 3rd series, xiii, p. xlvii; *Historical Notices of Scottish Affairs, Selected from the manuscripts of Sir John Lauder of Fountainhall, bart., one of the senators of the College of Justice* [Fountainhall *Historical Notices*], ed. D. Laing, 2 vols (Bannatyne Club, 1848), ii, 896–7. Fountainhall records that although the court of session sat during November 1688, yet by the Prince of Orange's arrival in England, no business was done, save on a few bills' (Fountainhall, *Historical Notices*, ii, 884).

2. R. Wodrow, *The History of the Sufferings of the Church of Scotland from the Restoration to the Revolution*, 2 vols. [Edinburgh, 1721–2], cited hereafter in the later edition ed. R. Burns, 4 vols (Glasgow, 1828–30), iv, 470–2.

3. D. Burnet, *Siege of Edinburgh Castle, MDCLXXXIX*. Presented by Robert Bell (Bannatyne Club, 1828), 13; G. Donaldson, *Scotland: James V — James VII*, The Edinburgh History of Scotland, 4 vols, (Edinburgh, 1969), 384.

4. W. Ferguson, *Scotland's Relations with England: A survey to 1707* (Edinburgh, 1977), 158–161; Paul Hopkins, *Glencoe and the End of the Highland War* (Edinburgh 1986), 68–71, 83–88.

5. James, duke of York arrived in Scotland in November 1679 (*Reg. Privy Council*, 3rd series, vi, 331,344) and left in February 1680 (ibid., vi, 392–3). He returned to Scotland in November 1680 (*Reg. Privy Council*, 3rd series, vi, 565–8) and became royal commissioner in July 1681 (*The Acts of the Parliaments of Scotland* [Acts Parl. Scot.] ed. T. Thomson and C. Innes (Edinburgh, 1814–75), vi, 406); *Reg. Privy Council*, 3rd series, vii, 148; he finally departed on 6 March 1682 (Fountainhall, *Historical Notices*, i, 349).

6. *Acts Parl. Scot.*, ii, 530–532; ibid., iii, 14,23, 36; ibid, viii, 238, c.2; 243, c.6; *The Works of John Knox*; collected and edited by David Laing, 6 vols. (Bannatyne Club, 1846–64), ii, 108–112.

7. Fountainhall, *Historical Notices*, 307.

8. Ibid, 307–8; *Acts Parl. Scot.*, viii, 242.

9. *Reg. Privy Council*, 3rd series, vii, 373.

10. Fountainhall, *Historical Notices*, 677.

11. *Acts Parl. Scot.*, viii, 459–60.

12. Ibid., viii, 459–60.

13. Ibid., viii, 460.

14. Fountainhall, *Historical Notices*, 715–718.

15. *Acts Parl. Scot.* viii, 579–81.

16. Ibid.

17. Fountainhall, *Historical Notices*, ii, 723–734.

18. Ibid., ii, 723, 734–5.

19. Fountainhall, *Historical Notices*, ii, 726–735.

20. Ibid., 735–6; *Reports of the Royal Commission on Historical Manuscripts* [*Hist. MSS Comm.*] (London, 1870–): *MSS of the Earl of Mar and Kellie* (1904), 217–19.

21. Fountainhall, *Historical Notices*, ii, 737.

22. *The Lauderdale Papers*, ed. O. Airy, 3 vols. (Camden Society, 1884–5), i, 172; iii, 36.

23. Fountainhall, *Historical Notices*, ii, 740–1, 748, 750–1.

24. Ibid., ii, 736–7.

25. Ibid., 745.

26. Ibid., i, 327.

27. 'Duke Queensberry was an atheist in religion, a villain in friendship, a knave in business and a traitor in his carriage to him' [James] (Melfort to the duke of Hamilton, 3 December 1685) *HMC* 11th Rep. App. VI, 171); Fountainhall, *Historical Notices*, ii, 675, 740.

28. Hopkins, *Glencoe*, 104.

29. Fountainhall, *Historical Notes*, ii, 713, 794, 822; Burnet, *The Siege of Edinburgh Castle*, 5–6; Hopkins, *Glencoe*, 107–8.

30. Donaldson, *Scotland: James V — James VII*, 383; Fountainhall, *Historical Notices*, ii, 733, 736, 772, 783

31. B. Lenman, *The Jacobite Risings in Britain, 1689–1746* (London, 1980), 28–9.

32. M. Dilworth, 'The Scottish Mission in 1688–1689' in *Innes Review*, xx (1969), 70–5.

33. A. Bellsheim, *Geschichte der Katholischen Kirche in Schottland*, 2 vols. (Mainz, 1883); English trans. with additions by Hunter Blair, 4 vols. (Edinburgh, 1887–90), iv, 128; P. Anson, *Underground Catholicism in Scotland* (Montrose, 1970), 76; D. Maclean, 'Roman Catholicism in Scotland in the Reign of Charles II' in *Records of the Scottish Church History Society*, iii (1929), 48–50.

34. A. MacWilliam, 'A Highland Mission: Strathglass, 1671–1777 in *Innes Review*, xxiv (1973), 82–4, provides evidence for the number of priests at work in the Highlands and Islands in this period.

35. *CSP Dom.* 1689–90, 383; W. Forbes-Leith, *Memoirs of Scottish Catholics during the XVIIth and XVIIIth Centuries*, 2 vols. (London, 1909), ii, 148–9.

36. Paul Hopkins, *Glencoe*, 105–6.

37. Fountainhall, *Historical Notices*, ii, 759; Hopkins, *Glencoe*, 106.

38. Ibid., 106; *Reg. Privy Council*, 3rd series, xiii, p. xlvii.

39. Hopkins, *Glencoe*, 106, citing *The Lockhart Papers*, ed. A. Aufrere, 2 vols. (London, 1817), i, 63.

40. Hopkins, *Glencoe*, 106.

41. Ibid., 106.

42. Fountainhall, *Historical Notices*, ii, 713, 759, 762.

43. Wodrow, *History*, iii, 304–6, 308.

44. Ibid., iii, 308–9.

45. Ibid., iii, 309.

46. *Acts Parl. Scot.*, viii, 245.

47. Wodrow, *History*, iii, 310; G. Burnet, *History of My Own Time*, ed. O. Airey, 2 vols. (London, 1897–1900), iii, 318–9.

48. Ferguson, *Anglo-Scottish Relations*, 160; Wodrow, *History*, iii, 310; I. B. Cowan, *The Scottish Covenanters, 1660–1688* (London, 1976), 109.

49. Ibid., 109.

50. Hew Scott, *Fasti ecclesiae Scoticanae. The Succession of ministers in the parish churches of Scotland from the reformation, 1560, to the present time*, revised edition, 8 vols (1915–50), 305, 307, 310, 312, 316, 318, 333, 344, 348, 353, 357, 363, 372, 389, 393, 397, 399.

51. Hopkins, *Glencoe*, 105, 117 n. 147.

52. Fountainhall, *Historical Notices*, ii, 670–1, 708–9, 717; *Historical observes of memorable occurrents in church and state from October 1680 to April 1686*. By Sir John Lauder of Fountainhall ed. A. Urquhart and D. Laing (Bannatyne Club, 1840), 243.

53. Fountainhall, *Historical Notices*, ii, 722.

54. Ibid., ii, 726, 728.

55. Ibid., ii, 735.

56. Ibid., ii, 775–6.

57. Cowan, *The Scottish Covenanters 1660–1688*, 50–55.

58. Ibid., 82–102.

59. Wodrow, *History*, iii, 94–5; Wodrow avers that this declaration was published and printed at Glasgow, but J. King Hewison, *The Covenanters*, 2 vols (Glasgow, 1913) ii, 308, claims that it was first affixed to the mercat cross at Hamilton and subsequently printed in Glasgow.

60. Wodrow, *History*, iii, 66–7.

61. The Queensferry Paper, 1680 (Wodrow, *History*, ii, Appendix, xlvi); Sanquhar Declaration, 1680 (ibid., ii, Appendix xlvii); *Reg. Privy Council*, 3rd series, vi, 265.

62. A Shields, *The Life and Death of. . . J. Renwick*, (Edinburgh, 1724) 52–3.

63. Wodrow, History, ii, Appendix cxxix; cf. *Reg. Privy Council*, 3rd series, xiii, 123–4; Wodrow, *History*, ii, Appendix cxxxiv; cf. *Reg. Privy Council*, 3rd series, xiii, 156–8.

64. Woodrow, *History*, iv, 428.

65. Ibid., iv, 431–3

66. Ibid., iv, 432.

67. Ibid., iv, 432.

68. King Hewison, *The Covenanters*, ii, 506.

69. Wodrow, *History*, iv, 431–3.

70. Ibid., iv, 473; Burnet, *The Siege of Edinburgh Castle*, 16–17.

71. Ibid., 17–19; Wodrow, *History*, iv, 472–4; *Memoirs touching the Revolution in Scotland, MDCLXXXVIII-MDCXC* by Colin Earl of Balcarres, ed. Lord Lindsay (Bannatyne Club, 1841), 38–43.

72. *Reg. Privy Council*, 3rd series, xiii, p. xiii; Hopkins, *Glencoe*, 120.

73. King Hewison, *The Covenanters*, ii, 518.

74. *An Account of the Proceedings of the Estates in Scotland*, ed. E. W. M. Balfour-Melville, 2 vols. (Scottish History Society, 1955), i, 1–15, 27, 32–3, 56–7, 105, 110, 125–6, 128–30; Hopkins, *Glencoe*, 120–1.

75. Fountainhall, *Historical Notices*, ii, 884; *Extracts from the Records of Edinburgh 1681 to 1689*, ed. M. Wood and Helen Armet (Edinburgh 1954), 256–8, 263–4; Hopkins, *Glencoe*, 121 (Edinburgh, 1968), 1–2.

76. W. Ferguson, *Scotland, 1689 to the Present*, The Edinburgh History of Scotland, 4 vols (Edinburgh, 1968), 1–2.

77. W. Fraser, *The Melvilles Earls of Melville and the Leslies Earls of Leven*,

3 vols (Edinburgh, 1890), iii, 193; Balfour-Melville, *Proceedings of the Estates in Scotland*, i, 1.

78. Ibid., i, 1; W. Ferguson, *Scotland, 1689 to the Present*, 2–3.
79. Balfour-Melville, *Proceedings of the Estates*, i, 4–5, 33, 47; *Acts Parl. Scot.*, ix, 9, 10n.
80. Balfour-Melville, *Proceedings of the Estates*, i, 25–6; *Acts Parl. Scot.*, ix, 37–41.
81. Ibid., ix, 45.
82. *Facsimiles of the National Manuscripts of Scotland* (London, 1867–71), iii, no. cvii.
83. *Reg. Privy Council*, 3rd series, xiii, 565–6; ibid., xiv, 82–4, 125–6; Balfour-Melville, *Proceedings of the Estates*, 183, 185–7, 220–5.

6

JAMES II, WILLIAM OF ORANGE, AND THE ADMIRALS

David Davies

Imagine an alternative 5 November 1688. Almost at the moment that the vanguard of William of Orange's invading army sets foot on the sands of Bridlington Bay, the mastheads of the English fleet are sighted, closing rapidly in line-of-battle from the south-east. The Dutch fleet, trapped between the enemy and a lee shore, and hampered by the need to defend several hundred transports clustered in the bay, struggles vainly to gain sea room. The battle is short, sharp, and decisive: by nightfall, most of the Dutch transports are ablaze and the shattered remnant of the escorting fleet is heading in disarray for Holland, bearing aboard it a sadder, wiser, and disheartened Prince of Orange. When news of the crushing victory reached Whitehall, James II gave orders for a Te Deum to celebrate the triumph of his fleet and the preservation of his throne. Provincial noblemen returned, dispirited, to their estates, and prepared to draft loyal addresses congratulating the king on his victory; colonels hastily burned incriminating correspondence and ordered their regiments to give three huzzahs for King James and the Prince of Wales; Anglican clerics agonised over drafts of sermons which would try to show that such a clear manifestation of God's providence was not proof that He was, after all, a Roman Catholic God; and generations of historians yet unborn were condemned to spend their professional lives considering just why James II had such unanimous support from the political nation in 1688.

Fantasy? Yes: but this 'fantasy' is what many people in England and western Europe in September and October 1688 expected to become the reality. That it did not become the reality in November and December was due above all to naval factors. It may be that James II's incompetence as king would have cost him his throne sooner or later; but the loss of his throne in 1688 was not due to the discontent of some clergymen with troubled consciences, nor to the plots of provincial noblemen, nor even to the schemes of certain ambitious army officers. James fell because William was able to land, and he was able to land only because James's fleet did not intercept William's fleet. Without the landing, there would have been no catalyst for provincial revolts, nor for the defection of the army. Therefore, any consideration of the question 'why did the Glorious Revolution succeed?' surely ought to take into account, if not to hinge upon, the answer to another question — why did James II's fleet not fight?

On 3 October 1688, a new admiral, George Legge, Lord Dartmouth, took command of the English fleet, then lying at the Buoy of the Nore. The fleet had been mobilised to defend against the alarming and as yet unexplained activity in the Dutch dockyards; the king's instructions to Dartmouth specified that he should prevent 'any approach of any fleet or number of ships of war from Holland', and 'to endeavour by all hostile means, to sink, burn, take and otherwise destroy and disable the said fleet and ships thereof'.[1] However, the achievement of this hypothetical victory depended on a correct anticipation of the Dutch plan of campaign, for none of the anchorages available to the English were ideal for covering all of the possible invasion routes. On 15 October it was decided to move the fleet to the Gunfleet, off Harwich. In the light of what subsequently happened, this decision has been criticised for allowing William to slip into the Channel while the English fleet lay immobilised behind a sandbank miles to the north.[2] Any such criticism depends very heavily on hindsight. Throughout October, all the intelligence pointed to a Dutch landing in the north or east, with Harwich, Yarmouth and Bridlington Bay the favoured landing sites, and it was also believed that the Dutch would fall in with the conventional naval strategy of using their warships to engage and neutralise the English fleet before attempting to convoy the invading army.[3] James's intelligence was in fact sketchy and unreliable, much of it coming from (perhaps deliberately) overheard remarks by seamen in Dutch ports, and passed on without critical comment by James's singularly inept ambassador in the Netherlands, the Marquis d'Albeville. Through his spies in England, William soon knew that James expected a landing in the north, and he was also aware of James's formidable defences along the Thames and in East Anglia.[4] In fact, William's naval advisers, headed by the renegade Admiral Arthur Herbert, had carefully researched all the potential landing sites on the east and south coasts from Tynemouth round to Falmouth. Herbert certainly favoured the south-west from the beginning, believing the anchorages there afforded better shelter and that it would be easier to seal the Channel against French reinforcements for James. William probably favoured the north, on the grounds that he could get more support there, but he was shrewd enough to adapt his strategy according to circumstances. The final decision, made just before sailing on 1 November, meant that the fleet's destination would depend on the latest intelligence from England and above all on wind direction. If the wind was from the east or north-east, the fleet was to aim for the west country, with Exmouth the favoured landing place.[5] Herbert would have known, too, that in an easterly wind the English fleet would be trapped at the Gunfleet; the question of using that anchorage in fairly similar circumstances had last been a live issue in 1666, when Herbert had been a young lieutenant in the English fleet, and its disadvantages in an east wind had been widely discussed in the fleet at that time.[6] By contrast with the English, William's intelligence was excellent. Just before sailing, he received accurate reports on the disposition of James's fleet and army: these confirmed him in the opinions that the west was less well defended, and that he could slip past the English ships while the wind remained easterly.[7]

For its part, the English fleet was faced with three possible courses of action. It could stay where it was, awaiting better intelligence; it could move to a new anchorage, either the Buoy of the Nore or the Downs, each of which had at least as many disadvantages as the Gunfleet; or it could move on to the Dutch coast and intercept William and Herbert as and when they sailed. The last of these courses was advocated by the king, but seventeenth century fleets were not autocracies: Dartmouth did not issue orders dictatorially, but relied on the consensus opinion of the council of war. At such councils on 26 and 28 October, the officers of the English fleet decided against crossing to the enemy's shore, ostensibly because of the danger to the fleet from the November weather. Dartmouth attempted to sail on 30 October, believing from new intelligence reports that William was about to sail. For once, the intelligence was reasonably accurate, but the stiff north-easterly gale which brought the Dutch out on 1 November made it impossible for the English fleet to round the Gunfleet shoal. Dartmouth finally sailed on 3 November after sighting some stragglers from the Dutch fleet, but by then the main invasion fleet was already passing Dover. When William came ashore at Brixham on 5 November, the English fleet was no nearer than Beachy Head, and at another council of war on that day Dartmouth's captains resolved not to attack what was believed to be a greatly superior enemy force. Storms forced Dartmouth back to the Downs on the seventh, and he did not re-emerge until the sixteenth, when the fleet again sailed west. By the nineteenth, Dartmouth actually had the Dutch fleet in Torbay in sight, but the storms which had already decimated his fleet in its slow progress down the Channel blew up again and forced him back to Spithead. There James II's fleet remained, increasingly insignificant in the course of events of the Revolution, until it tamely surrendered to William's authority on 13 December.

So much for the chronology of what so nearly became the fourth Anglo-Dutch naval war. Yet was this chronology determined by something other than a saga of hopelessly inadequate intelligence and the vagaries of North Sea squalls? To almost all historians, the notion of a tightly knit and successful Orangist conspiracy among the captains of the English fleet has proved irresistible: the fleet did not fight because it did not want to fight, not because it could not fight. The basis of the conspiracy theory is William's determination to avoid battle with the English fleet at almost any cost. Even a successful engagement would have destroyed the illusion of William as liberator, rather than conqueror. The strategy which James expected William to follow, namely deliberately seeking an engagement between the two fleets, had been debated by the Dutch and finally abandoned, and Herbert's secret orders instructed him to avoid battle, unless, of course, he had to fight in self-defence.[8] Therefore, every effort had to be made to subvert the loyalty and morale of Dartmouth's officers and men. Two declarations, one by William and one by Herbert, were aimed specifically at the English fleet, both stressing the message that it was being used by James as an instrument of 'Popish slavery'.[9] By mid-October, certainly, controversial pamphlets and newsletters were circulating around the ships at the Gunfleet, and Dartmouth complained of 'caballing' among his captains.[10] By that time, Captain Matthew Aylmer and Lieutenant George Byng were active in the Orangist cause, having been recruited by the senior army officers Percy Kirke and the Duke of Ormonde, and they informally sounded several captains.[11] Also in October, another leading army conspirator, the Duke of Grafton, went surreptitiously to the fleet to subvert the captains' loyalty.[12] Dartmouth was aware that something suspicious was going on: he was wary of Grafton's visit and of the 'very pert' activities of Captain Lord Berkeley of Stratton, who 'infused strange notions into the seamen and a great part of the commanders of ships', and whom Dartmouth placed in the ship next to his own in order to keep a closer watch on him.[13] Berkeley and the fleet's rear-admiral, Sir John Berry, were involved in a plot to kidnap Dartmouth aboard Captain Anthony Hastings's ship, after which the command would have been given to Grafton: however, this scheme had to be aborted after Dartmouth got wind of it.[14] According to the various accounts of the conspiracy, all of this covert activity bore fruit at the councils of war which took the decisions not to attack. James

D

II himself believed that two-thirds of his captains had decided not to fight for him.[15] Other accounts were more conservative: probably the best informed estimate, that of William's other English naval adviser, Edward Russell,[16] put the figure at eight who were 'resolved to . . . come over to our side', including Berkeley, Berry, Aylmer, and Hastings.[17]

Despite the conspirators' apparent success, James II's fleet remained in being and remained under the staunchly loyal Dartmouth. Therefore, during November, while William was advancing through Devon and Dorset, the conspirators in the fleet decided to make direct contact with him. Byng obtained leave to visit relatives ashore, promptly disguised himself as a farmer, and set off across country, escaping recognition and capture in a scrape with some royal troops. On 28 November he reached William's headquarters at Sherborne and delivered an assurance of support from the Orangist officers in the fleet. William sent him back with an answer for the officers and a letter for Dartmouth, assuring the admiral of William's regard for, and good intentions towards, him. On his return, Byng gave the letter to Aylmer, who smuggled it into the admiral's toilet.[18] Dartmouth's initial response was cool, but in the first fortnight of December his position shifted considerably. In particular, he protested loudly to James against the sending of the infant Prince of Wales to France, and refused to assist in this venture, arguing that he might be guilty of treason if he did so.[19] James's own attempt at withdrawal was the last straw for Dartmouth: 'this looks like so great mistrust of me that many could witness it hath almost broke my heart', the admiral wrote, and his other letters of this time show his anguish and astonishment at his king's actions.[20] One of those letters was written on 12 December, addressed to William of Orange, and carried to the prince by Matthew Aylmer, 'who is my very good friend, and is entirely devoted to your highness'.[21] Dartmouth had given in, and a council of war on the following day rubber stamped the surrender of the English fleet.

The story of the 'naval conspiracy' possesses a satisfying combination of drama, farce, and pathos, and it appears in the form outlined above in practically every modern account of 1688. Unfortunately, it is a story which begs several critical questions: what were the motives of the conspirators? how great was their influence in the fleet? above all, to what extent, if at all, did they influence the outcome of events in the naval campaign of 1688?

When Byng won over Captain Wolfran Cornwall to the conspiracy, he did so by naming 'some persons that were engaged in it that was his most intimate and particular friends as Mr. Herbert, Kirk, Russell, & c.'.[22] From 1679 to 1683, Arthur Herbert had been commander-in-chief

of the Mediterranean fleet, based at Tangier and fighting a war against
the corsairs of Algiers. Edward Russell had been Herbert's second-in-
command; Percy Kirke, Herbert's boon companion, had been deputy
governor of Tangier; and Wolfran Cornwall had then been a young naval
officer desperate for his first commission. That reward finally came his
way in 1682, when he became lieutenant to Herbert himself through the
admiral's patronage.[23] Cornwall's rise was far from atypical, for the late
1670s and early 1680s were yet another time of severe retrenchment of
naval expenditure, and the Mediterranean was the only station on which
an officer could hope for rapid advancement. However, such advancement depended largely on gaining the favour of one man — Herbert.
The admiral's many critics, notably Samuel Pepys, grumbled about the
dominance in the fleet of Herbert's 'young fellows', and complained that
'no man can expect to get anything but those who are his favourites'.[24] By
1688, the 'young fellows' who owed their early advancement in the navy
to Herbert were all holding important commands in James II's fleet: they
included Cloudesley Shovell, Matthew Aylmer, Anthony Hastings, Sir
Francis Wheeler, and several others.[25] One of Herbert's closest followers
from the days at Tangier, David Mitchell, had actually turned down a
command from James in the summer of 1688 and followed his patron
into exile in Holland, where he confidently stated that many of the
English captains would abandon James.[26] By appointing Herbert to
command his fleet, therefore, William plainly hoped that past loyalties
would compel many of the English captains not to fight.[27]

Other ghosts of the Mediterranean fleet of the early 1680s returned to
haunt the quarterdecks of 1688. Not long after Herbert had finally sailed
home from Tangier, Dartmouth had sailed out with a fleet and orders to
demolish the useless and expensive colony. It has been suggested that
Herbert and the other Tangier veterans, the so-called 'Tangerines',
hated Dartmouth thereafter for destroying their playground,[28] but
this interpretation is untenable — Herbert had been a stern critic
of Tangier's failings as a naval base.[29] In fact, the quarrel of Herbert
and Dartmouth had its roots in the complex factional struggles at the
courts of both Charles II and James II in the 1680s. The two men were
among the closest friends of James both before and after his accession,
but they regarded themselves as competing for his favour; to complicate
matters, one of Herbert's other close friends was John Churchill, the
future Duke of Marlborough, whom Dartmouth had always detested.[30]
In James's reign, observers invariably had the fortunes of Dartmouth
on the one hand, and Herbert and Churchill on the other, rising and
falling in tandem. When Dartmouth's friend, the Earl of Rochester,

lost the lord treasureship, it was believed that Dartmouth would be the next out of office; when Churchill made some remarks that offended the king, it was observed that this would stand Dartmouth in good stead.[31] Above all, Burnet believed that the real cause of Herbert's stand against James was 'his private quarrel with the Lord Dartmouth, who he thought had more of the king's confidence than he himself had'. The 'private quarrel' led, in September 1688, to Dartmouth's astonishing challenge to Herbert to meet him at Ostend 'at what time & with what armes' he desired for having 'said very reflecting things of him'.[32] Therefore, any historian who suggests that Dartmouth wanted to avoid fighting Herbert ignores one crucial fact: the two men hated each other to a degree which did not preclude mortal combat.[33]

One of Dartmouth's peculiar misfortunes in 1688 was to be hated so whole-heartedly by the two men who were conceivably capable of turning the fleet against him, for Herbert was not the only influential enemy Dartmouth had made in the early 1680s. Henry, Duke of Grafton, the elder illegitimate son of King Charles II and the Duchess of Cleveland, had been made Vice-Admiral of England in 1682 on the strength of two Mediterranean cruises, and had been in command of the fleet in 1683 when he was suddenly recalled and replaced by Dartmouth, who then took the fleet to Tangier. Grafton and his mother looked on the removal as a personal insult and never forgave nor forgot it.[34] In 1687, Grafton had commanded a fleet in the Mediterranean and impressed James by his command of it. Because of this and his high honorific rank, Grafton expected the command of the 1688 fleet, but when James appointed Dartmouth at the end of September he dealt with this problem by abolishing the offices of Vice- and Rear-Admiral of England altogether, a move which one observer in the fleet correctly interpreted as 'a wile to be rid of the duke'.[35] It was probably within days of receiving this new affront that Grafton paid a secret visit to William in the Netherlands; the visit was discovered by James's agents and reported to the king, who exposed Grafton in public and then took no further action. As the Earl of Ailesbury noted sadly, after he had begged James to deal with those, like Grafton, who were believed to be in the conspiracy, 'the King could not resolve'.[36]

Following his lucky escape, Grafton went to the fleet on at least one occasion in what was seen both at the time and since as a transparent attempt to subvert the captains' loyalty.[37] Grafton's intention to spend one of these visits aboard Anthony Hastings's ship reveals another ingredient of the naval conspiracy, for Hastings was a captain in Grafton's regiment of foot guards.[38] Historians have tended to assume that in 1688 the army and navy were entirely separate institutions with no overlap in personnel.[39] However, the uncertainties of naval employment in an age of retrenchment had driven many naval officers to take out the insurance policy of purchasing an army commission as well. Eleven of Dartmouth's captains and lieutenants also held army commissions in regiments whose commanders, and in some cases other ranks, were to defect to William during the land campaign: this number included several names which have recurred frequently in this study, including Lord Berkeley, Matthew Aylmer, Wolfran Cornwall, and George Byng.[40] Several of these officers had been with their regiments in the camp at Hounslow Heath until mid- or late October, by which time the army conspiracy was already well established, and would therefore have been well aware of opinion in the army at that time.[41] Because of their reliance on military service in the intervals between sea employment, they, too, would have been influenced by those issues which had created widespread discontent among James's soldiers: the purge of the Irish army's officer corps, with all its implications for the property rights of commission holders, and the related matters of opposition to an army declaration in favour of the repeal of the Test Act, and the increasingly widespread promotion of Catholic officers at the (apparent) expense of Protestants.[42]

An influx of Catholics into the army may have affected some naval officers; an influx of Catholics into the navy affected them all. James had made no blatant moves in this direction for the first two years of his reign, partly because there were hardly any qualified Catholic candidates for naval command.[43] However, over the winter of 1686–7 Sir Roger Strickland, former Rear-Admiral of the Mediterranean fleet, publicly announced his conversion.[44] Strickland can hardly be bracketed with the opportunists and place-seekers who succumbed to the king's missionary campaign in 1686–7, for he came from one of the staunchest Catholic families of northern England, and his true faith had long been suspect.[45] Even so, the impact of his conversion was considerable. His naval clients promptly converted, as did a number of other officers, and in the appointments to commands for 1687 James rewarded them with significant promotions; above all, Strickland became vice-admiral in Grafton's Mediterranean fleet, and then succeeded the disgraced Herbert as Rear-Admiral of England. It is possible that the rapid rise of Strickland and the other Catholic naval officers contributed to Herbert's spectacular fall in March 1687. Herbert had refused, on the grounds of conscience, to agree to James's plan to repeal the Test Act: this stand stunned everyone, especially the king and the admiral's own family, both because Herbert's dependence on the income from his offices was well known and because his immorality and total lack of conscience were considered shocking even by the standards of post-Restoration England. As one poet remarked,

> Murders and Rapes his honor can digest–
> Boggles at nought but taking off the Test.[46]

However, the end of the Test could only have led to further honours for Strickland, whose influence on naval patronage had been increasing rapidly. Even more alarming for Herbert was the fact that Strickland's closest friend in the navy and at court was his *bête noire*, Lord Dartmouth.[47] In the spring of 1687, therefore, the prospect of Dartmouth and Strickland coming to dominate naval affairs must have seemed very real indeed.

The influx of Catholics into the fleet had other repercussions. Several historians have dismissed the number of Catholics in the navy as insignificant, and in absolute terms they are quite correct: only nine Catholics served as captains or lieutenants in 1687, and eight in 1688, before mobilisation began. The real importance of these figures lies in relative terms, for the commissioned officer corps of the navy was always much smaller than that of the army. In 1687 the Catholics comprised 12% of the navy's officer corps, and in 1688 10% — figures almost identical to those suggested for James's army by recent research.[48] With employment opportunities in the navy still few and far between, the sudden creation of this privileged elite was bound to create resentment. Grafton warned James that many naval officers opposed the promotion of Catholics, and Sir John Berry told the king bluntly that if he put Catholic officers into the 1688 fleet, 'the seamen would knock them on the head'.[49] As usual, James displayed a total disregard for sensible advice and appointed Strickland to command the summer fleet of 1688. Strickland, in turn, tactlessly allowed Catholic priests to say mass openly on the ships, and Berry's prophecy came true: one seaman was hanged 'as a terror to the rest for endeavouring to cause a mutiny against the priests and Catholic officers'.[50] Strickland's attempt to organise an abhorrence from the captains against the acquittal of the seven bishops ended abruptly when 'one of them swore bloodily at him and threatened to beat him'. James himself had to go down to the fleet for two days in July to calm tempers.[51] Even so, he retained the detested Strickland in command, and even when he replaced him with Dartmouth at the end of September he retained Strickland as vice-admiral; moreover, there were still nine Catholic captains and lieutenants in the fleet throughout the naval campaign of 1688. Therefore, when Aylmer tried to win over Captain John Ashby to the cause of the conspiracy, he overcame Ashby's initial reluctance (epitomised by the famous remark about naval officers that 'in their profession they were not taught to turn against the King') by persuading him of the need to fight popish oppression.[52] For the officers of the fleet, 'popish oppression' was not just an abstract concept — it also meant Strickland, and the loss of plum commands to Catholics. Similarly, William's and Herbert's declarations to the English fleet both stressed the religious issue, with William's warning the officers and men that they were

> being made but instruments to bring yourselves and your cuntry under the Popish slavery of Irish and forrigners who are in readinesse to compleate your destruction.[53]

The reference to the Irish may not have had the desired impact on a fleet in which several of William's own agents were Irish, but that to foreigners was a telling reference to one of the other vital concerns of naval men in 1688. For much of the year, there had been talk that James had secretly entered into an alliance with France, and that French ships and troops would come to his assistance if William threatened to invade. The French had done nothing to dispel these rumours,[54] and James himself had made soundings of the sea officers since at least the beginning of 1687 to find out how they would react to the idea of a new Dutch war and a French alliance. Herbert, before his dismissal in 1687, and Berry and Grafton in 1688, had all told him the same thing: the fleet would not fight alongside the French.[55] James himself believed that Grafton 'industriously fomented the natural aversion the English have to the French' among the officers of the fleet, and when Dartmouth took command he found widespread criticism of the policies emerging from 'the old conduit of Whitehall'.[56] When the crisis finally came, James found a 'general aversion' among his captains to the notion of French reinforcements, and only two — of whom Strickland was one — were reported to be willing to take French troops aboard their ships.[57] The fleet's reaction against the French appears particularly strong, even by the normal standards of seventeenth century Englishmen's francophobia. The explanation for this probably lies in the memory of the last occasion when the English and French had fought jointly against the Dutch, the battle of the Texel in August 1673. On that occasion, the French squadron had disobeyed Prince Rupert's signal to engage and had stayed clear of the action, exposing the two English squadrons to a hammering. The incident prompted an outburst of violent and intense criticism of the

French from the men of the fleet, a reaction which was rapidly echoed ashore.[58] The memory of the Texel lingered long in the navy. Among those who had commanded ships in the battle were Herbert, Russell, Berry, William Davies (Dartmouth's flag captain in 1688), John Ashby, and even Dartmouth, who was himself a vigorous opponent of French assistance to James in 1688. Several other captains in Dartmouth's fleet had held commands or more junior posts at the Texel.[59] Therefore, the prospect of a new French military alliance was not alarming simply because of concern about the extent of Louis XIV's power, or because of the belief of contemporary and later writers that the seamen did not want to fight their fellow Protestants, the Dutch:[60] the French could be perceived on a purely professional level as at best incompetent and unreliable, at worst incompetent and treacherous.

The prospect of war *against* the French, a likely outcome of any successful invasion by William, was rather different. Any such war would entail a massive expansion of the fleet, which would bring the concomitant benefits of opportunities for employment and promotion, and for enriching oneself through prize money. These were considerable enticements after the retrenchment of the 1670s and 1680s, and Herbert and Russell may have made specific promises of future preferment. Herbert's address to the fleet promised 'all marks of favour and honour' to those who changed sides, and after their triumph he and Russell were careful to mention the services done for William during the revolution by the likes of Aylmer and Ashby.[61] Indeed, the survival rate of naval officers after the revolution was remarkably high, suggesting a rapid and widespread acceptance of the new regime in order to preserve and promote one's own career. Of the captains of the main fleet in 1689, 87% had held commissions from James II, and most of them had been in Dartmouth's fleet; in 1690, despite very high casualty rates in the first year of war, the figure was still almost 75%.[62] Between December 1688 and April 1689, only about 10–15% of the 157 commissioned officers of Dartmouth's fleet resigned or were dismissed, about half of whom were Catholics who were bound to be removed.[63] This situation is best compared with that in the army, where, according to the latest research, only a third of James II's officers went on to serve William and Mary.[64] It was hardly surprising, therefore, that James himself believed the main motive governing the officers' behaviour in November 1688 was 'fear of loosing their command',[65] or that the Earl of Ailesbury should have labelled the officers of Dartmouth's fleet as 'so many scabby time-servers'.[66] Perhaps the best statement of this safety first attitude, in which the preservation and enhancement of one's career was paramount, was made by a lieutenant who had just gained his first commission after years of working his way up through the ranks. When asked in March 1689 to help defect with his ship to France, Thomas Jennings replied that

> he would not ruin himself and family in that cause, for as the representative of the nation had made King William their King, he was his servant, & that . . . (he) was sorry for King James, but 'twas not he that drove him out of the land, but himself & his priests . . . he could not take part with a French or an Irishman against his own country, & soe refused to goe.[67]

The abiding influence of Herbert and Grafton; the connections with the army; anti-Catholicism and francophobia; professional ambition — the officers of Dartmouth's fleet certainly had ample motive for conspiring against James and for William. However, motive alone does not prove guilt. For it to be proved that the conspiracy was the decisive factor in preventing a naval battle in 1688, it would need to be shown that the conspirators' influence was paramount in determining the outcome of the councils of war on 26 and 28 October, and 5 November, when the crucial decisions not to attack were taken, and in preventing the fleet's sailing from the Gunfleet between 30 October and 3 November.

On 26 October Dartmouth was under pressure from the king and the court to sail to the Dutch coast and wait for William's fleet there. That afternoon, the council of war debated this option and decided to remain at the Gunfleet while the nights were comparatively light; the latest intelligence, as presented to the council, stated that the Dutch intended to land either at Harwich or in the Thames Estuary. The alternative strategy of sailing to the enemy coast, advocated only by Captain Sir William Jennens, was rejected on the grounds of the lateness of the year and the consequent uncertainty of the weather, which might imperil the fleet.[68] This decision was reiterated on the twenty-eighth after the king had sent another suggestion that the fleet should sail.[69] When the next council of war met, on 5 November, the fleet was off Beachy Head. Dartmouth had already ordered the fleet to form line-of-battle, and the ships had cleared their decks for fighting.[70] When the council met, it possessed new intelligence gleaned from the officers of a stray Dutch transport which had been captured on the third: according to this intelligence, the Dutch fleet comprised 45 capital ships.[71] Therefore, as each captain entered the council two points were put to him: first, that the Dutch fleet was greatly superior in size ('it is thought they are almost double our force', one captain observed), and second, that it was almost certain that the Dutch had already landed. Not surprisingly, perhaps, given that they had been presented with two such loaded assertions, each captain replied that 'it was not thought fit to hazard the fleet at such odds and to no purpose'.[72] It was a comprehensive admission of defeat.

How did the councils of war reach these declarations? Each council actually consisted of two meetings: the first was a private meeting of the flag officers and senior captains, which would then present its views to the full council of all captains. It was therefore natural for the full council to accept an interpretation presented by the elite council, and at each of the crucial councils of war in 1688 this is exactly what happened. William's agent, Byng, recorded that in the council of 26 October 'the chiefest and most considerable' captains persuaded the others not to sail to the Dutch coast; on 5 November, the two bald statements of defeat presented to the captains had been agreed on beforehand by the elite council.[73] In these circumstances, in the previous Dutch wars, a bold and experienced admiral could carry both the elite council and the full council by force of personality. Dartmouth was neither bold nor experienced. His entire military, naval and political career had been characterised by lack of self-confidence and caution; moreover, his total time in command of ships of war consisted of 23 months out of 22 years as a dilettante naval officer, and his time in command of a fleet totalled eight months, much of which was spent at anchor before Tangier.[74] Therefore, it was inevitable that he would have to defer to his more experienced subordinates in the elite council. At each of the crucial meetings, this body consisted of the same men. Dartmouth and his vice-admiral, Strickland, were present. Berry, the rear-admiral, was (as we have seen) one of the most vigorous opponents of Catholics and the French in the fleet. He had refused to join the jury to try the seven bishops, and, despite his long standing hatred of Herbert, he had a very personal reason for opposing James — he had bought up some former abbey lands in Kent, and was worried that they might be reclaimed by a resurgent Catholic church.[75] Lord Berkeley, present by virtue of social rank rather than naval seniority, was one of the most active conspirators — James himself later described him as one of the 'most factious and disaffected officers of the Navy'.[76] The other senior officer present was William Davies, Dartmouth's flag captain. In addition to being an officer in the queen's regiment of foot, whose field officers defected to William early in the land campaign, Davies had been briefly dismissed by James in 1687 for smuggling Huguenots out of France in the royal yacht under his command.[77] Therefore, the elite council on which Dartmouth relied for guidance was dominated by a majority of men who were either actually or potentially disaffected to James II.[78]

Some other pieces of evidence also suggest that the conspirators might have had an active influence on events during the critical period at the end of October and beginning of November. Other meetings of officers, at which possible attitudes to be adopted in general councils of war could have been discussed, were taking place at the Gunfleet, though very little evidence of them survives: one such took place on 27 October, when Berry consulted privately with the captains of his division.[79] The intelligence from the captured Dutch transport might be suspect: the captured Dutch officers certainly exaggerated the number of large ships in the Dutch fleet, which was in fact roughly equal in strength to Dartmouth's if transports and lesser rates are discounted.[80] It might just be significant, therefore, that the boat was captured by Captain Thomas Hopson, one of Herbert's Tangerine cronies, and its officers were taken to the flagship for interrogation by Captain Matthew Aylmer.[81] Unfortunately, it is at this point that it becomes too easy to read conspiracy theories into everything. For instance, the fact that Sir William Jennens was the leading advocate of the strategy of sailing to the Dutch coast at the council of war on 26 October may seem to take on a new significance when it is learned that he refused to accept the outcome of the revolution, and became one of the leading naval Jacobites of the 1690s. In fact, in what was a long and bizarre career even by seventeenth century standards, Jennens had the knack of unfailingly making the wrong decision at the wrong moment. During his naval career, he successfully offended virtually everyone of importance in the service: he was court-martialled twice, on one occasion for taking his wife with him on a Mediterranean convoy, and he got into many other scrapes with authority for drunkenness, lying, embezzlement, and immoral acts with both sexes. On 26 October 1688, therefore, his fellow officers ignored Jennens not because he was Jacobite, but because he *was* Jennens.[82]

Notes of caution must also be applied to other aspects of the conspiracy theory. On 26 and 28 October, rejection of an expedition across the North Sea was not sinister, it was simply professional common sense. Although the wind was from the west and therefore suitable, the weather as a whole was unsettled and often stormy, threatening to drive the fleet into the shallows and lee shore of the Netherlands.[83] In 1672, Dartmouth, Strickland, Berry, and Davies had all been at the council of war at which a motion to go over to the Dutch shore had been rejected because of the lateness of the year over six weeks before the same scheme was mooted in 1688, while in 1673 all four had been with the fleet when it was battered by storms off the Texel — in mid-August.[84] Adverse weather conditions, conventional naval thinking, personal experience, and professional common sense, combined with the poor intelligence coming to the fleet, would have been more than sufficient to keep it immobile off the Essex coast. When Dartmouth tried to sail on 30 October and 1 November, the east wind which brought William out made it impossible for the fleet to round the sandbanks. The logbooks of the English ships make it clear that they did make every effort to sail, at considerable risk to themselves: had they succeeded, they would certainly have intercepted William. Perhaps the most persuasive witness to this particular period is a man who probably had much to gain in later years from stressing the importance of a conspiracy in determining events in 1688: Sir Roger Strickland. When in exile at the Jacobite court, Strickland stated that 'the winds would not allow the fleet to come out, on account of some sand banks', while on 5 November he fully accepted the argument that the fleet should not fight a superior Dutch force.[85] Unlike Dartmouth, Strickland was very experienced both as a captain and a flag officer: the conspirators would have been most unlikely to have deceived him with exaggerated fears of the weather, and deliberately cautious strategies.

Nevertheless, although the English fleet did not fight for James, it did not defect to William either, despite all the subsequent Jacobite jibes about its disloyalty.[86] Admittedly, an English fleet doing nothing was immeasurably better for William's cause than it was for James's, but the continued existence of an English fleet of uncertain attitude was hardly ideal for the invaders. The single most apparent characteristic of the behaviour of the fleet as a whole, and of individual officers and men, in November and December 1688, is caution. Even those who were placed in a position to defect when it was clear the advantage had swung William's way behaved with great circumspection. According to almost all accounts, Captain George Churchill, brother of John, and his ship, the *Newcastle*, made a premeditated defection to William at Plymouth in mid-November 1688; indeed, Churchill was one of the eight captains named by Russell as being ready and willing to defect. In fact, the *Newcastle* was forced into Plymouth by a bad leak which flooded her powder room; once safe in harbour, Churchill hastily wrote to Dartmouth and the Admiralty to inform them of his problems, to request money for repairs, and to assure them that he would make every effort to get his ship seaworthy as soon as possible.[87] Although Plymouth's governor, the Earl of Bath, had already secretly assured

William of his support before Churchill's arrival, and publicly took the garrison onto the Orangist side shortly afterwards, it was some days before Churchill announced his defection.[88]

Those, like Churchill, who could have and should have defected, did not do so, while the decisions of the councils of war were so much in line with what any normal council of war would have decided in any normal war that it is hard to discern any real influence of the conspirators at all. The explanation for this conspiracy that lost its nerve lies in the realities of seventeenth century naval warfare, realities which have been generally ignored by historians of 1688, but which also help to explain some of the differences between the behaviour of the army and navy in that year. In the first place, a captain could not decide to defect, or refuse to fight for his king and country, and then expect his ship to sail magically to the other fleet. He would need to persuade his lieutenant and warrant officers, who, unlike the subordinate officers in an army regiment, formed a clearly defined hierarchy, any member of which could in given circumstances take command of the ship. Even if the subordinate officers concurred, they would still need to persuade the crew, who would need a very great deal of persuading that arrears of wages due from the government they were about to desert would not be lost to them forever.[89] These were the circumstances in which Lieutenant Thomas Jennings, as cited earlier in this study, refused to go along with his captain's scheme to defect to France, and they also explain Churchill's circumspection at Plymouth — Herbert was quick to inform William of the advantages to be gained by paying Churchill's crew quickly, and they soon received a month's wages 'gratis from his Highness'.[90] Moreover, Jennings's concern to preserve his career cut both ways. As no-one could foresee the likely outcome of the 1688 campaign, especially not before William landed, it would have been exceedingly foolish for any except the most committed to act overtly in a manner likely to offend James, who could well have come to an accommodation with William and kept the throne, and Dartmouth, who could well have retained a prominent place in naval affairs. Indeed, following Herbert's disgrace many of his old clients, such as Aylmer and Sir Francis Wheeler, had been promoted by Dartmouth,[91] and it never made good sense to desert any patron when competition for naval places was so intense.

Such caution was made even more necessary by the disunity and suspicion among the conspirators themselves: men might think twice about any action which could lead to the advancement of a professional rival, and many such rivalries existed in 1688. The relationship between Herbert and Russell had been thorny ever since they fell out in the

Mediterranean in 1681, and by the summer of 1689 they had returned to their accustomed state of mutual loathing.[92] Russell was also an old friend of Dartmouth, and was trying to repair his bridges with him as early as Christmas 1688; at the same time, Russell attacked Lord Berkeley, who had risen rapidly to rear-admiral.[93] Grafton and Berry had long records as opponents of Herbert, and Berry had been one of the staunchest critics of Herbert's 'young fellows' among the Tangerines, including his fellow plotters Shovell and Aylmer.[94] The conspirators were no 'band of brothers', but a loose alliance of competing and mutually antagonistic factions whose unity broke down almost before James II had fled. Moreover, the conspirators' behaviour was constrained by the Articles of war, embodied (unlike those for the army) in statute law by an act of 1661. It could have been argued that the sort of activities in which the conspirators had engaged or might have been plotting to engage would have infringed the third, sixteenth, and nineteenth articles, all of which carried mandatory death sentences, and the fourth, tenth, eleventh, twelfth, fourteenth, and twentieth articles, all of which carried optional death sentences. Dartmouth had read the articles to the captains at the council of war on 11 October, and thereafer a copy was nailed to the mainmast of each ship as a salutary reminder to her officers and men.[95]

In the light of all these constraints, it is surprising that the conspirators should even have contemplated something as extreme as kidnapping and replacing Dartmouth; that they were prepared to contemplate it at all is surely a sign of the extraordinary level of resentment which they felt towards James II's policies. Analysis of the kidnap plot is complicated by the fact that the only two accounts of it give two totally different dates: according to James II, the plot was to be carried out just before William was due to land, which would place it in late October or early November, while according to Byng it took place after his return from Sherborne at the end of November.[96] However, there are good grounds for preferring James's dating, though with certain reservations. Above all, there was simply no point in replacing Dartmouth with Grafton at the end of November, when the fleet could no longer influence events and when Grafton had already defected to William, but there was every point in replacing him at the end of October, when the outcome of the naval conspiracy was very much in doubt. According to both Byng and James II, Dartmouth was to be invited to dinner aboard Anthony Hastings's ship, the *Woolwich*, and there seized. Credence is given to this account by Dartmouth's own statement that the plot was revealed to him by Hastings's lieutenant, William Tollemache —

perhaps significantly, the younger brother of one of the leading lights of the army conspiracy, Colonel Thomas Tollemache.[97] Unfortunately, it is very hard to construct a satisfactory chronology from these isolated facts and rumours. The *Woolwich* did not join the fleet until 12 November, having been delayed in the Thames by a shortage of manpower and supplies. Moreover, Grafton's movements are shadowy: he had certainly paid one, unofficial, visit to the fleet early in October, and gained official permission to rejoin it as a volunteer with Hastings at the very end of October, but the complete lack of any reference to Grafton in the ships' books and letters of the period provides considerable, if negative, evidence to suggest that the duke never carried out his intention of returning to the fleet.[98] Perhaps the fleet's departure from the Gunfleet, or the delays to the *Woolwich*, forced him to turn back; perhaps the journey had already become pointless as a result of some form of communication between Tollemache and Dartmouth. It is, therefore, just possible that Dartmouth knew about the kidnap plot before the councils of war of late October, and more likely that he knew about it before that of 5 November; any such discovery would have made the conspirators far more cautious in any future measures, and might explain the lack of discernible influence of the conspirators on the strategy determined at the vital councils of war.

Even if Dartmouth did not learn of the plot before Tollemache's arrival on 12 November, the knowledge would have strengthened his position in time for the fleet's remarkable change of strategy during the following week. By 13 November the elite council had received intelligence from Pepys which showed that the Dutch fleet was much weaker than had been thought. Caution remained the order of the day, with the council resolving only to sail to St Helen's Bay to await reinforcements. However, on the next day the council met again following the receipt of a royal order under the sign manual, which Dartmouth interpreted as an express command to attack the Dutch immediately. Dartmouth advocated sailing at once, but the others overruled him and the fleet only left the Downs on the sixteenth, following another full council at which the king's order was read to all captains.[99] The fleet moved down the Channel, despite severe storms, and actually had the enemy fleet in sight at one point, but the weather prevented any attack. If the conspirators and a great majority of the captains had made an earlier, premeditated decision not to fight, this behaviour was eccentric to the point of perversity: risking their ships and their lives in remarkably severe weather, when William was already firmly established ashore, made little sense. Yet James's order only reinforced the point which had

already been made apparent to the officers through the king's continued
concern for such matters as the issuing of commissions and the plans for
his 1689 fleet, despite the crisis facing his throne: James was king still.[100]
For captains concerned with preserving their careers and uncertain about
the political outcome, making some gesture, however futile, on behalf of
the king was only prudent. Dartmouth was acutely aware that he had
failed by letting the Dutch evade him, and among uncommitted captains,
and perhaps even the conspirators, there seems to have been something
of a sense of shame in the navy's performance which the foray to the
west might have been designed to assuage.[101] Endeavouring to keep in
with both sides, while doing as little as possible for either, had proved
a remarkably difficult course to steer.

Despite their gestures and their circumspection, the officers of
the fleet certainly did offend James. When, at the end of November,
a delegation of captains went to beg the king to call a free parliament,
he noted how their address contained 'their resolution of standing by
the Protestant religion but not one word of standing firm by their
king'.[102] Both at the time and subsequently, James and the Jacobites
expressed nothing but surprise and bitterness that he, a king who had
done so much for the navy, had been betrayed by the very instrument
he had created for 'the mistaken notions of religion . . . so managed
by angry men, as to stifle all those former sentiments of honour and
duty'.[103] His initially charitable attitude towards Dartmouth, whom at
first he believed to have done his duty as far as he was able, gave way
in exile to the paranoid suspicions of the deposed head of state: 'whether
it was religion, faction, or interest, that weighed most heavily with him
[Dartmouth], tis certain his loyalty was worsted in that conflict'.[104] In
one way, James was right. It was indeed ironic that the navy should fail
to protect him, of all kings: as Lord High Admiral from 1660 to 1673,
and afterwards, he had sponsored a great increase in the strength of the
fleet, had supported Samuel Pepys's important administrative reforms,
and had taken a genuine personal interest in the careers and welfare of
his officers and men. Moreover, he had personally commanded many
of those who served in 1688 in two hard-fought naval battles, Lowestoft
in 1665 and Solebay in 1672, and not long after coming to the throne
he had told his sea captains of his pride in having been their admiral
before he was their king.[105]

However, this remark, and James's surprise that his seamen should
have placed religion before honour, suggests the fundamental error
which he made in his dealings with the navy in 1688. James saw
the world in simplistic, black and white terms: when a man took his

commission, he forsook all other concerns and formed an unbreakable bond of honour and duty to his king, for whose favour he ought to be ever grateful. When, in July 1688, James spoke to the captains about Herbert's recent departure for Holland, he accused him, significantly, not of treachery or cowardice, but of 'ingratitude'. The captains replied that they would always behave themselves as men of honour, but that the king was the only judge of their truthfulness in this.[106] James believed them. On 22 October 1688 Dartmouth wrote to inform him of he suspicious activities of Grafton and Berkeley, and added that he was glad Henry Priestman, a close friend of Russell's, was not with them, 'for he sets up for a leading politician'. Despite such a clear warning, James granted Priestman the command of the powerful new seventy gunner *Hampton Court* on 8 November.[107] This apparently incredible disregard for advice, manifested also in his refusal to act on all the accusations made against Grafton, John Churchill, and the other leading conspirators, only becomes explicable if viewed in the light of James's straightforward and naive perception of the concept of military honour. He had granted the officers of the navy their commissions, therefore they would be loyal to him. Even years later, in exile, he could not accept that of all men Sir John Berry, whose career he had nurtured for quarter of a century, could have changed his opinions so radically as to forsake his duty to his king.[108] James simply did not understand.

His attempt to blame Dartmouth for the failure to intercept William was both an unfair indictment of a man who had genuinely tried to do his best, despite his own limitations, and a negation of James's own responsibility for what happened. In both the second and third Dutch wars James, as admiral, had complained of indecisive and contradictory instructions from London, but he had evidently forgotten these lessons by 1688. Theoretically, he gave Dartmouth unlimited freedom of action, but he often added riders which set out his own preferred strategy. On 17 October, for instance, Pepys told Dartmouth that James had 'resolved to put no restraint upon you by any advice of his in a matter where he judges himself so safe, in his committing it entirely to your prudence'; he then added James's private remark that, regardless of this, he thought it was not wise to move to the Gunfleet at that time. On 27 October, James strongly advised Dartmouth to sail to the Dutch coast, though adding that he left the matter entirely to his judgement.[109] Such advice was the last thing Dartmouth needed when faced with the sort of men in his council of war. Moreover, James's personal intervention in strategy could only have been justified if that intervention was decisive: as it was, he only gave Dartmouth an unambiguous order to attack when it was already too late. James must also accept the responsibility for accepting uncritically the dubious intelligence he was receiving from the Netherlands. In particular, by accepting the unlikely notion that the Dutch planned to attack the heavily defended Thames Estuary or the north, James predetermined Dartmouth's strategy in a way which allowed William to get into the Channel unhindered. James's refusal to accept the possibility of the Dutch adopting a different strategy, even after they had done so,[110] suggests that his appreciation of the situation was governed above all by his recollections of the Dutch wars. The Dutch had attacked Harwich and Chatham in 1667; therefore they would do something similar in 1688. William was flexible enough to adapt his strategy to circumstances, James was sufficiently inflexible to believe that the circumstances had not changed in twenty years.

Through his own misunderstanding of the concerns of the officers of the fleet, through his contradictory advice to Dartmouth, and through his unfailing ability to do the wrong thing at the wrong moment, James brought what happened in the North Sea and English Channel in November 1688 down on himself. His memories of 1673 should have told him how his officers would react to the prospect of French reinforcement in 1688, but James still seemed genuinely surprised when they objected. It would have been sensible and tactful to have removed Strickland from command in July 1688, but James did not realise the loathing which his Catholic admiral and other Catholic officers generated. There were good reasons for giving the command of the fleet to Grafton, rather than Dartmouth, but by placing personal friendship ahead of seniority of rank and support in the fleet, James both pushed Grafton wholeheartedly into the conspiracy and saddled himself with a less decisive admiral. James (and, indeed, Dartmouth) did not appreciate the extent of Herbert's abiding influence in the fleet, and the extent to which its officers were influenced by political and religious developments ashore. A better admiral and a less discontented fleet *might* have taken different resolutions at councils of war, *might* have chosen different anchorages, *might* have attacked even after the Dutch had landed. Ultimately, the responsibility for all this has to rest with James II. He lost his throne because he failed in the one capacity in which he was undoubtedly experienced, competent, and successful: he fell because he failed as an admiral.

I wish to thank the Master and Fellows of Magdalene College, Cambridge, and the Warden and Fellows of All Souls College, Oxford, for granting permission to consult manuscripts in their care; and the Marquis of Bath and the Earl of Dartmouth for granting permission to consult the manuscripts of their respective families. Versions of this paper were given to a meeting of the Devon History Society and South West Maritime History Society at Brixham, and to the seminar chaired by John Morrill and Mark Goldie at Cambridge; thanks are due to those who attended on those occasions for their valuable comments and suggestions. Above all, I owe a particular debt of gratitude to John Anderson, Paul Hopkins, Sari Hornstein, and especially Peter Le Fevre, for providing me with references, advice, and access to their articles and theses; and to Josephine Newton of Bedford Modern School for her invaluable assistance with translation from foreign sources.

NOTES

1. E. B. Powley, *The English Navy in the Revolution of 1688* (1928), 28–9. Unless otherwise stated, this and the following paragraph is based on the narrative in Powley, chs. 2–6, which remains the standard account of the movements of the fleets; for a broader perspective it should be supplemented by J. Childs, *The Army, James II and the Glorious Revolution* (Manchester, 1980), ch. vii.

2. Powley, *English Navy*, 62. For more recent and comprehensive, though contradictory, treatments of the Dutch strategy and the weather situation in the 1688 campaign, see C. Jones, 'The Protestant Wind of 1688: Myth and Reality', *European Studies Review*, iii (1973), 201–21; J. Anderson, 'Combined Operations and the Protestant Wind: Some Maritime Aspects of the Glorious Revolution of 1688', *The Great Circle*, ix (1987), 96–107.

3. N. Luttrell, *A Brief Historical Relation of State Affairs, from September 1678 to April 1714* (Oxford, 1857), I, 465, 466, 469–70, 473; *HMC Dartmouth*, I, 183–4; BL, MS. RP.630; Childs, *Army*, 168–174.

4. Add. 34,510, ff. 152v, 169; *HMC 7th Rep.* 422–3; J. R. Jones, *The Revolution of 1688 in England* (1972), 286–7; Childs, *Army*, 169–70, 181–3; W. A. Speck, 'The Orangist Conspiracy against James II', *Historical Journal*, xxx (1987), 455–62.

5. NUL, PWA 2188, 2202; G. Burnet, *Bishop Burnet's History of his Own Time*, ed. J. Routh (Oxford, 1823) iii, 291; H. C. Foxcroft, *A Supplement to Burnet's History of my Own Time* (Oxford, 1902), 285; N. Japikse, ed., *Correspondentie van Willem III en van Hans Willem Bentinck* (The Hague, 1928–35), ii, 607–24; Anderson, 'Combined Operations', 96–107. Weather and tide conditions forced the abandonment of Exmouth for Torbay: Anderson, 'Combined Operations', 103.

6. Jones, 'The Protestant Wind', 215, 219–20; J. R. Powell and E. K. Timings, eds, *The Rupert and Monck Letterbook 1666* (1966), 227–8, 283.

7. *HMC 7th Rep.*, 422–3; Anderson, 'Combined Operations', 102.

8. Foxcroft, *Supplement*, p. 285; Japikse, *Correspondentie*, ii, 616–17.

9. Japikse, *Correspondentie*, i, i, 59–60; A. Herbert, 'A Letter to all Commanders of Ships and Seamen' in *An Impartial Account of Some Remarkable Passages in the Life of Arthur Earl of Torrington* (1691), 12–13. Cf. Japikse, *Correspondentie*, i, i, 46–7.

10. *HMC Dartmouth*, i, 259.

11. J. K. Laughton, ed., *Memoirs Relating to the Lord Torrington* (Camden Society, new series xlvi, 1889), 27–8.

12. Bodl., Rawlinson MS. D.148, f. 10v; J. S. Clarke, *The Life of James the Second* (1816), ii, 208.

13. *HMC Dartmouth*, i, 260–1; *Memoirs of Thomas, Earl of Ailesbury, Written by Himself* (Roxburghe Club, 1890), i, 186.

14. *Torrington Memoirs*, p. 32.

15. Clarke, *James the Second*, ii, 208. For similar estimates see Add. 34,510, f. 170v; Arconati Lamberti, *Mémoires de la Dernière Revolution en Angleterre* (The Hague, 1702), i, 599.

16. The total absence of private Russell papers prevents the postulation of any interpretation of his motives other than that traditionally accepted, namely that he sought revenge for the execution of his cousin Lord Russell: Burnet, *History*, iii, 263; Sir J. Dalrymple, *Memoirs of Great Britain and Ireland* (1771), i, 133.

17. B L Egerton MS. 2621, f. 47. Even the conservative estimate would suggest that the navy conspiracy was more extensive than that in the army, for eight captains would have been 10% of those in commission at that time: PRO, Adm. 8/1, fos. 238–9. For the small number of army conspirators see Childs, *Army*, 85, 140, 162.

18. *Torrington Memoirs*, 30–2; letter is in *HMC Dartmouth*, i, 219.

19. *HMC Dartmouth*, i, 220, 275, 277.

20. *HMC Dartmouth*, i, 226, 279–80, 282; F. Devon, *Vindication of the Right Honourable the First Lord Dartmouth from the Charge of Conspiracy or High Treason brought against him in the year 1691, and Revived by Macaulay in his 'History of England'*, 1855 (1856), 50–1.

21. Devon, *Vindication*, 51.

22. *Torrington Memoirs*, 28.

23. P. Le Fevre, 'Tangier, the Navy and its Connection with the Glorious Revolution of 1688', *The Mariner's Mirror*, lxxiii (1987), 188.

24. E. Chappell, ed., *The Tangier Papers of Samuel Pepys* (1935), 186; *HMC Finch*, ii, 185.

25. P. Le Fevre, 'Tangier', 187–90.

26. Add. 34,510, f. 145; Add. 41,816, f. 209v.

27. Burnet, *History*, iii, 285–6. Suggestions that Russell had more influence in the fleet than Herbert cannot be sustained: J. D. Davies, 'The Seagoing Personnel of the Navy, 1660–89: Political, Religious and Social Aspects' (unpublished University of Oxford D.Phil. thesis, 1986), pp. 246–7.

28. J. Carswell, *The Descent on England* (1969), 167n.

29. S. Hornstein, 'The Deployment of the English Navy in Peacetime 1674–88' (unpublished University of Leiden D.Litt. thesis, 1985), pp. 158–66.

30. Add. 28,053, ff. 291–2; Add. 51,511, f. 9v; S. W. Singer, *The*

Correspondence of Henry Hyde, Earl of Clarendon, and of his Brother Laurence Hyde, Earl of Rochester (2 vols., 1828), i, 92; A. Browning, *The Memoirs of Sir John Reresby* (Glasgow, 1936), 294.

31. NUL, PWV 53 (unfol.), Blathwayt to Southwell, 'Whitehall Satterday' (1686), 3 Dec. 1687.

32. Burnett, *History*, iii, 261; BL Egerton MS. 2621, ff. 9–10.

33. For contemporary suspicions of Dartmouth see Add. 34,510, f. 166; Add. 51,511, f. 9v; *Ailesbury Memoirs*, i, 186. For more recent suspicions of his conduct see M. J. Sydenham, 'The Anxieties of an Admiral: Lord Dartmouth and the Revolution of 1688', *History Today*, xii (1962), 714–20.

34. Bodl. Carte MS. 40, f. 108.

35. Magdalene College, Cambridge, Pepys MS. 2860, p. 404; Bodl. Carte MS. 217, f. 201; Marquise Campana de Cavelli, *Les Derniers Stuarts à Saint-Germain-en-Laye* (Paris, 1871), ii, 345.

36. Bodl., Rawlinson MS. D.148, fos. 1–2; *Ailesbury Memoirs*, i, 185; Childs, *Army*, 142; Speck, 'Orangist Conspiracy', 457.

37. Bodl., Rawlinson MS. D.148, f. 10v; Lamberti, *Mémoires*, i, 526–7, 599; Dalrymple, *Memoirs*, ii, 319; *Ailesbury Memoirs*, i, 185; Jones, *Revolution*, 232.

38. *HMC Dartmouth*, i, 176; C. Dalton, *English Army Lists and Commission Registers, 1661–1714* (1892), ii, 129.

39. See e.g. Jones, *Revolution*, 228–9.

40. Davies, 'Seagoing Personnel', 247.

41. *HMC Dartmouth*, i, 141–2, 166, 171; Childs, *Army*, 144, 158–9.

42. Jones, *Revolution*, 229–30; Childs, *Army*, 48–9; Speck, 'Orangist Conspiracy', 455–6.

43. Davies, 'Seagoing Personnel', 226–7.

44. *Reresby Memoirs*, 582.

45. H. Hornyold, *Genealogical Memoirs of the Family of Strickland of Sizergh* (Kendal, 1928), 264–67; Davies, 'Seagoing Personnel', 131.

46. G. M. Crump, ed., *Poems on Affairs of State*, iv (1968), 167; PRO, PRO.31/3/168, ff. 51v–53; Dr. Williams's Library, MS. 31Q, pp. 81–2; Burnet, *History*, iii, 95–6.

47. *HMC Dartmouth*, i, 132–3.

48. PRO, Adm. 8/1, ff. 219v, 232–3; J. Miller, 'Catholic Officers in the Later Stuart Army', *EHR*, lxxxviii (1973), 47; Childs, *Army*, 22. Cf. Jones, *Revolution*, 232.

49. Dr. Williams's Library, MS. 31Q, p. 338; NUL, PWA 2142.

50. Longleat House, Thynne MS. 42, ff. 156–7; Burnet, *History*, iii, 248–9; *Reresby Memoirs*, 503–4; C. R. Markham, ed., *The Life of Captain Stephen Martin 1666–1740* (1895), 6.

51. PRO.30/53/8, f. 67; Add. 34,487, f. 17.

52. *Torrington Memoirs*, 27–8.

53. Japikse, *Correspondentie*, i, i, 59–60.

54. NUL, PWA 2110, 2166, 2168; Jones, *Revolution*, 179–83, 255–7, 272–4.

55. Bodl. Carte MS. 130, f. 313; Dr. Williams's Library, MS. 31Q, pp. 320–1; Foxcroft, *Burnet Supplement*, 223; Lamberti, *Mémoires*, i, 589; Campana de Cavelli, *Les Derniers Stuarts*, ii, 332–3. It was believed in April 1688

that several sea officers had refused to accept commands in such circumstances: NUL, PWA 2160.

56. Clarke, *James the Second*, ii, 187; *HMC Dartmouth*, i, 261.

57. Clarke, *James the Second*, ii, 186; Bodl. Carte MS. 130, f. 313.

58. Davies, 'Seagoing Personnel', 185–7.

59. R. C. Anderson, ed., *Journals and Narratives of the Third Dutch War* (1946), 310–11, 400–02. On Dartmouth's attitude to the French in 1688 see Devon, *Vindication*, 38.

60. For this belief see, *inter alia*, Add. 34,510, f. 172v; Add. 34,512, ff. 95, 108, 114; Burnet, *History*, iii, 248–9.

61. Herbert, *A Letter to All Commanders*, 13; *CSP Dom. 1689–90*, 40; *HMC Finch*, ii, 245, 270–1.

62. Analysis based on PRO, Adm. 8/2, fleet lists of 1 Aug. 1689, 1 July 1690.

63. Davies, 'Seagoing Personnel', 249–53.

64. Childs, *Army*, 85.

65. Clarke, *James the Second*, ii, 233–4.

66. *Ailesbury Memoirs*, i, 212.

67. PRO, Adm. 1/5253, f. 132.

68. PRO, Adm. 51/384, pt 3, *Garland* log, 26 Oct. 1688; National Maritime Museum, DAR-16, pp. 66–7.

69. N.M.M., DAR-16, pp. 66–7; *HMC Dartmouth*, i, 175.

70. Bodl., Rawlinson MS. C.976, Jeremiah Johnson's journal, 5 Nov.; PRO, Adm. 52/22, pt 1, *Dreadnought* (Thomas Stollard's journal), 5 Nov.; Adm. 52/7, pt. 3, *Bristol*, 5 Nov.

71. PRO, Adm. 52/88, pt. 1, *Plymouth*, 5 Nov.

72. PRO, Adm. 51/384, pt 3, *Garland*, 5 Nov.; Adm. 51/4322, pt 2, *Ruby*, 5 Nov.; Adm. 51/4160, pt. 1, *Deptford*, 5 Nov.; Bodl., Rawlinson MS. C.976, *Elizabeth* (Capt. Nevill's journal), 5 Nov.

73. *Torrington Memoirs*, 26; N.M.M., DAR-16, pp. 66–8, 84–6.

74. Davies, 'Seagoing Personnel', 215–24, 237–8.

75. Longleat, Thynne MS. 42, ff. 134, 138; PRO, Prob. 11/398, f. 294.

76. Clarke, *James the Second*, ii, 233–4.

77. Dalton, *English Army Lists*, ii, 27; All Souls College, Oxford, MS. 317, ff. 22, 41; Magdalene College, Cambridge, Pepys MS. 2860, pp. 88–9.

78. Grenvill Collins, the master of the flagship, who was present only at the council of 26 Oct., had risen to the post of hydrographer to Trinity House through Grafton's patronage: J. R. Tanner, ed., *Samuel Pepys's Naval Minutes* (1926), 189, 388.

79. PRO, Adm. 52/35, pt. 1, *Foresight*, 27 Oct.; Bodl., Rawlinson MS. D.752, f. 12v.

80. See Bodl., Rawlinson MS. A.186, ff. 438–9.

81. PRO, Adm. 52/35, pt. 1, *Foresight*, 3 Nov.

82. Bodl., Rawlinson MS. A.186, f. 368v. I hope to be able to produce in due course a fuller account of the career of this colourful later Stuart character.

83. See the weather reports in the relevant ships' journals in PRO, Adm. 51, 52; Bodl., Rawlinson MSS. C.198, C.969, C.976 & D.752.

84. *Journals and Narratives*, 23–4, 53–4, 309–13.

85. C. Petrie, *The Marshal Duke of Berwick* (1953), 41–2; *HMC Dartmouth*, i, 264. This argument was also accepted by other senior captains. When, at the full council on 5 Nov., the apparently gloomy strategic situation was put to each captain individually as he entered the cabin, the first three to agree with the defeatist elite council propositions were the highly experienced captains Richard Carter, John Tyrwhitt (a Catholic) and Sir William Booth (a staunch Jacobite loyalist): N.M.M., DAR-16, pp. 85–6.

86. And contemporary jibes: one pamphleteer in Oct. 1688 believed that 'not a captain, & scarce a man in all our fleet will fire a gun against the Dutch', and warned the mariners of the avarice, religious hypocrisy, lies, and 'brutish lust', of the 'great greasy Dutchman': Staffordshire Record Office, MS. D(W)1778/Ii/1502.

87. PRO, Adm. 52/75, pt. 1, *Newcastle*; N.M.M., ADM/L/N89; *HMC Dartmouth*, i, 210; PRO, Adm. 106/383, f. 210; Magdalene College, Cambridge, Pepys MS. 2862, p. 422.

88. Japikse, *Correspondentie*, iii, 69–70.

89. See Clarke, *James the Second*, ii, 276; PRO, Adm. 1/5253, ff. 131–2; Davies, 'Seagoing Personnel', 253.

90. Japikse, *Correspondentie*, iii, 74; PRO, Adm. 52/75, pt. 1, *Newcastle*, 21 Dec. 1688.

91. Magdalene College, Cambridge, Pepys MS. 2858, pp. 366–7; *HMC Dartmouth*, i, 211.

92. Bodl., Rawlinson MS. A. 183, f. 190; Rawlinson MS. A.228, f. 123; *HMC Finch.*, ii, 117; J. Ehrman, *The Navy in the War of William III* (Cambridge, 1953), chs. ix, x.

93. Staffordshire RO, MS. D(W)1778/Ii/1747, 1767.

94. Davies, 'Seagoing Personnel', pp. 216–21.

95. N. A. M. Rodger, ed., *Articles of War* (Lavenham, 1982), 13–19; PRO, Adm. 51/384, pt. 3, *Garland*, 11 Oct. 1688.

96. Clarke, *James the Second*, ii, 208; *Torrington Memoirs*, 32.

97. Clarke, *James the Second*, ii, 208; *Torrington Memoirs*, 32; Add. 51, 511, f. 10; E. D. H. Tollemache, *The Tollemaches of Helmingham and Ham* (Ipswich, 1949), 83–91. Byng's suggestion that the plot was revealed to Dartmouth by the future Jacobite agent Captain David Lloyd is untenable. Lloyd only returned to Plymouth from the Mediterranean in his ship, the *Sedgemoor*, as late as 17 Dec. 1688: PRO, Adm. 52/75, pt. 1, *Newcastle* log.

98. *HMC Dartmouth*, i, 176; Lamberti, *Mémoires*, i, 526–7; *HMC Rutland*, ii, 122; *HMC 10th Rep.*, pt. iv, 397.

99. N.M.M. DAR-16, pp. 107–8, 113, 115–16, 127–8; PRO, Adm. 51/384, pt. 3, *Garland*, 16 Nov. It may be significant that, although the minutes of the councils of 14 and 16 Nov. show Sir John Berry as having been present, he was in fact inexplicably absent from both meetings: Bodl., Rawlinson MS. D.752, ff. 13v, 14.

100. See e.g. *HMC Dartmouth*, i, 144, 171–4, 188, 206–7.

101. *HMC Dartmouth*, iii, 62–3; *HMC 7th Rep., Appendix*, p. 416.

102. Clarke, *James the Second*, ii, 233–4.

103. *HMC Dartmouth*, i, 226; Clarke, *James the Second*, ii, 235.

104. Clarke, *James the Second*, ii, 207–8 (quotation from p. 208); *Ailesbury*

Memoirs, i, 186; Dalrymple, *Memoirs*, i, 325; *HMC Dartmouth*, i, 220.

105. Dr. Williams's Library, MS. 31P, p. 585.

106. PRO.30/53/8, f. 67; Clarke, *James the Second*, ii, 204.

107. *HMC Dartmouth*, i, 260–1; J. R. Tanner, ed., *Catalogue of the Naval Manuscripts in the Pepysian Library at Magdalene College, Cambridge*, I(1903), 395.

108. Clarke, *James the Second*, ii, 233–4. Cf. Jones, *Revolution*, 231–2.

109. Magdalene College, Cambridge, Pepys MS. 2862, pp. 198, 254–5.

110. Add. 34,510, f. 169; Childs, *Army*, 177–8, 182–3.

7

REPRESENTING THE REVOLUTION:
POLITICS AND HIGH CULTURE IN 1688

Steven N. Zwicker

In the constellation of British politics the Glorious Revolution occupies a notable place. The role of that revolution in securing parliamentary liberty and in the foundation of personal freedom has long been argued. Of late there has been revision: historians are now agreed on the revolution's conservative character; some suggest that the term 'revolution' itself is a misnomer for the events of the late fall and winter of 1688/89;[1] one historian has recently argued the unruffled continuity of patriarchalism, deference, and divine right ideology for the whole of the late seventeenth and eighteenth centuries.[2] However revised, the character and history of the events of these months remain rightly fixed as of high importance. And yet the standard histories of English literature, even studies of Augustan writing, hardly acknowledge the events of these months; the indices of these books often contain no entry for the revolution. Was the revolution with all its long-lasting consequences for the structure of politics, foreign relations, and economic organization simply unremarked in the high culture of those who witnessed and participated in the deposition of one monarch and the installation of another? The events of 1688 would seem to offer promising materials for a literature of defense and celebration, especially in an age when the actors in high politics were more than occasionally the creators of high culture and when literary forms were used not only to contemplate events in politics but often to precipitate political change. And yet there is some justification for the traditional indifference of literary histories to the revolution. Indeed, it is hard to think of a political crisis in this century so unremarked in literary form. There is good reason to consider *Macbeth* a meditation on the accession of a Scottish clan to the English throne;[3] the execution of Charles I and triumph of militant puritanism called forth a notable literature of political meditation, defense, and celebration. Simply to name the *Horatian Ode* is to remark how brilliantly high cultural forms could act to interpret the meaning of political change.

The constitutional struggle that most directly precedes the revolution —
the Popish Plot and Exclusion — is examined and contested and partly
enacted in writing of quite substantial energy and art. But a reading of
the literature of 1688/89 produces no immediate analogues.

I want to speculate on the reasons for literary silence partly for
what it might tell us about the revolution and in part for what it
suggests about the cultural absorption of 1688. Both issues will involve
us in thinking about the character of the revolution, its representation,
and what effect the political habits of the revolution — habits of
obliqueness and innuendo — had on the literary imagination. In turn,
I want to examine the revolution through its only literary masterpiece,
Don Sebastian. The aesthetic and popular success of Dryden's Jacobite
drama raise questions about the force and identity of Jacobite ideals
and values in 1689 and about the political identity of cultural forms.
Throughout this century the idioms of high culture were used to
express political values and to lend them prestige and authority; the
rather sudden and wide literary silence that surrounds 1688 has its own
political and expressive significance.

We might well assume that on the eve of the revolution and directly
in its aftermath the work of literature would have been obvious and
extensive. The events of 1688 were in need of defense, interpretation,
and celebration. Less polemically, the function of literature is also to
represent the complexity and anxiety of the moment, to calibrate the
fluidity of events, the possibilities of subversion and reversal, the moral
and ethical consequences of political action, the dangers of resistance
and passivity. Slightly more than a year before the revolution we have
an example of a literary text that does exactly this kind of work.
Dryden's *Hind and the Panther* expresses the very great sense of danger
and instability that marked James's last year. What is communicated
in this intricate and evasive work is the difficulty of achieving political
credibility for a monarch much in need of credibility and explanation.
A fair amount of the energy of this work is expended in arguments for
the rectitude and high-mindedness of the regime. But there are other
facts about James's rule that the poem also suggests: the anxiety of
those charged with its defense, the precariousness of its political and
religious aims. Obliqueness and fright run through the poem, and its
defensiveness conveys an idea of how significant must have been the
resistance to James's monarchy by the middle of 1687.

The achievements of the revolution found no such expression
or exaltation. The only great literary text from these months, and
it comes rather late, almost a year after the landing at Torbay, is

a blank verse tragedy that exalts the high courage and principles not of the leaders of the Revolution but of the Monarch who had fled the Revolution and was by then pawn and dependant of Louis XIV. Rather than a revolutionary text, *Don Sebastian* is a reactionary creed, an irony that raises the occasional coincidence of revolutionary action and reactionary art; but more directly, *Don Sebastian* reveals the terms of resistance that could be assembled in 1689, the cultural resources that could be summoned on behalf of a deposed and discredited regime, and the issues that needed to be conjured with in any work either defending or deploring the revolution. As literature of the Glorious Revolution, *Don Sebastian* tells us a great deal about the fabric of ideals that could be spun around failure and deposition and about why such ideals might have endured the revolution and indeed played very well to London audiences in 1689 and after.

Citing *Don Sebastian* as the only great literary text of the revolution must also raise questions about generational shifts among writers in the late seventeeth century and the possibility that is was merely an accident of literary history that the former laureate should have been trapped in his Roman Catholicism and Jacobitism in 1689, that the greatest exponent and exemplar of high culture in the 1690s — translator of Horace, Homer, Juvenal and Virgil — should have been an adherent of Stuart monarchy and Stuart policy (not to say principles); and, in turn, that the closest student of his art, Alexander Pope, should also have been a Catholic and Jacobite and in his first major work, *Windsor Forest*, have identified himself as an acolyte of Stuart monarchy. Was it solely chance that high culture should have been so firmly attached to Stuart monarchy, and that the revolution should have been attacked in cultural terms as boorish, illiterate, and dull;[4] that William's first laureate was Thomas Shadwell, dunce of *MacFlecknoe*; and the Williamite epic should have been Blackmore's *Prince Arthur* rather than Dryden's *Virgil*. From this perspective Clarendon's *History of the Rebellion* seems emblematically and nostalgically poised in 1702, casting a long backward glance at Stuart personalities and principles.

In fact, the links between the Stuart court and high culture are deep and complex in this century.[5] It was no accident that those panegyrists who welcomed a returning Stuart in 1660 should so insistently have linked the Restoration with the revival of arts and letters.[6] The patronage and production of high culture in the decades following the Restoration are impressive, not least so under James II. But it is to simplify the sources of that productivity to suggest that wit and luxury were the exclusive model, precondition, or main support of literary art. We should not forget that *Paradise Lost, Paradise Regained,* and *Samson Agonistes* were products of the first years of the Restoration, or that Bunyan and Baxter, spiritual writers who have abundant claims on our literary attention, could hardly have found the court a source of inspiration. Clearly, both patronage by and resistance to the court have a significant role in restoration culture. The sudden demise of the center of that patronage with the flight of James must have been a source of some consternation in 1688, but the patronage system itself not only continued — and often in the same hands — new patrons emerged on the market together with a gathering force of patronage deployed for specifically political aims and purposes in the 1690s. The sudden flurry of new editions of Milton's works following the revolution suggests the increasing role of politics in the formulation of literary canons.[7] Indeed, republication and translation are more characteristic of this decade than is literary invention, a fact about the decade that returns us to the center of the problem, the literary silence surrounding the revolution.

One of the most interesting verbal documents of the revolution is the set of debates engaged in by members of the convention that settled the crown on William and Mary.[8] Those who have studied the language of the convention have noted the detailed and careful exchanges surrounding the choice of words for describing James's absence and William's presence in England. The scrupling over language had an immediate and important political rationale. On the careful choice of words rested a cornerstone of the revolution. If the debates could satisfy the conscience of those who had sworn allegiance and passive obedience to James II, the revolution might be swiftly secured. Hence, the careful deliberation over a vocabulary that would neutralize and pacify, that would suggest James's abandonment of the throne, its subsequent vacancy and William's entry into England as an effort to secure and preserve parliamentary liberty. A whole array of words was examined and debated; the deliberation was an effort at discovering a way of representing the revolution that would cause the least disturbance to the civic fabric, that would raise the fewest qualms, legal scruples, and ethical anxieties. Such a discovery was made in the language of demise and vacancy. Of course, some regarded the debates as exercises in hypocrisy or self-delusion. But the efforts to fix a neutralizing vocabulary were in fact successful; the nation as a whole allowed the revolution without hesitation. It helped of course that James had conducted an increasingly vigorous perhaps desperate campaign to install his religion and co-religionists and secure the throne for Roman Catholicism in perpetuity, and the revolution was of course accompanied by a flood of anti-catholic propaganda.[9] But the linguistic activities of the convention should not be underestimated in calculating the success of the revolution.

What also needs to be remarked is that in the story which these debates tell not only do we find a neutralizing and pacifying vocabulary but also a language that suggests the remarkable passivity of the nation. This is a revolution not of heroic endeavor and godly militancy but of deep impassivity, retreat and negation. James withdrew from office, the nation sat passively obedient (or disobedient as the case may be), and William was blown across the channel by a Protestant wind.[10] To cast the nation as victim at once of Jesuit machination and Protestant redemption clears the people of complicity both in Roman Catholic intrigue and Dutch usurpation. And the passivity is to be found not only in the debates but everywhere in the verse celebrating the deliverance. For the nation to have played a passive, if willing, role in the rescue means that some of the scrupling over passive obedience can be put to rest and that a de facto acceptance of William and Mary can be taken as the route of least political resistance. Passive obedience was a banner that flew high over the camp of nonjurors and Jacobites;[11] it was an idiom of considerable moral capital and authority. National passivity allowed the mysteries of providence to wipe clear the crimes of rebellion and abjuration of oaths. So long as the revolution was acquiesced in rather than effected, the politics of conspiracy and rebellion could be eased into the principle of happy deliverance. None participating in or acquiescing to the revolution could have desired to revive the memory of civil war, and if we miss Old Testament ethical vigor and moral urgency in the language of this Protestant revolution, if we are surprised by the supineness of this foundation of liberty, we need to be aware that the civil wars remained part of the context of any constitutional change in the seventeenth century. It was after all James's father who had gone to the block and some of those who had witnessed the execution would still have been alive in the revolution.

If the revolution of 1688 is glorious then in part because it is bloodless, cultural silence may have been one of the minor expenses incurred along the passive way. Not that the conventional effort is entirely absent, but it seems hampered, confused in its handling of themes, caught out for an idiom, a language of revolutionary exaltation, nervously suspended between the claims of conscience and expediency. Of course a respectable amount of verse was produced, although by comparison with the restoration, a comparison that panegyrists tactfully avoid, the amount of celebratory verse is surprisingly small. And though the quality of writing is below even what we would expect for corporate and occasional exercises — university volumes from Oxford and Cambridge as well as show pieces by individual entrepreneurs — the panegyrics taken as a whole have an interesting story to tell about the engagement of high culture with this revolution. What comes immediately clear from the body of this verse is that both the character of the revolution and the ways in which it was represented work against the creation of an heroic idiom for 1688. Not simply that the events of the revolution were indeed bloodless, that the reigning monarch fled the country in fear, but also that the revolution was hardly the result of a national effort. This revolution was deliverance from outside and above, a "providential revolution" effected by a foreign prince governing a former military and current commercial rival, stadtholder of a nation that had effected a tremendous national humiliation in 1667. This prince was now chosen out by a mysterious providence to spare a luckless people from the miseries of popery and slavery; a Dutchman was needed to rescue the virgin from the dragon's jaws.[12] Of course, the language of deliverance allows large sway for providential readings of this event, and sermon after sermon as well as nearly every panegyric celebrates the unpredictable and miraculous ways of providence. We need of course to allow that the conventions of panegyric include such elevation and agency, but this heavenly rescue was effected neither by a martial hero nor by a fearsome God, rather by a cool and distant intelligence. Zeal and enthusiasm are figures not welcome in this Protestant recovery; while miraculous, the revolution was no levelling or overturning but a victory of piety and moderation.

From the central fact of national passivity and acquiescence there seems to be no escape. Nor perhaps was one wanted. Quite consistently in the panegyrics, the nation is depicted as confused, unhappy, reluctant, and recumbent. England lies wasted and dismal; justice has withdrawn, the laws lie broken and trampled, the nation is prey to insulting foe.[13] The rescue is effected, however, not by arms but by 'looks'.[14] This revolution is a triumph of virtue, its hero praised not for martial valor but for prudence, his breastplate stamped with 'truth' and 'love'.[15] Although more than one of these pieces nervously acknowledges conquest and invasion, even usurpation, those disagreeable idioms are transformed, pacified, Europeanized.[16] Indeed, some of the offending vocabulary drifts from the point where it might most cogently or immediately be applied to quite different targets; in the panegyrics we hear of 'usurping France . . . invading English rights';[17] more than once kingship by blood and immutable divine right are elided for merit and *salus populi*:[18]

> Kings differ not from Men of baser blood,
> But in the Godlike Pow'r of doing Good,
> When some brave Spirit did the rest outshine,
> The Ancients bad him reign, and thought his Race divine;
> That being inthron'd, as in his proper sphere
> The lustre of his Worth more sparkling might appear;
> For Objects are not seen by being nigh,
> But plac't at a fit distance from the eye.

The theory of divine right kingship and sanctity of lineal descent are here traded wholesale for kingship of the common good. In this account, the optics of godlike ascendancy are simply a device to enhance political prestige; divine right kingship is a trick of public relations rather than immutable civic or sacred truth.

One panegyrist mixes theories of kingship in order to account for and give credibility to William's unexpected and perhaps illegitimate presence in the kingdom:[19]

> No dull Succession sanctifies his Right,
>   Nor conquest gain'd in Fight,
>   But o're the Peoples minds, and there
> Does *Right Divine* triumphantly appear.
>   The mind, impassible and free,
> No pow'r can govern, but the deity,
> Howev'r o're Persons, and o're Fortunes, may
>   A bold Intruder sway;
> The *Right Divine* is by the people given,
> And 'tis their Suffrage speaks the mind of Heav'n.

The address is an odd mixture of providentialism, election, *jure divino*, and contract. It toys with but dismisses lineal descent and conquest only to rescue divine right from the language of contract and donation. What we have here is not an exercise in high strung ambiguity and paradox but an irresolute and contradictory mixing of constitutional idioms. The lines, colored ever so slightly by a Miltonic rhetoric, suggest an absence of theory and a failure of idioms — heroic, legal, dynastic — by which one might indeed figure the meaning of the revolution or the person of its hero.

Nor is it difficult to understand this reluctance to allow succession since the son-in-law and nephew displacing the father-in-law and uncle could hardly claim much protection from that model. Nor is the shyness over conquest difficult to grasp. Conquest as a source of legitimacy carries a heavy price. What is worth observing about a number of these efforts is the very difficult and indeed contradictory circumstance which the revolution and its consented to representation put those who would address and vindicate the event and its principal actors. Miraculous redemption and business-as-usual are difficult points of view to argue simultaneously. I have not touched on the very many references to William as savior of religion and the law, dwelling rather on the difficulties of model, office, and legitimating language because both redemption and continuity had to be addressed, and while the rhetoric of liberty and property is much and on occasion energetically deployed, the circumstances of the revolution, the nature of William's entry, the very real as well as useful passivity of the nation, and the ambiguity of James's status created a troubled circumstance for a literature of heroism and high principles. It was a difficult task to adjudicate such a language in this revolution, but 1688 was not without parallels, analogues and types that might explain the happy conquest.

It helped of course that the landing at Torbay took place on November 5, and that 1688 was the hundredth anniversary of the English triumph over international Catholicism. The defeat of Marian persecution, Elizabeth's glorious reign, and the humiliation of the Spanish armada are precursors and predictors of William's Protestant triumph. But the defeat of the Armada, the centerpiece of such analogues, had its own mildly subsersive subtext. 1588 was an English triumph over threatened foreign invasion; 1688 was a triumphant foreign invasion and routing of an English monarch. Of course, the ironies of the analogy are partly hidden under the shadow of its more happy application, but they could hardly have been invisible in a literature that everywhere allows, indeed embraces, passivity. And the problem of claiming an English identity both for the revolution and its resistance was of course a real difficulty. In fact, what seems to be at the center of the revolution is absence: a throne that lies vacant; a king that has disappeared in the night; a people reluctant to act in defiance of or on behalf of William's entry. That set of circumstances — literal and metaphoric — suggests some of the difficulty of those who might have produced a literature of the revolution.

The highest forms of literature are then either in difficulty or in the hands of an opposition, but there is another literary mode, satire, not quite so fallow. I want to exclude for the moment some satiric forms that lie close to popular literature: broadside and lampoon. That public response belongs to a different category than that of high culture. But 1688 does not of course go unnoticed in the traditional forms of satire where both Roman Catholic rapacity and Dutch boorishness and usurpation form topics of steady interest not only in 1688 but throughout the coming decade. The modern edition of *Poems on Affairs of State, 1688–1697* runs to over six hundred pages and concerns itself with works that might be thought of as literature, although even the editor of this volume — one might have thought a partisan of the decade — begins his preface by regretting the 1690s as 'one of the dullest decades in English literature'.[20] In his commentary on the formal verse satires, W. J. Cameron remarks their narrowness of vision, the redundancy of personal attacks, the reductiveness of their caricature. While we would expect and indeed hope for such bluntness and hardness in lampoon and broadside — and there the reductiveness is not only imposed by formal demands, brevity and speed remark the alliance to jingle and litany, but also part of its appeal — the traditional appeal of satire also includes complexity, disinterestedness, commentary from beside or above the fray — qualities that are more often absent from than characteristic of the satires of 1689 and after. Elsewhere I have suggested that fable and translation are particularly characteristic and brilliantly practised in this decade because so much about its public and political life seemed contingent, transient, and unstated.[21] The debates in the convention parliament can be read as an emblem of such uncertainty; they suggest as well that obliqueness and indirection follow from such a circumstance. Fable and translation not only offered the direct protection of cover and indirection in the expression of political aims and principles — and a number of writers in this century were caught holding difficult or embarrassing positions after a shift of power had taken place — but also and more expressively, fable and translation are indicators of the mood and circumstance of the whole culture. The political and intellectual uncertainty and obliqueness of the 1690s were hardly propitious for the growth of satire which can happily flourish as opposition, but for such an opposition values and limits must be fixed as a point of reference, moral and civic ideals need to be taken for granted rather than newly charted with each shift of the political tide. The first years of the restoration were ideal for panegyric and satire; moral and political landmarks were visible, celebrated, idealized even if not adhered to. Such a case can be made well into the 1680s; the 1690s seem by contrast a moment of high political and cultural uncertainty; and that uncertainty communicated itself to satirists, indeed to all who undertook literary venture. It was in fact a circumstance in which fable, translation, and a drama of masking, indirection, and innuendo would thrive.

Let me sharpen the case slightly. 1688 might well be read as a

E

revolution of compromise and collusion. Rather than a trumpeting of high ideals, of a new social and political order, protection and retrenchment were its aims. This was a moment in the political culture when wary hesitation and cool distance marked much of the behavior of the political nation. Out of this circumstance, and more, out of disappointment, bitterness, and no little sense of irony came the literary masterpiece of the revolution, *Don Sebastian,* a play whose aesthetic and popular success must raise questions about the force of Jacobite and nonjuring sentiments in the 1690s. The popular success of the play in 1689 is particularly puzzling, for the fall of that year was a time when both the former laureate and his former master were under savage attack.

What then was the play articulating? For one thing, it is a feast of dramatic conventions and devices, of heroic rhetoric and high ideals, of double plots, concealed identities, hidden morals, interlocking rings, incestuous longings, and spurned honor. It is a play whose conventions Dryden knew well how to handle, and their somewhat nostalgic display in *Don Sebastian* must have provided a good deal of pleasure for those with a taste for heroic drama. But rather more was at stake for the former laureate than shuffling a familiar if brilliant hand of dramatic conventions. Dryden wanted very much to enter the public debate over the revolution and he wanted to enter it on his own ground, in forms of which he was a master, with conventions and codes whose meaning he might shape, with a language whose resonance he might control. *Don Sebastian* gave him a format that could provide not only artistic and financial rewards but also a means of vindicating his personal and political honor while minimizing the damage of his religious conversion and exposing the hypocrisy of the revolution, the bankruptcy of its ideals, the hollowness of its slogans. In its own way, *Don Sebastian* is as steady and sharply directed a political argument as are the satires of the 1680s, but it is an argument conducted in so very different a set of circumstances that its very articulation has been denied and ignored in favor of what is read as timeless and universal in the work.[22] Needless to say, there is much that is timeless and universal in a play that announces a dramatic ancestry including Sophocles and Shakespeare. But we also need to recognize that the high ground of literary affiliation and literary history was itself a crucial vantage point for Dryden after 1688. The play steadily entertains and arranges a set of political arguments so that eternal verities might be argued out of an historically potent and particular set of political events, positions, platforms, and claims. This is a play that is in steady colloquy with the arguments posed in defense of the revolution.

The aim of that colloquy is to embarrass and debase the revolution and to assert the heroic and tragic character of a Catholic prince vanquished by a cruel and unsurping infidel. There is some irony in the fact that the very success of *Don Sebastian* as timeless literary masterpiece argues Dryden's ability to cover the polemical with claims of high principles, to soften and universalize difficult particulars, to divert attention away from polemical values and political conclusions that were fixed in the revolutionary moment. But first and foremost *Don Sebastian* is a piece of very high culture indeed.

Tragedy is the genre of this play and it is so announced in bold letters that cross the title page. Under this rubric, we are invited to contemplate conquest, usurpation, betrayal, and retreat as the very stuff of high art. Generic identification not only elevates the materials of 1688 to a high pitch but lends to them a particular interpretation, for *Don Sebastian* centers on a hero flawed but majestic whose fall was not a cowardly flight but a tragic inevitability, a reversal cruel and ironic but beyond comprehension and following from sins concealed in distant generations. Such tragedy cannot be averted, particularly in the realm of politics, and the pattern of conquest, betrayal, and retreat is one lent tragic dignity by the play. Thus are the principles of the drama imagined and thus is the fate of the conquered portrayed. Altitude and dignity are in fact the argument not only of genre but also of the prefatory materials that accompanied the printed play. *Don Sebastian* was dedicated to Philip, third earl of Leicester. The dedication to Leicester allowed Dryden to do a number of interesting things; most obviously, the long and deep connections of that family with literature and patronage is itself a claim to aristocratic privilege and protection.[23] At one point in the dedication, Dryden poses as Spenser to Leicester's Sidney. But a more elaborate argument about politics and art is folded into the dedication, for not only were the Sidneys a family of aristocratic lineage and dignity, they were also one of republican principles, nowhere more shockingly asserted than in the execution of Philip's brother Algernon for complicity in the Rye House Plot. The third earl of Leicester was himself at one time a 'zealous republican,' counsellor of Cromwell as well as member of Cromwell's 'House of Lords'.[24] He had since 1660 lived in retirement, having put away politics in favor of patronage, wit, and art. But Leicester's political career could not have been entirely absent from Dryden's mind nor could the important role that Leicester's younger brother, Howard, earl of Romney, played in the revolution been unknown to Dryden.[25] This dedication is then a claim to protection from a patron of Whiggish principles and republican lineage.

There is yet a more complex argument developed in the dedication about such a patron's significance, and that argument is twofold. First, Dryden develops, indeed dwells on, the virtues of the retired life which his patron exemplifies and which is extended through analogy to the Roman aristocrat and patron Titus Pomponius Atticus. That analogy allows Dryden to play Cicero to Leicester's Atticus, giving ample scope to the dignity and moral virtues of patron and protégé. Both Roman figures exemplify the meaning of retirement from politics: 'What a glorious Character was this once in *Rome*; I shou'd say in *Athens*, when in the disturbances of a State as mad as ours, the wise *Pomponius* transported all the remaining wisdom and vertue of his Country, into the Sanctuary of Peace and Learning'.[26] Dryden's citation from Cicero's letters at the close of the dedication sharpens his own appropriation of Cicero's exile for a figure of his own condition after the revolution, the analogy suggesting that Dryden's dislocation bore no faint resemblance to Cicero's purge. Both sets of figures, Roman and English, have turned away from the turmoil and disappointments of politics toward contemplation, self-knowledge, charity, and constancy. Moreover, this motif, the retreat from politics, is crucial to the play which closes as its hero departs for voluntary exile, and such a theme is of course a way of thinking about the circumstance of James II, that exemplar of piety and virtue who was cultivating self-knowledge in the gardens of Louis XIV.

There is one additional argument to be drawn out of the dedication to Leicester. Not only does the noble aristocrat retreat from politics to practice contemplation and self-knowledge, he is also to be found exercising patronage without regard to partisan affection. Such an exercise of patronage exemplifies a principle that not only allows a Jacobite to benefit from patronage without regard to politics but indeed expresses the true principles of patronage and thus articulates a whole system of moral, familial, and civic ties. Leicester's patronage is an example of the fullest meaning of charity and constancy not despite Dryden's political principles but because of them. The application of this ideal of patronage and charity to national politics is not difficult to make. The subjects of constancy and beneficence are repeatedly examined in the play, in the behavior of its principals, in the comic inversions, in the relations of subject to sovereign, in the inconstancy of the mobile. Those who have shunned and betrayed the former laureate are practising a brutality very much exemplified by the acts of betrayal and usurpation depicted within *Don Sebastian* and presumably visible everywhere since the revolution. The dedication to Leicester argues the meaning of charity and constancy on the local and at the national levels; the play suggests the eternal verities of such an argument, and it does so with no lack of suggestion how such verities might be seen in the events of the months prior to the staging of the play in November of 1689.

Perhaps because the dedication is laid at the feet of a republican aristocrat, Dryden can dare the arguments he indulges, nor could the principles of charity and constancy be faulted. Indeed, the high-minded display of such principles is steady throughout the play, and while such principles have not only a moral but also a sharp polemical meaning, I need to allow that the application of such materials to personal and national politics in 1688 was not quite so simple as my description of the dedication might suggest. Dryden was quite aware of the potential applications from the play, and he both invites and shields the play from such. Part of the shield is to be found in the very complexity of materials within the play, that unsteady system of analogies and parallels, proximities and disparities, that defeats any simple allegorical arrangement and, in part, is meant to discourage historical applications.[27] This is, moreover, an important argument of the *Preface* which suggests in other ways how generic issues insulate the play from too easy a political reading. For in this preface the playwright insists that the substance of his work is pure fiction. Many poems and plays of this century are eager to appropriate the honorific of history, to marshal its qualities, to claim significance through veracity. Dryden's argument is quite the opposite: 'As for the story or plot of the Tragedy, 'tis purely fiction; for I take it up where the History has laid it down. . . . declaring it to be fiction, I desire my Audience to think it no longer true, than while they are seeing it represented. . . I must likewise own that I have somewhat deviated from known History in the death of *Muley-Moluch*, who, by all relations dyed of a feaver in Battel, before his Army had wholly won the Field; but if I have allow'd him another day of life, it was because I stood in need of so shining a Character of brutality, as I have given him'.[28] The intermixing of comic scenes, subplots, hidden identities and delayed discoveries enlarges the scope of Dryden's claim that *Don Sebastian* is purely the matter of fiction. To those resources we must add the quite ostentatiously fictional element of the plot — the discovery of incest committed between hero and heroine. Whatever applications we might be invited to make from the play, no one was suggesting that incest was a crime either contemplated or committed by James II or William III. I suppose that there might be a slight titillation in the fact that William III was both James's son-in-law and nephew, but the charge of incest is one of the few that was not levelled against William in the satiric literature of the 1690s where just about every other natural and unnatural vice is charged to his person.

The *Preface* aims then to situate the play within the realms of romance, pathos, and tragedy; it shields the play against too quick an application — it would have us contemplate its politics philosophically as well as historically. It has one additional and rather important argument to make about the character of the work: its lineage and its author's position within that lineage. The literariness of the work is underscored by the argument about fiction; it is also very much the subject of the discussion of technique. The play, Dryden confesses, came after a long absence from the theater; it is rather too long for the stage, a fact that he learned from opening night. And yet as a printed work, its beauties and proportions are everywhere visible. The writing has 'a noble daring in figures, a loftiness in subject, propriety of thought'; it displays 'secret beauties in the decorum of parts and uniformity of design'; those who have read it, among them the Earl of Dorset, think it 'beyond any of my former plays'.[29] Dryden both commends its qualities and gives his readers the terms in which they are to appreciate the play. He is also insistent on the tradition to which this work belongs, the line of writers in which he might claim a position: Euripides and Sophocles, Lucan and Sallust, Shakespeare and Corneille. The *Preface* closes with a citation from Virgil, *Aeneid* 6, 'But thou, secure of Soul, unbent with Woes/The more thy Fortune frowns, the more oppose,' which recalls the use of Cicero at the end of the dedication and forms part of a complex, defensive and rather delicate argument about literary identity and moral authority in a changing and hostile political world.[30] The exalted literary tradition and the lofty literary character of his work both shield Dryden from some of the dangers of that world and give him an authority to speak of its character and values. This may at first strike us a rather naive or wishful argument, but in fact the very altitude of the work — claimed and real — may have been part of its success in the 1690s. Both Dryden's writing in the prefatory materials and the highly wrought, self-conscious character of the work suggest that he knew quite well what the polemical values of altitude were, what protection they might offer, and what argumentative advantage they allowed. The invocation of high culture, even the explicit denial of historical accuracy and intent, offered a polemical advantage; it was one of the few that Dryden could easily claim after 1688.

Part of the polemical argument of *Don Sebastian* is then the connection between high culture and the values of the play: the meaning of principles, the nature of oaths, the quality of honor, the uncertainties of fate. The play also provides explicit political materials and arguments which it would harness to the loftiness of its enterprise; they suggest not only the abstract polemical situation of the work but also indicate very much how it is doing business with the claims made on behalf of the revolution and its settlement. Dryden's handling of themes and plots, verbal and dramatic idioms is in fact an excellent guide to the polemics of the revolution, and it is these that I would for the moment explore.

Any writer choosing the Portugese king for his subject had by the late seventeenth century a wealth of histories and legends to sift among. The centerpiece of the histories was a sixteenth-century king of Portugal, a Catholic gallant who apparently entertained fantasies of a glorious reign dedicated to military triumphs in the cause of his religion, a mystic and fanatic.[31] This history intersects Moroccan politics in the battle of Acacerquivir which closed an ill-fated campaign that Don Sebastian had conducted on behalf of a slight heir to the Moroccan throne — but one incident in a saga of political and familial intrigue and treachery, fratricide, assassination, and rival claims to the throne. In fact, Moroccan history, which forms the immediate background to Dryden's play, might itself be taken as an emblem of divided ruling houses, conquests, and usurpations. The military crusade that Don Sebastian conducted on behalf of the injured heir resulted in his own death and the decimation of the Portuguese army. For Portugal, what followed the defeat was years of decline and domination by Spain, and the growth of the Sebastian legend which held that the king had not died in battle but would one day return from exile to claim his throne. A political force known as Sebastianist battened on the legend and grew to form a substantial force in Portuguese national politics.

It is not difficult to see what this history of political mayhem, Catholic gallantry, and Sebastianist hopes for an exiled prince might have offered Dryden in 1689. The parallels are so obvious that it may be surprising that Dryden chose to dramatize the legend at all. A version of the story dramatized by Philip Massinger had been suppressed on political grounds in 1631,[32] and though we do not know if Dryden was aware of this, he must have been aware of the parallels to be drawn out of his subject in 1689, parallels which he of course orchestrates, complicates, and heightens himself. He must also have been aware of the danger of doing so, and we have seen some of the steps that he took both to excite the applications and to distance himself from them, to dehistoricize and neutralize the politics of the legend while allowing the obvious inferences to be drawn. He not only indulged these parallels and applications, he wove so complex a system of such parallels that their variety and number is slightly dizzying. If, for a moment, we take 1688 to be the center of *Don Sebastian* — a proposition that Dryden and some of his explicators would I think vigorously contest — we are offered parallels to English politics from both Moroccan history and from Portugese history; these are mixed and indulged in scenes of straight fiction and scenes based on history. What the multiplicity first suggests is that revolution, usurpation, exile, and retreat are something like the inevitable conditions of politics, a conclusion amply illustrated in all the histories indulged and implied by the play. Such a display of confusion and revolution leads us to understand that good men are forced by tragic circumstance beyond their control and understanding to retreat from the turbulence of politics and to embrace stoic retirement. Self-knowledge, charity, beneficence are virtues that we can know and practice, they are beyond the reach of political revolution which is after all simply an instrument of blind fate. A number of local examples are then offered to illustrate this pattern: there is Philip, Earl of Leicester, his Roman counterpart, Pomponius Atticus; there is the former laureate and his Roman pattern, Cicero; there is the Don Sebastian of history and the Don Sebastian of Dryden's play who closes the work with renunciation and retreat; and there is of course James II who is following such a pattern of retreat and piety at St. Germain. To abjure empire, to hold property and power in moral contempt, offers the final example of piety and elevation: Christ of the gospels. Dryden may not be explicitly asking us to draw the analogies among all these parties, but the materials for constructing such a pattern and abstracting such a meaning from the play and its legends are obviously there. Given such a moral argument, we can see how the dedication, *Preface,* and the play itself might be read as a thematically linked and continuous text pointing a repeated stoic moral, one quoted from Cicero and Virgil and expressed by the hero himself:[33]

> The world was once too narrow for my mind,
> But one poor little nook will serve me now;
> . . . .
> A scepter's but a play-thing, and a Globe
> A bigger bounding Stone.

Politics is the prime example and inevitable stage of such instability: crowns and empires are slippery things; conquest and usurpation simply beget more such; once a rent is made in the fabric of bonds, oaths, and gratitude the state unravels. Political activism is clearly not Dryden's aim in *Don Sebastian,* but the consoling moral of endless fluctuation is repeatedly drawn in dramatic colloquy over such topics as title, empire, conquest, providence, and fate. Although William and Mary have been crowned, James deposed, and his former laureate dispossessed, the victory is but a momentary variation in the larger scheme of instability and change. It is hardly surprising given the moral and political comfort of such a philosophy to find Dryden translating Lucretius in the 1690s; it is, if not with a vengeance then certainly with pleasure that Dryden embraced the Lucretian flux in *Fables,* and it is a moral and political consolation already obvious to Dryden in 1689.

The histories that form the background to *Don Sebastian* provide both frame and consolation. The play itself engages more directly in polemical work, although we ought not to underestimate the polemical value in Dryden's handling of the large frame of providential histories. Providential rescue was a theme crucial to a revolution which argued the divine right of providence as a handsome alternative to the divine right of kings. Dryden is careful to engage that theme at various moments in the play so that we have both a general devaluation of the politics of providence and a rather more specific refutation of providential arguments applied to conquest and tyranny within the play itself. Indeed, rather than lift the play above the revolution, such philosophical material situates *Don Sebastian* in the midst of that great political event, steadily engaging the themes, the principles, the banners and the catchwords of the revolution and its apologetics. The attack is aimed at the theory of the revolution and its language, at the claims of necessity and high-mindedness, at the character of its principles. *Don Sebastian* steadily inspects the rationale of the Glorious Revolution, the action of the rabble and its political and religious leaders, the slogans of popery and slavery, property and religion. Through comic scenes that slight the principles of the revolution, through soliloquy that heightens nonjuring values, through a steady examination and deflation of such terms as title, slavery, conquest, tyranny, and sovereignty Dryden offers an alternative reading of the revolution, its justification, its rhetoric and its principle actors so that we might see 1688 not as the high-minded and selfless rescue of religion, property, and the law from the hands of a reckless and bigoted innovator but as an act of political betrayal motivated by greed, argued with lies, a revolution that everywhere revealed the cupidity, cowardice, and moral indifference of the nation.

The polemical engagement that I have been describing takes place in several ways. Most abstractly, the play spins out philosophical and moral principles: the universe is in flux, providence is inscrutable, title is mere vanity; only an indifference to the things of this world can guarantee nobility of character and purity of soul. Less abstractly, the main characters in the play are allowed through language and circumstance to suggest, often in momentary, fleeting and almost always partial ways, the principle characters of the revolution. The Moroccan shereef, a bloody tyrant, martial and heroic yet cruel and morally indifferent flits in and out of focus as William III; the hapless, noble and stoic hero, Don Sebastian, "Brave,/pious, generous, great and liberal . . . no other could represent such suffering majesty" offers us an idealized James, a portrait that may strain credulity and is obviously intended as flattering suggestion rather than careful delineation; a virtuous princess loyal to her murdered father and brother's ghost, who upbraids the nephew of her father, a man who seized his throne, is obviously an inversion of Mary; and a set of secondary characters whose actions suggest momentary analogy with either the principle actors of the circumstances of the revolution.[34] Dryden also fits out the debates and exchanges in the play with a set of political idioms that were crucial to the Williamite representation of 1688. For example, playing out a scene in which real slaves are bought and sold at market, the drama literalizes the meaning and conditions of slavery in a manner intended to puncture and ridicule the political uses of that word. The steady cry of popery and slavery was crucial to the rhetoric of the revolution; *Don Sebastian* insists that slavery is a word that has, first of all, a literal meaning and a political provenance; slavery is the direct result of conquest, and the Catholic slaves in this play are bought and sold at the whim of a conquering infidel. By literalizing the word and depicting slavery as the result of military conquest and by suggesting that conquest is indeed the condition of William's triumph, that retreat and retirement acknowledge such conquest, Dryden uses a set of political circumstances implacably to argue the meaning of national conquest: the people are now quite literally slaves of a conqueror, to be bought and sold at his whim.

The scenes and colloquies that analyze slavery as language and condition have the effect first of all of insisting on root definitions and political preconditions. None had argued that James had taken the throne by conquest; many were troubled by the title of conqueror as it applied to William. This was in fact a crucial issue, and by linking conquest and slavery in both comic and serious scenes Dryden entered the debate, argued its language and suggested that the most important political consequence of conquest was in fact slavery.

And so it is with other crucial words of the revolution. Repeatedly characters in this play examine and debate the word title, always to the detriment of that word as fixed indicator of virtue or proprietary right: 'Thou wouldst have Titles/Take 'em then, Chief Minister, First Hangman of the State . . . . By what title, Because I happen'd to be born where he happen'd to be a King?'[35] Not only is this a philosophical disquisition on the relations of words and things, it seems direct refutation of the debates over title in the Convention Parliament. Dryden's argument that title is mere cypher, that qualities of honor and sovereignty are more deeply fixed than the language denominating those terms, is at once philosophical and political argument. No one should fool himself into believing that the mere application of title would legitimate the deposition of James and the installation of William and Mary in his stead. Nor of course was Dryden the only one to raise such scruples; the nature and meaning of title was an issue of some significance in the wake of the revolution and scrupling over language engaged in by the convention was a subject of long-standing debate.[36] Dryden entered this particular debate quite early and staked out the Jacobite position with apparent ease. Having himself lost title to the laureateship Dryden was in no mood to be overawed by title, to allow that a mere shift of name would in fact confer authority and preeminence. This was at once a personal, political, and philosophical argument, and it is part of the interest of this play that several venues can be simultaneously engaged, that the complexity and varied applications can be handled through the different modes of the work: tragic, comic, satiric, and ironic. The importance of the comic to the tragic action in *Don Sebastian* is nowhere better seen than in the variety of polemical tones that the two modes allowed; balance and disinterestedness suggested by the comic writing strengthen the pathos and philosophical elevation that define such topics as fate, providence, fortune and title.

Scenes of mistaken identity, accidental appearance, and displaced lovers play out in a comic vein the rather portentous political and philosophical arguments of *Don Sebastian*. Fate itself, the comic scenes argue, is hardly a source for the authority or virtue of either action or agency. Thus the lottery scene early in the play in which the fates of hero and heroine are supposedly decided is a scene covered by whim and accident. That debunking of fate and fortune is then followed by repeated scenes of accidental and mistaken action and identity that alone seem to determine turns of plot and fortune. Arguments that based the revolution on analogy with 1588 or likeness with other Protestant redemptions are engaged in specious polemic; justification by providence is an argument made from whimsy dressed as legitimating divinity. Dryden also understood the power of images of mob rule and civil anarchy in treating of the revolution. In scenes both of high principle and episodes of ridicule and burlesque, he derides the clergy and the mufti who are seen alike as bent on profit and self-promotion, who wilfully incite riot and tumult, who play on the greed of the multitude and the chimera of consensual politics to ride the crest of revolution to new heights of power and property. The repeated image of mob rule stalks the play as does the suggestion of a physics of revolution run toward chaos and destruction. Of course, the politics of fear were very well understood by publicists both for and against the revolution, and indeed those defending the revolution had a rather more immediate arsenal of images with which to conjure rape, murder, and plunder. But figures of political tumult and social levelling were still forcefully to be deployed in 1688 and the evocation of the revolution as 'Chaos of Power, and privileg'd destruction' must have been potent in the months following the revolution.[37] Exclusion had partly been defeated through the association of Whiggery and The Good Old Cause; and this play manages scenes of mob instability to excite the meaning of the revolution as social dismemberment. Once conquest and tumult were embraced, the play argues, all stood in danger: 'when Kings and Queens are to be discarded, what shou'd Knaves do any longer in the pack?'[38] The language neatly combines the figure of chance — politics as gaming — with the argument that revolutions, once begun, are difficult to control; all parties should have an interest in social stability. This revolution, the play argues, is a dangerous unhinging of social and political order.

Certainly self-interest as an engine of the revolution played an important role in the rhetoric of those who regretted 1688, and Dryden displays his mastery of the topic. In an extremely witty scene where the mufti excites opposition to tyranny and absolutism — the charges of course repeatedly hurled against James — he mingles self-interest, fantasies of a glorious national history, and religious hokery in order to rouse mob allegiance. The mufti's speech is riddled with ironies nowhere more tellingly expressed than in the mufti's three P's: 'Self-Preservation, Property, and our Prophet'.[39] These are of course a debased and ridiculed version of the slogans of 1688; none embracing the revolution was eager to raise the standard of self-preservation with its Hobbesian overtones, and Dryden repeatedly contrasts self-preservation as low self-interest against the bonds of nature, family, and society. By fixing self-interest as the first principle of the revolution, he aims to expose greed and cowardice as its principles. As one of the characters who comically plays out the role of thief and principal of the new order admits: 'Not very heroick; but self preservation is a point above Honour and Religion too'.[40] This, from a character who cheats his father-in-law by stealing his daughter and using his property to found a new regime. The application to English politics is not simply obvious it seems wilfully so.

Indeed, the whole handling of property as a principle of the revolution is extremely imaginative in the play. The topic allowed Dryden to debase the motives of the rabble as plunder and tumult and simultaneously to undercut the rhetoric of the revolutionary settlement. The steady reach in *Don Sebastian* is for the moral high ground and nowhere does this reach allow Dryden more play than in his handling of property as a principal motive of the revolution. Property addressed in various terms was indeed part of the apologetic rhetoric of 1688, but it was not a principal term, mainly I think because it was not indeed very heroic matter. Dryden sensed the vulnerability of the term and exploited its weakness as moral and social principle. This exploitation allowed him to arrange the political principles of the play so that property and self-interest and 'our prophet Mahomet' vindicate 1688 and trust, loyalty, and the bonds of family and society suffer defeat. The old bonds of family and society are intended of course as a foil against which the poet can display the politics of plunder and property. If one might begin the argument that the revolution was theft, and property its mainspring, then the authority of the entire action is undercut. From property springs the violation of familial bonds, social disorder, contempt for duty, trust, and gratitude; 1688 was a revolution driven by appetite, contemptuous of the polity, fixed in a brave new world of opportunism, craft, and greed. Over and against the engine of property stand honor, trust, charity, and self-knowledge, virtues that can best be exercised independent of property, whose distribution is after all dictated by the whims of fortune.

Don Sebastian has of course more to argue than the hollowness of revolution principles and more ways of arguing that theme than I have suggested. What wants observing is how thoroughly the apologetics of the revolution are engaged, how carefully structured, scene by scene, is this high drama of the Sebastian legend. The play was engaging in a contest for moral and cultural authority and Dryden brought to that contest not only his gifts as a stylist of the heroic drama, a keen ear for political rhetoric, but also an understanding of how historical romance could be used to orchestrate a political argument. The matter of Don Sebastian allowed Dryden to indulge in a brilliant display of hints, allusions, and innuendo; it also allowed him to construct an allegory of moral principles and in such a construction he is of course holding the

winning hand. Honor and obligation, loyalty and gratitude, the spare
soulfulness of Atticus and Cicero, these are the properties of a Jacobite
position; needless to say, such a conclusion did not altogether fit the public perception of either the Jacobite cause or the playwright himself.

For whom did Dryden think he was writing this play in the summer
and early fall of 1689? He argues in the *Preface* that he was forced back
to the stage by financial need; one could think of a number of topics,
themes, and histories that might have offered more promise of wide
popularity in 1689 than *Don Sebastian*. And yet what is most puzzling
is not the apparent contradiction between stated motive and performance
— one would have thought however that a more grateful audience could
have been discovered in the antechambers of St. Germain than on the
London commercial stage — but the actual success of the play in 1689 and
thereafter. This is not a play of occult politics; argument and innuendo
are clear throughout. Of course, an audience might always ignore or
deny the applications — Algernon Sidney had made a noble defense of
his purity of motive in writing Roman history — but the idioms of the
revolution are so clearly handled in *Don Sebastian* that it would have
taken not simply a willing suspension of disbelief to ignore or elide
the politics but an active denial of much of the language of the play to
achieve an apolitical reading of *Don Sebastian*. It might well be that the
philosophical materials of the play — and they are elegantly displayed
in both dedication and text — are more immediate and attractive for
us than are its politics. But for contemporaries, the political currents
would have been extremely difficult to ignore. That the politics of 1688
are provided with an overlay of philosophical meaning makes them not
only more attractive but also deepens their argumentative coherence;
philosophy gives the politics an altitude and a dignity that are in fact
one of the principle polemical aims of the work.

To whom then could such a play have appealed? That it did
appeal is a fact that we can gather from its stage history. If this were
simply published verse, one might argue that the venue may not have
been commercial success but rather the admiration of posterity. But
the claimed motives are at least in part popular and commercial, and
we need to think for a moment about *Don Sebastian* playing to cheers
and applause in the London theater. Could an audience some of whose
members had not simply accommodated the revolution but embraced it
have been flattered by the portraits and arguments of *Don Sebastian*?
What might they have seen in its exposition of revolutionary folly and
greed; its condemnation of the new political morality; its debasement of
the rhetoric of the revolution? I have no certain answer to this puzzle

but we might think that the political and moral values which this play celebrates — stoic indifference to fortune, gratitude, loyalty, honor, trust, beneficence — could not have been willingly abandoned by the nation in its rapid acquiescence to a convenient revolution. Although Dryden was in control of the action and language of his play, he could not entirely regulate its reception and understanding. One might well imagine an audience that both embraced the revolution and proclaimed its allegiance to the values that this play honors. Although Dryden might hope to deny an audience this ground, the embrace of paradoxes is not easy to forbid nor can the playwright insists on scrupulous self-knowledge among his audience. The very success of the play does not inevitably argue the acceptance of its political meaning; one might indeed embrace the principles of *Don Sebastian* while regretting the politics of its author and the misbehavior of James II. More than one panegryric to William attempts to shuffle James beneath the cover of wicked advisors and evil Jesuits. In fact, the very success of *Don Sebastian* makes the now widely accepted point about the conservative nature of the revolution in a new form. So eager was the political nation to deny the revolutionary character of 1688, so eager was it to underscore the continuity, indeed return to, ancient principles, to argue James as aberration, that it might go to the theater, witness a production of *Don Sebastian* and vigorously assent to the values of the play without allowing the playwright's application of those principles. In fact, the success of *Don Sebastian* seems to me one rather interesting piece of evidence about the continuity of political values in the 1690s, or at least the moral and psychological advantages for Dryden's audience of professing such a continuity of values and forms.

What might an art of the new order have looked like? Perhaps *Robinson Crusoe*, that allegory of acquisition, might be taken to represent a new order. One might also speculate on the shaping of a poetics that could exalt property as a moral principle, celebrate cunning and manipulative power as political skills. But the formulation of new cultural forms and values, the validation of those forms in literary expression would be some decades in coming. In historiography we have come to understand the new form as the triumph of the Whig interpretation of history; in high culture we would have to include the development of the novel as part of the new aesthetic, a form that allowed ample room for a poetics of property. But on the eve of the revolution and directly in its aftermath, there were no forms for the new order, nor was the order really new. Although dramatic political events had taken place, the best that could be said of them was their augury of a return to older ways. In rhetorical terms, 1688 was a triumph of the past. Understanding the values of the revolution and their cultural implications, untangling the meaning of the revolution from its apologetic and distracting rhetoric were difficult tasks. It is hardly surprising that the muses were reluctant to speak in 1688. They were, I think, uncertain of what to say and what forms to say it in. From that perspective, the silence surrounding the revolution seems to have its own logic. The Glorious Revolution, we are told, ushered in the dullest decade in English literature; although this is not altogether true, it was a difficult decade for literary invention, and given the perplexity of values and events, it is not surprising that Dryden could have found in the repeated display of old principles a quite adequate base on which to run his shop. For one Jacobite, at least, there were no contradictions to solve although there were ironies enough to savor in the principles and careers that were promoted by the revolution.

NOTES

1. See J. P. Kenyon, *Revolution Principles* (Cambridge, 1977), 1–4; J. R. Jones, *Country and Court* (Cambridge, Mass., 1978), 252–253; J. G. A. Pocock, ed. *Three British Revolutions* (Princeton, 1980), 13 and L. Stone in the Pocock volume, 63–64; Gary Stuart de Krey, *A Fractured Society* (Oxford, 1985), 45–47.

2. J. C. D. Clark, *English Society, 1688–1832* (Cambridge, 1985), esp. section 3, "The Survival of the Dynastic Idiom," 119–189.

3. David Norbrook, "*Macbeth* and the Politics of Historiography," *Politics of Discourse*, ed. Kevin Sharpe and Steven Zwicker (Berkeley and Los Angeles, 1987), 78–116.

4. The satiric verse in *Poems on Affairs of State*, V, 1688–1697, ed. William J. Cameron (New Haven and London, 1971), gives some idea of the reception of the Revolution.

5. These links can be profitably studied at moments of crisis and celebration, as, for example, in the elegies lamenting the execution of Charles I and in the panegyrics on the restoration and coronation of Charles II.

6. See, for example, the verse in the Oxford volume, *Britannia Rediviva* (Oxford, 1660); R. Brathwait, *To His Majesty upon his Happy Arrival* (London, 1660); A. Brett *The Restauration* (London, 1660), or Waller's and Dryden's panegyrics.

7. I have tried to deal with this topic in "Lines of Authority: Politics and Literary Culture in the Restoration," *Politics of Discourse*, 216–247; see also Stephen H. Daniel on Toland as biographer and editor of Milton, *John Toland* (Kingston and Montreal, 1984); and Bernard Sharratt, "The Appropriation of Milton," *Essays and Studies* (London, 1982).

8. The debates can be followed in William Cobbett's *Parliamentary History of England*, 36 vols. (London, 1806–1820), v.

9. See, again, *Poems on Affairs of State*, v, esp. 19–36; and such volumes as *The Design of Enslaving England Discovered* (London, 1689); *London's Flames Revivi'd* (London, 1689); *Sidney Redivivus* (London, 1689); the verse panegyrics on William are filled with references to bigotry, superstition, and Egyptian slavery.

10. The "amasing concurence of Providences, which have conspired to hatch and bring forth, and perfect this extraordinary Revolution," was a repeated theme in sermons and panegyrics on the revolution; see, Gilbert Burnet, *A Sermon Preached . . . the 23rd of December, 1688* (London, 1689); Simon Patrick, *A Sermon Preached . . . January 31, 1688* (London, 1689); W. Sherlock, *A Sermon Preached before the Right Honourable The Lord Mayor* (London, 1689); Symon Patrick, *A Sermon Preached in the Chappel of St. James* (London, 1689).

11. See Kenyon, *Revolution Principles*, chapters 5 and 6.

12. Cf. the satire, "Mall in her Majesty," *Poems on Affairs of State*, V, 25–29.

13. "On the late Happy Revolution, A Pindarique Ode," *Musae Cantabrigienses* (Cambridge, 1689), sig. av.

14. "On the late Happy Revolution," "The Land with dire confusion thus o'respread,/Call'd the Great Nassau to its aid,/The peacefull Warriour quickly came,/And struck it not, but look't it into Frame;/He came and took a pittying view,/the Conscious heap his meaning knew/And the unruly motions quickly drew/Into an Order regular and true," sig. a2v.

15. "A Panegyrick upon their Majesties King William and Queen Mary," *Lux Occidentalis* (Oxford, 1689), 12.

16. See, for example, John Herbert, "To the King," *Musae Cantabrigienses*, "Great Prince, what Glories do's Thy Name deserve?/What Praise? who only Conquer'st to preserve . . . ." sig. b3v; or the reference in Rich. Stone's panegyric in *Musae Cantabrigienses*, c3r, to William's "kind Invasion"; or B. Cudworth's verse in *Musae Cantabrigienses*, "No more the ancient Conquerour's splendid Name,/Shall fill alone the Glorious Rolls of Fame;/Whose Arms, Revenge, or vain ambition lead,/And rais'd their bloody Trophies on the dead;/Your Pow'rfull Name the Mighty Work compleats,/And over willing minds an easier Conquest gets," c4v.

17. Cf. Rob. Smythies, "On the late Happy Revolution," *Musae Cantabrigienses*, a2v and W. Bisset, "Great Heroe!" *Musae Cantabrigienses*, d2v.

18. P. Sayve, "To the King," *Musae Cantabrigienses*, b2v.

19. John Guy, *On the Happy Accession of Their Majesties . . . A Pindarique Ode*, (London, 1699), C2v-D1r.

20. *Poems on Affairs of State*, V, vii.

21. Zwicker, *Politics and Language in Dryden's Poetry* (Princeton, 1984), 123.

22. See, especially, the commentary of Earl Miner in *The Works of John Dryden*, ed. by Miner (Berkeley and Los Angeles, 1976), xv, 404–408.

23. See Miner, *The Works of John Dryden*, xv, 408–409.

24. See Cokayne's *The Complete Peerage*, edited by H. A. Doubleday and H. de Walden, 12 vols. (London, 1910–1959), vii, 556–557.

25. The Earl of Romney was a 5 guinea subscriber to Dryden's *Virgil*; he

was given a particularly compromising plate for his subscription; see Zwicker, *Politics and Language in Dryden's Poetry*, 195–196.

26. *The Works of John Dryden*, xv, 60.

27. For a full discussion of parallel and analogy in *Don Sebastian*, see David Bywaters, "Dryden and the Revolution of 1688: Political Parallel in *Don Sebastian*," *Journal of English and Germanic Philology*, lxxxv, No. 3, 346–365.

28. *The Works of John Dryden*, xv, 67–70.

29. *The Works of John Dryden*, xv, 67, 70–71.

30. *The Works of John Dryden*, xv, 72.

31. For an excellent summary of the historical materials, see Miner, *The Works of John Dryden*, xv, 391–392.

32. *The Works of John Dryden*, xv, 385.

33. *The Works of John Dryden*, xv, 211.

34. See Bywaters, 'Dryden and the Revolution of 1688,' 358–359.

35. *The Works of John Dryden*, xv, 82.

36. See, for example, Robert Jenkin, *The Title of an Usurper* (London, 1690).

37. *The Works of John Dryden*, xv, 85.

38. *The Works of John Dryden*, xv, 175.

39. *The Works of John Dryden*, xv, 173.

40. *The Works of John Dryden*, xv, 151.

8
THE REVOLUTION AND THE DEVELOPMENT
OF ENGLISH FOREIGN POLICY

Jeremy Black

'It is much for the honour of the English nation, that they are become the arbiters of the publick differences in Europe, and that their forces are employed in all countries to bring exorbitant and oppressive powers to reason.'

Observator 23 May 1702

'The affairs of Germany are in no great state at present, but the resolutions of the Parliament, may give some new life to the allies. In truth, the German princes will not stir, till they are forced to it, for self preservation.'

Sir Rowland Gwynne, a Whig agent in Hanover, 1703.[1]

If the Tory view on the foreign policy of Hanoverian Britain has not been probed adequately,[2] the same is also true of 1688 and its consequences. This essay seeks to probe a number of related questions in order to throw light on the criticisms made during the reigns of William and Anne that the Revolution had had detrimental consequences in the field of foreign policy. Of necessity many of the points that will be made involve counterfactual questions and are not subject to proof. However that did not prevent them from being raised by contemporaries and if the Revolution is to be rescued from teleological perspectives that rescue must extend to one of the principal and most significant fields of political action and debate in the period, foreign policy.

Bruno Neveu has recently drawn attention to the role of national myth-making in the historical treatment of the Jacobites. He has suggested that the expulsion of James II and his son's failure to prevent the Hanoverian accession, events seen by contemporaries as violent ruptures and extreme developments, have been transformed into irresistible manifestations of a general aspiration by British society for progress and liberty. Neveu added that foreign historians have possibly a more acute perception than their British colleagues of the seriousness both of the overt crises and of the ideological, political and diplomatic tensions of the period.[3] These suggestions could be expanded and qualified by considering foreign policy, for in that sphere two linked abrupt changes have been discerned as stemming from the Revolution. The first is a supposed shift from compliance towards France, which is commonly held to have characterised the restored Stuart monarchy, to marked opposition to her. The second serves both as proof and consequence of the first. It is the shift from peace to war. England had last fought France in the 1620s and last fought a European conflict in the early 1670s: the third Anglo-Dutch war 1672–4. In contrast, between 1689 and 1713 England was at war with France in the Nine Years' and Spanish Succession wars, a precarious peace pertaining only in 1697–1702. There is little doubt that such a shift from peace to war did occur and that it had significant economic, financial and political consequences. The two wars with France were costly in men and money and the economic and financial burdens they created became a political issue, as the conduct and purposes of the wars had been throughout their course. What is less clear is that the purposes of these wars were not free from criticism. It could be suggested that France posed little threat to England prior to 1688, that James II was not excessively pro-French and that the wars with France were not in the national interest, ambiguous as that term obviously is. Such suggestions lead to the possibility that the balance of advantage over the Revolution was definitely with William of Orange not England, that an abrupt break can be discerned in 1688–9, but should not be seen as advantageous to the invaded country.

Central to any assessment of later Stuart foreign policy, 1688 and the post-Revolution wars is the view that is advanced of French policy, of Louis XIV's plans and their feasibility. There was no shortage of contemporaries willing to criticise Louis in Parliament, in the press and in private. The boldness of French action during the War of Devolution, at the beginning of the Dutch war and in the early 1680s had helped to make France the central issue in English foreign policy and the prime topic of public discussion, a position from which it had displaced Spain and the United Provinces. The note of widespread English hostility to France had been sounded by numerous commentators including French diplomats, such as Cominges in 1663.[4] Four years later Charles II admitted to a French envoy, concerned about the prospect of parliamentary agitation in favour of Spain and against France, that it would be necessary to display the advantages England could gain from her French alliance.[5] Charles' attempt to make the United Provinces the centre of English animosity once more failed. France was seen by relatively few as an ally during the third Anglo-Dutch war and the end

of the war was followed by an upsurge of criticism of Louis. The image
of Louis was one of overwhelming and overweening ambition,

> The phaeton of France (who hath set all Europe in a flame, and
> whose unbounded ambition will still continue that unnatural heat till
> the divine compassion shall strike him from his chariot) begins now to
> move towards the Spanish borders . . . His councels are dark; they are
> like a flint, where the fire is not visible till the steel be drawn, and the
> stroke be given . . . Like a true phaeton he consumes towns, burns up
> the fruits of the earth.'[6]

The need for an English response to Louis' expansionism became an
issue both in ministerial politics and in parliamentary debate, the two
ultimately focussing on the person of Thomas Osborne, Earl of Danby.
There were, however, cogent reasons for arguing that Louis' position was
not as threatening to England or the rest of Europe as some suggested.
In April 1675 Sir Edward Dering noted in his parliamentary diary,

> Sir Thomas Littleton began a set speech against the growing greatness
> of the French, how dangerous and formidable he was, what enlargement
> he had made of his empire in Flanders, Germany, Alsace, the Franche
> Comté and elsewhere, now threatening all Sicily, but concluded that he
> did not say this to engage us in a war with France, but only to forewarn
> us, that we might not at least lend our own hands to raise him so high,
> and therefore that an address should be made to the King to call home
> his forces that are now there.

> Secretary Williamson said that it was under consideration already . . . that
> . . . the King of France was in no such grandeur as was apprehended, that
> he had got but two towns by this war and they had cost him fourscore
> millions of money.

The following month Dering informed the House that 'the Dutch
have recovered all their own, both strength and vigour, and are able
to put the French upon the defensive.'[7] It did not cease to be credible
to debate the nature of French intentions and strength in 1675, but the
debate was complicated by its relationship to, indeed location in, that
over the succession, the constitution and religion. The intervention of
foreign powers in English politics increased this relationship,[8] making
it impossible to present a debate about English foreign policy in the
abstract. James Duke of York sought French support to bolster his
position.[9] At one level English politics became a battleground for
foreign powers, French influence opposed by that of Spain and of
William of Orange.[10] Statements attacking supposed French schemes

emanated from the partisans of the latter, discussion of English foreign policy was political in its nature and intentions.

Though James sought the support of Louis XIV it would be misleading to suggest that he simply acted in response to French interests. Instead James sought to create a position in which it would be credible for him to receive French Support. The fundamental basis of this policy in the latter stages of the Franco-Dutch war was French moderation in the conduct of the war and in the peace negotiations. As France was by this period substantially fighting Spain and the Emperor this did not entail James urging restraint on Louis in order to help the Dutch. James was convinced that French restraint would make it easier for Charles to preserve his domestic position and that the absence of it would lead Charles to oppose Louis in order both to quieten domestic political opinion and to obtain money from Parliament. In July 1676 he warned Courtin, the French envoy, that Louis must demonstrate that he sought peace; the following year he pressed Courtin on the need to stop Anglo-French disputes in the Channel, because they inflamed opinion in England.[11] By the summer of 1677 James' fears about the deteriorating position in the Spanish Netherlands and his anger Louis' unwillingness to offer conciliatory peace terms led him not only to abandon his support for Louis, but also to show increasing favour to Danby's scheme for bonding crown and people in French blood. James does not appear to have opposed the marriage of his eldest daughter Mary to William of Orange on 4 November 1677, a step that Louis could not have been expected to welcome, and which, taking place in the midst of a major conflict, sent a clear message about a possible change of policy by England. As it was swiftly followed by the death of James' newborn son, the Duke of Cambridge, the marriage also had clear implications for the English succession. It was followed by the presentation to Louis by Lord Feversham of a set of proposals, agreed by Charles, James and William, which would have led to France ceding more of her conquests than she had hitherto offered to do. Louis offered instead an armistice, which Barrillon, the French envoy, presented to Charles as a clear sign both that France was not out to conquer Flanders and that Louis was determined to allow Charles to show English opinion that he heeded Charles' views. Charles and James were unimpressed, fearful that France would still overrun the Spanish Netherlands and increasingly interested in seeking the domestic political benefits of confrontation with Louis.[12] James was particularly eager and showed considerable interest in commanding in Flanders against Louis. He saw war with France as a solution to his domestic unpopularity, an obvious demonstration that anti-Catholic polemic was inaccurate. One unintended consequence was a French attempt to intrigue with parliamentarians in order to oppose any war with France.[13] Another was the alignment of James and William of Orange, both eager to fight France and each thwarted by domestic opposition.[14]

If James' views on French foreign policy were variable prior to his accession this situation did not cease when he became king. His diplomatic inheritance was very mixed: a treaty of mutual assistance with Spain negotiated in 1680, treaties with the United Provinces, renewed by James in August 1685, and an agreement between Charles II and Louis in 1681, by which subsidies were given in return for Parliament not sitting. James sought to retain this mixed inheritance. It gave him greater flexibility, offering him more options, and, in particular, allowed him to avoid being dependent either on France or on Parliament. Sensible from the domestic point of view, this policy was also reasonable in diplomatic terms. France was no more or no less reliable as an ally than most other powers in this period, but that was little recommendation to any dependence on Louis, a course of action that would also be dishonourable. French diplomatic pressure on James not to align with other powers indicated that alliance with Louis would entail a position of dependence in which England would be unable to develop links elsewhere and to respond to events.[15] Rather than surrendering his capacity for diplomatic initiative, James sought to maintain links with Louis by stressing common interests, not least in 1685 the supposed cooperation of Huguenots and the Duke of Monmouth, both allegedly backed by Protestant powers.[16] He also suggested to Barrillon in the autumn of 1685 that it was unnecessary for him and England to choose between Louis and his opponents. In part the reasons James advanced were reasonable. Pointing out that Spain and Austria were not in a state to break the Truce of Regensburg (1684), he suggested that even when Austria and Turkey negotiated a peace, the Emperor Leopold I would not lightly begin a war with France, and continued with the unrealistic statement that he would be able to block such a project, as Leopold would not attempt it without consulting and seeking to engage James in a project which was entirely opposed to his designs and interests.[17] James discerned correctly that England could play a major role in any serious conflict and that the continental powers were therefore interested in English politics, but he was mistaken in assuming that this would necessarily accord with his views and he arguably exaggerated the significance of England to the major European powers, a mistaken path in which he followed his grandfather. Possible the suppression of Monmouth's rising in July 1685 increased James' confidence about England's international position excessively. William of Orange's support for James during the rising, which contrasted with Louis' decision to refuse to provide a subsidy, suggested that foreign powers would not meddle in English domestic politics in an unfriendly fashion. The success of the 1685 elections and the prorogation of Parliament in November 1685 appeared to close a major sphere of foreign intrigue.

James thus followed an independent policy and sought to keep both England and Europe at peace. If in September 1685 he declared that he would openly support France if Spain broke the Truce of Regensburg and in the following January he rejected Spanish pressure to renew the 1680 treaty, stating that it would be neither advantageous nor necessary, and that Louis seemed in favour of peace, James repeatedly pressed Louis in late 1685 to recognize William's right to the recently annexed Principality of Orange.[18] If in 1686 James' interests were identified more closely with those of Louis,[19] he did not display a willingness to cooperate with France comparable to those of Cromwell in the late 1650s or Charles II in 1672. Instead, James wanted peace, peace that would enable him to pursue domestic schemes, avoid the difficulties that calling Parliament might bring and evade the problems of commitment that war on the continent would entail.[20] Usson de Bonrepaus, a French special envoy sent to negotiate commercial matters, reported that James was not in a state to try anything against the Dutch unless Louis lent support.[21] Reports that James wished in alliance with Louis to attack the Dutch in 1687 were inaccurate. In fact that spring James sought to persuade William to support the repeal of the penal laws and Test Acts. James did not believe it necessary to align with Louis in order to obtain his domestic ends; indeed, as in the late 1670s, he thought that this might make matters more difficult, by arousing domestic and foreign opposition. However, his room for diplomatic manoeuvre was narrowed by William's growing unwillingness to keep out of English domestic affairs.[22] Most monarchs encountered problems with the reversionary interest, the standing question mark against all policies. For James the position was complicated by the fact that the reversionary interest was based abroad, enjoyed an independent international position and represented Protestant aspirations in Britain more obviously than the monarch. He became convinced that William was seeking to form a Protestant league.[23] However, his response was not a slavish adherence to Louis, but rather pressure for Louis to moderate his policies and, in particular, settle his differences with other Catholic rulers.[24] Believing that war would serve the interests of his domestic rivals,[25] James was uncertain as to how best avoid it, other than by avoiding public identification with Louis, and he misunderstood the nature of the developing international crisis in 1688.[26] It is fair to point out that this was a common failing.[27]

Aware that William was seeking to enlist allies against Louis, including crucially the leading Catholic ruler, Leopold I,[28] James was unsure about the attitude he ought to adopt towards Louis. He feared that close support would encourage other powers to help William, while Louis' pressure for expansion of the English fleet could be seen both as justifying accusations of joint Anglo-French schemes against the United Provinces and as a possible cause of war in a period when the issue of predominance at sea was a major source of tension.[29] Sunderland told Barrillon that James was against the cost of naval armaments and would require French financial help.[30] James' attitude to naval preparations, at a time of increased Dutch naval activity, was as aggravating to the French as his refusal to commit himself to them diplomatically. In March 1688 Bevil Skelton, English envoy in Paris, reported, '. . . some discourses I heard yesterday at Court from some of the ministers, who making reflections upon the States ill usage of his Majesty in the matter of his subjects in their service and other affairs, say that they would not dare to do it were they but made more sensible of the amity and good understanding that there is between the two Crowns, and 'tis the assurances which his Majesty sometimes gives the Spanish minister of his being in no manner of engagement with France, that makes the States thus insolent; I have nothing more to say to it then to tell you what are the discourses of the most considerable men here, as well as of Monsr de Croissy, who again told me his Majesty might depend upon all the services this Crown was able to do him'.[31]

In the Baltic crisis of the spring of 1688 James refused to follow Louis' lead. At the beginning of June Louis was concerned as to whether Viscount Carlingford, sent to Vienna to congratulate Leopold on the election of his son as King of the Romans, had anything else to negotiate. Carlingford himself had to deny rumours that he was negotiating an Austro-Turkish settlement.[32] Unhappy about James' attitude, Louis nevertheless offered him assistance in order to repel any Dutch invasion.[33] If this offer of French naval help identified James with Louis in the public mind, James' support for the French candidate in the contested election to the Archbishopric Electorate of Cologne had a similar effect in diplomatic circles.[34] James found it difficult to appreciate that conflict was imminent both with William and over Cologne. Neither wishing to commit himself, nor believing it necessary, James' misunderstanding of William's schemes led him to respond in an equivocal fashion to Louis' offer of naval assistance. The Dutch were informed that James and Louis were not allied and that James did not wish to be treated by Louis in a similar fashion to the French protégé in Cologne.[35]

Thus James was far from being a client of the French. His presentation thus during his reign owed much to propaganda. That he was forced into the role of French client after William's invasion encouraged his presentation thus and a consequent rewriting of his political career, consistency being intertwined with polemic. However, it is reasonable to point out that the Protestant Succession did not necessarily lead to opposition to France. That it did in 1689 was due substantially to William. It was clear that William's invasion was intended not only as the deciding move in a British war of succession but also as an essential preliminary to a successful war with France. It was the latter that had enabled William to build up the powerful diplomatic and military support without which he would not have invaded.[36] However, the inconclusive Nine Years' War led William to welcome the opportunity to negotiate in the late 1690s a settlement by which conflict would be avoided over the Spanish succession. Had the Partition Treaties been negotiated by James and Louis then it is likely that contemporary and subsequent English commentators would have criticised them bitterly for their territorial concessions to France. Instead they failed, but William was prepared to acknowledge Louis' grandson Philip, as Philip V of Spain. More obvious as a qualification of the thesis that the Revolution of 1688 led a Protestant Britain into opposition to France, indeed a second Hundred Years' War, was the alliance between the two powers between 1716 and 1731 and the subsequent care to avoid conflict until 1743.

If William's negotiations with Louis and the alliance of 1716–31 can be presented favourably as responses to changing circumstances, then a case can indeed be made for James on the same basis. This can be further advanced if attention is drawn to recent reinterpretations of Louis' foreign policy.[37] The harsh criticism of Louis that characterised much of the nationalist historiography of other western European states has been declared redundant. French vulnerability has been stressed, a vulnerability made more serious by the objectives of France's enemies. In an age when pretensions were retained, the treaties that enshrined French victories were not regarded as final settlements of disputes. The manipulation of legal claims and judicial institutions and/or the use of force to seize disputed territory, all activities for which Louis was castigated both by contemporaries and subsequently, were both resorted to by a large number of powers and characterised the essential means by which many disputes, particularly those over contested successions, were conducted. Furthermore, it was and is by no means clear that France in the 1680s was the threat to continental Europe, still less to England, that opponents such as William claimed. The Dutch war had been a failure for Louis. Not only had the Dutch not been crushed, but the war had revealed the weakness, both of France's alliances and of the strategic situation on her eastern frontier.[38] If the Spanish succession was a continual question mark against Louis' achievements, by the mid 1680s this had been joined by the fate of the Austro-Turkish struggle. Louis has been accused of self-deception over the struggle,[39] but, aside from the understandable wish to credit bad news about the Austrians, it is worth pointing out that by 1688 French diplomats were stressing the threats posed by both Austria and William. An element of justification is clearly apparent,[40] but it is worth pointing out that from the 1680s until the 1790s a clear trend is apparent in European international relations, in which central and eastern European powers, Austria, Prussia and Russia, grew in power relative to their western counterparts. In territorial terms this was readily apparent. Louis' conquests, in territory or population, were trivial compared to those of Leopold I, Charles VI and Peter the Great. In terms of influence the shift to the east was apparent in the growth of Austrian influence in Italy and the Empire and Russian in the Baltic. French allies, actual or potential, were defeated or intimidated. The Marquis de Villars, sent in late 1688 to win the alliance of Max Emanuel of Bavaria, reported that the Bavarian government was frightened by Austrian ministers who said that the Electorate would be overrun if it opposed Leopold.[41] In the war of the Spanish Succession this threat was to be accomplished.

There is little evidence that James should be credited with a prescient assessment of international affairs. The policies of the Regent Sophia scarcely suggested that Russia was about to burst on the European scene. However, it was already clear by the mid-1680s that Louis could not dominate western and central Europe. The crucial issue in dispute in 1688, and one over which James was prepared to lend Louis diplomatic assistance, the Cologne succession, was not one in which Louis was successful. Indeed, rather than supporting a dangerous threat to the balance of power, James was loosely aligned to a ruler who was increasingly isolated. This was partly through choice, in that James both sought subsidies, which only Louis was in a position to provide, and felt that a Catholic ally was best suited to a monarch seeking to improve the position of British Catholics. However, James' position, which by late 1688 entailed sharing Louis' increasing isolation, arose partly from necessity. As alternatives to Louis he could have sought to ally with other Catholic powers, principally Leopold I and Charles II of Spain, or with the most influential Protestant rulers. Not all of the latter welcomed William's invasion, Christian V of Denmark being particularly unhappy about it.[42] This was a significant qualification of Williamite propaganda that presented a Protestant camp united against James and Louis. However, for James a 'Protestant' foreign policy entailed alliance with William, partly because the interests of the other leading Protestant rulers, Sweden, Denmark, Brandenburg and the Dukes of Hanover, were centred on the Baltic,[43] a volatile region in which James did not wish to commit himself, as he made clear in early 1688. As other Protestant rulers were linked, though not always closely or reliably, to Leopold or Louis,[44] the possibility of James creating a Protestant alliance system excluding William was limited. James' failure to produce a male heir capable of surviving for more than a few months ensured that the succession would pass to his eldest daugher Mary and that effective control would be wielded by her husband, William. The foreign policy that England was to follow from 1689, hostility to France and alliance with the United Provinces, appeared as an obvious future prospect throughout most of James' reign due to his failure to father a son. Given that William was likely to control English policy soon, there was little incentive for Protestant powers to seek James' alliance exclusive of William. Furthermore there was no real basis for such an alliance. James' position was not dissimilar to that of his father in the 1630s, his grandfather in the 1610s and British ministries in the 1760s. Though willing to ally with other powers, he did not wish to commit himself to their interests insofar as these might entail military action and thus force James to turn to Parliament in unpropitious circumstances. In the volatile diplomacy of the 1680s, with its unpredictable crises producing a heady atmosphere of opportunity and fear, opportunism and anxiety, James had little to offer as an ally. While thus repeating the position of his grandfather, father and elder brother in the early 1680s and prefiguring that of the 1760s,[45] James was placed in a different situation in 1688 by the possibility of invasion. Whereas that of 1685 had been rendered less serious by an absence of international support and the untrained nature of Monmouth's forces, in 1688 the prospect was bleak on both grounds.

If James' unwillingness to commit himself in international affairs limited the prospect of Protestant alliances, it had a more serious effect on the possibility of improving relations with the Catholic powers that were opposed to Louis. For both Spain and Austria an alliance would have required James' guarantee against French attack, a guarantee that James was neither able nor willing to provide. If in 1678 James had been eager to join both powers and William against Louis, thus prefiguring the anti-French alliances of 1689 and 1702, this had been dependent on a compliant Parliament, able and willing to vote necessary sums and ready to avoid anti-Catholic measures. By the time James became king France and her neighbours were at peace, there was no pressing reason to arouse animosity by declaring himself in continental affairs and the encouragement and protection of Catholicism, so that the Catholics would not suffer again a persecution akin to that of the Exclusion years, was James' main priority. It is possible to advance the hypothesis that had James not fallen out with Parliament in 1685 the latter would have voted the funds necessary to permit an expansion in the army and a peaceful session would have provided the basis for future cooperation to lend substance to any agreements that James might negotiate with Austria and Spain. Several criticisms of this hypothesis are apparent. The policy had been attempted without success in 1678 and was to be followed by William and Anne only with considerable difficulty. If the suppression of the Argyll and Monmouth risings in 1685 and the response to the anti-Huguenot measures of the Edict of Fontainebleau produced propitious circumstances for a royal-parliamentary alliance offering support to France's enemies, Parliament was not willing to accept James' agenda in 1685. The army, the basis for any effective interventionist foreign policy, was the crux of the problem. In his speech opening the session on 9 November 1685 James made it clear that he wanted both a substantial standing force and no limitation on his right to employ Catholic officers, 'There is nothing but a good force of well-disciplined troops in constant pay that can defend us from such as, either at home or abroad, are disposed to disturb us'.[46] Both houses made it clear that they wanted neither a larger army nor Catholic officers. Barrillon had indeed warned in 1678 that any attempt to reconcile crown and Parliament at the expense of France would be short-lived, initial enthusiasm and financial support being followed by parliamentary exploitation of royal needs, to the particular detriment of both Catholics and the royal choice of ministers.[47] The attitude of Parliament in 1685 made it clear that James could not pursue an anti-French 'parliamentary' foreign policy or indeed any foreign policy that entailed significant expenditure. It was possible for the king to enlarge the army, but any use of it abroad would have created a substantial financial commitment that James alone could not meet.

Arguably James was therefore of little value as an ally to either Louis or his rivals. Domestic preoccupations and a lack of domestic support made interventionism unattractive and unworkable for the king. This was certainly true of any warlike situation, but, until the very end of his reign, western Europe was at peace and it was possible to resort to inexpensive diplomacy. It is certainly possible to argue that James could and should have made a greater effort to woo the Catholic powers other than France, particularly as Leopold was not without considerable influence with the north-German Protestant rulers. However, James could not dictate the manner in which other rulers regarded him. England was at best a second-rank power, the triumphs and energy of Cromwellian foreign policy a distant memory on the Continent. Knowledge of the weak domestic position of Charles II had handicapped the Earl of Middleton's mission to the Emperor in 1680. Philippe-Johan Hoffmann, the Imperial envoy in 1688, who was unsympathetic to James, presented his policies as unpopular.[48] England in the 1670s and early 1680s had followed the opportunistic and often inconsequential or unsuccessful tergiversations of other second-rank powers, such as Brandenburg, albeit with the additional handicap of domestic unrest, a succession that was called into question and a political system that facilitated and made worthwhile foreign intervention. It was not surprising that other states viewed England, like other minor powers, primarily in terms of whether she could and would help or hinder their policies. At the beginning of James' reign Leopold was relatively uninterested in him. Thereafter Leopold was chiefly influenced by James' likely attitude in any renewed Habsburg-Bourbon conflict. In May 1687 Count Andreas Kaunitz, the Austrian envoy, supported by the nuncio Count Ferdinand d'Adda and the Spanish envoy Don Pedro Ronquillo, pressed James to guarantee the truce of 1684 and thus to lend his political support to the existing peace settlement in Western Europe. James, who replied that he was working for the security of the Catholic religion and for his own domestic concerns, refused, as he declined the renewal of an alliance with the Elector of Brandenburg.[49] It was clear that James was unwilling to respond to diplomatic initiatives that might be anti-French in their intent if not in their letter. Any stabilisation of western-European frontiers at a time when Austria was advancing in the east could be thus regarded. It was not surprising if for Leopold James' apparent attitude to the Austro-French struggle took precedence over James pro-Catholic policies and vitiated both James' attempts to elicit sympathy on this basis and Louis' proclamation in 1688 of the need for a Catholic league in the face of Protestant aggression.[50] Had William not been committed to opposition to Louis, then Leopold's attitude to William's invasion might well have been different and Catholic internationalism might have been more important. Arguably William's clear stance was more important to Leopold than his assessment of James' views. Kaunitz, by November 1688 Austrian envoy in Munich, made clear his wish for the success of the invasion, which he spoke of as if simply to maintain the Peace of Nijmegen. Kaunitz told Max Emanuel that Leopold hoped William would succeed in his invasion. Similar enthusiasm was displayed by other Austrian diplomats.[51] The prospect of James pressing Louis to moderate his German policy in return for Austrian pressure on William was mentioned,[52] but Leopold was unwilling to oppose William's invasion. On 28 November Carlingford reported from Vienna,

> I have had a pretty constant account of what passed in Holland in relation to their preparations for the invasion of England, and of their declarations, and libels, for the promotion of that affair, which I have not failed to represent to the ministers here, as the thing deserves, and to show the contradictions there are between the public pretences they give out at this court, and in other places, and those they in these papers design to communicate to their friends and partisans, especially since I have the declaration of the Prince of Orange in my hands, in which the Prince of Wales, his birth is so scandalously questioned that it must be put to the judgment of his free Parliament; this My Lord does astonish, and strike with horror, all indifferent men, so that the most considerable here express a just sense of the dismal consequences such violent proceedings may have, and as I am told none can be more concerned than the Emperor himself, but was he willing he cannot in this exigence assist us, and he must conclude here that the preservation of Holland is more necessary for the conservation of the Empire, and therefore though they do not love these undertakings, they will not disoblige them.

Carlingford continued by complaining that he had no instructions for over a month and was therefore unable to represent James' views concerning Louis' breach of the peace. On 24 September Louis had issued a manifesto justifying his decision to begin hostilities. By the time Carlingford complained on 28 November, the French siege of Philippsburg, begun on 27 September, had been successful and the German princes, many of them supporters of William's invasion, were lining up in opposition to Louis. The envoy informed Middleton, 'all I can do here is only in general to represent that I do not question the King, when at liberty will most readily do all things the treaties oblige him unto, and that he will not encourage an unjust violation or infraction of a truce in any potent neighbour, had I any particular instructions at these points it might prove much more satisfactory.'[53]

Carlingford was whistling in the wind. Even had James been at liberty to act, Leopold would not have been swayed by any instructions Carlingford might receive. For the Emperor, action against France was not simply the first priority, but the perspective in which international affairs were regarded. Though he was both profoundly unhappy about William's plan for usurpation, to the prospect of which he allowed the Dutch envoys to close his eyes until after the invasion had begun, and concerned about the position of the British Catholics, Leopold was prepared to subordinate his fears for the sake of seeing William triumph. In this his position corresponded to that of Innocent XI and of the Spanish government. Religious considerations complicated the responses of both, but each was primarily concerned with Louis as their opponent, not as a friend of James and with William as an enemy of Louis not James.[54] Furthermore, Leopold, Innocent and the Spaniards had no way of gauging what was likely to happen in Britain. Its politics had long been volatile, and the prospects for a successful invasion were uncertain. Major amphibious operations were rare in seventeenth-century Europe and the French had had mixed fortunes when they sought to take advantage of Sicilian unrest in the 1670s. If Louis' attack on Philippsburg helped William by directing French military attention away from the United Provinces and its vulnerable neighbour the Spanish Netherlands, the Dutch invasion of England could be seen as a dangerous diversion of forces that should have been directed against Louis, a diversion made more hazardous both by the chance of failure and by the possibility that the invasion might take a long time to succeed. Avaux urged the movement of French troops to the Dutch frontier though he reported that William had told the Spaniards that any losses of territory to France would be reversed. Rebenec claimed in Spain that William would be unable to help in the defence of the Spanish Netherlands.[55] The invasion was a gamble in military terms, not only in England,[56] but with regard to the strategic situation in western Europe in 1688.

It can be argued that Louis did not pose a significant threat to English interests, except insofar as defined in terms of Protestant internationalism. It can be suggested that James should not be seen as a client of France,[57] and attention can be directed to the willingness of post-Revolution monarchs to reach understandings and eventually ally with France. In 1700 the French diplomat Tallard could suggest, in terms reminiscent of foreign envoys under the later Stuarts, that

Louis would have to reach an agreement with William prior to the meeting of Parliament, because of likely criticism of William there for being too accommodating to French interests.[58] Similar criticisms were to be directed against the Tories in 1712–13 over the Utrecht terms and the abandonment of Britain's allies and against the ministerial Whigs in 1726–30 for allowing the Anglo-French alliance to harm British and continental interests. If the rhetoric of national interests and ministerial betrayal, always a part of public discussion of foreign policy, had become centred on Anglo-French relations and was often unrealistic in its assumptions and prescriptions in terms of British capability and early eighteenth-century international relations, then it is possible to argue that the same is true of the position under the later Stuarts. Charles II and James II have lacked for their foreign policy defenders as persuasive and scholarly as Ragnhild Hatton, who has managed to justify George I, a monarch criticised bitterly by contemporaries for harming British interests, not least by alliance with France, his concern for Hanover serving as a source, justified and otherwise, for accusations, rather as James' Catholicism did. Indeed, it could be suggested that, insofar as comparisons can be made, the post-Revolution monarchs 'distorted' foreign policy to serve personal interests to a greater extent than James had done. In the case of both William and the Georges Britain's fortunes were linked to those of a foreign state with interests and problems of its own in the person of a ruler who was willing to direct British resources to the furtherance of his conception of the interests of the other state. In the case of William, Anne's ministers, George I and George II, post-Revolution governments interpreted Britain's interests in light of international circumstances and possible developments in a fashion that made an active interventionist foreign policy, resulting in guarantees, confrontation and/or conflict, the central feature of Britain's position. To that extent the Revolution represented a sharp break in foreign policy. It is too sweeping to state, as Graham Gibbs has done, that 'under Charles II and James II British foreign policy had been characterised by a fundamental unconcern for French advance in Europe' and that the two monarchs 'turned away from Europe'.[59] The complexities of 28 years foreign policy cannot be thus simply summarised, and Gibbs statement must be qualified by a consideration of policy in the late 1660s and in 1678. However, there is no doubt that Charles in his last years and James had both striven for peace, James making a marked effort in 1688 to reduce tensions over Cologne and to avoid being associated too closely with Louis. No similar effort was made in 1688 by William, which was scarcely surprising as the purpose of the expedition by the childless prince was not dynastic aggrandisement, but immediate benefit in European power politics. News of his success was promptly followed by reports of English participation in attacks on France. Indeed Sir Robert Holmes had reported in early November 1688 that William's fleet was designed for an attack on the French Channel coast rather than on England.[60] Louis was correct to argue that William's invasion would be a great obstacle to peace,[61] because in place of the territorial compromises that had characterised the two previous western European wars, William sought a non-negotiable gain. Leopold's subsequent hope that William would permit a succession by James II's son was misplaced.[62]

William declared war on Louis in May 1689, but he was to be swiftly disabused of his hopes that his allies, or indeed the western and central European powers, would unite against Louis. William was unable to bring either Sweden or Denmark into the anti-French alliance, 'the necessity of devoting all available energies to the defeat of France, which was so clear to William, was by no means so clear to Swedish statesmen'. The mutual jealousy of Sweden and Denmark was a serious handicap to William, as was the failure to negotiate an Austro-Turkish settlement. Lord Paget, English envoy in Vienna, warned of pro-French undercurrents at Vienna and complained of the recall of Austrian troops from the Rhine in order to deploy them against the Turks.[63] The problems of alliance politics were the principal topic of English diplomacy during the Nine Years and Spanish Succession wars. At the same time Williamite propaganda sought both to disguise the problems now confronting England and to vilify critics as pro-French and/or Jacobite in sympathy. Stuart foreign policy was presented as a distortion both of English national interests and of the development of English foreign policy, Williamite propagandists looking back to Elizabeth I. Her policy was defined in 1696,

> that England should always make itself the head and protection of the whole Protestant interest. . . By making all true Protestants, ie all true Christians, her friends she enabled England to make good her oldest maxim of state, which was to keep the balance of Europe equal and steady. . . Our allies of the Roman communion must allow this Protestant maxim to be truly Catholic, because their safety from the power of France was wrapped up in it together with our own.

A congratulatory poem of 1697 declared

> Just wars are made, to make unjust wars cease,
> King William's war was thus the means of peace.[64]

It was scarcely surprising that William and his supporters should seek to influence public opinion, given the importance of winning parliamentary support, both in order to further his foreign policy and to influence foreign powers. Paul Methuen wrote from Lisbon in 1701, 'I know not what good effects the proceedings of our Parliament may have at home, but I am afraid their resolutions concerning the Treaty of Partage, will be very much for our discredit abroad, and that all foreign princes will be very cautious how they deal with us for the future.'[65] It was scarcely surprising that William found it impossible to unify the country in support of his foreign policy. There was no defined sense of national interests, the war was both unsuccessful and costly and William was both a poor communicator and an indifferent manager of English politics. To a certain extent these problems were lessened under Queen Anne. However aggressive they may have been, Louis' moves in 1701 were judged provocative,[66] helping to reverse the isolationist trend of the late 1690s. Anne's ministers were more astute communicators than William, more willing to try to influence public opinion through press and pamphlets and more skilful in cooperating with Parliament. Possibly as important were the successes of the early stages of the war. Again the reign of Elizabeth I served as a period of comparison, and not only in public debate. In January 1703 Sir John Chardin wrote to Thomas Pitt, 'The reign of the Queen proves as successful glorious and beloved as that of the renowned Elizabeth and England saw nothing like since her in point of reciprocal confidence and love between the sovereign and the people and her Majesty's is like to be as fatal to the King of France as the other to the King of Spain.' Success helped to divert attention from the refusal of allies to co-operate, a refusal that did not arouse outrage in England alone.[67]

Victory was a lubricant both for the alliance and for English public support for the war, but its effects could not counteract indefinitely the impact of divergent interests among the allies and of the domestic costs of war. Indeed victory exacerbated both by raising expectations and enlarging demands. Differences with and between allies over objectives and methods constituted an incessant theme of British diplomatic correspondence,[68] a situation aggravated by the removal of the Williamite link with the United Provinces, the greater contribution of English resources, the absence of a security threat comparable to that in Scotland, Ireland and the Channel in the early stages of the Nine Years' War and the determination of the Habsburgs to press their dynastic claims to the Spanish inheritance. George Stepney advanced

Anglo-Austrian differences as one of the reasons why he sought his recall from Vienna in 1704,

> . . . I have had repeated orders to sollicit earnestly in favour of the Malecontents in Hungary, which I have done with all the zeal I could, and thereby have lost the good looks of most of the Ministry, though I barely discharged my duty, which is and ought to be my first consideration: However I perceive a change in the Imperial Court towards me upon that account, and for that reason am of opinion it may be no less for her Majesty's service than for my private satisfaction, that somebody else be found for that employment.[69]

Stepney's complaint was ironical, not so much because of the difference in the alliance that it revealed, as because this centred on the persecution of Protestants by one of England's major allies. The Revolution, the Revolution settlement and the Revolution wars had been presented in religious terms, but they had brought little comfort to the Protestant minorities in the Habsburg lands. Ideology in international affairs commonly entails hypocrisy. Revolutionary France was to be challenged for threatening the international system at the same time as Poland was being partitioned. The distribution of power and the exigencies of alliance politics led and lead to such inconsistencies. While William and his successors did make representations to their allies on behalf of Protestant minorities, including the Waldensians of Piedmont,[70] their success was mixed.

As repeated victory neither brought peace nor eased differences between the allies, war weariness grew in Britain. This was focussed on the seeming endlessness and heavy cost of the conflict, a problem that subsidies to allies contributed to.[71] Whig spokesmen, such as Robert Walpole, were driven to defend the cost of the war. Justifications of the purpose of the war and of Britain's role in it appeared increasingly unconvincing and unrelated to public opinion.[72] At the same time the prospect of peace intensified differences between the allies.[73] In October 1706 Hedges had written to Marlborough, pointing out that the war had been fought for the sake of 'an honourable and durable peace', and suggesting that military success had brought a fair prospect of such a peace,

> In order therefore to adjust the particular terms of it so as that the same good friendship and correspondence in which Her Majesty has lived with the States General ever since her accession to the Crown, and which she desires to cultivate, and improve with the greatest care, may continue as firm and inviolable after the peace, as it has been during the

war, her Majesty is of opinion, that the first proper step would be for herself and the States General to concert and agree betwixt themselves upon such a scheme of a peace, as may be honorable and safe both for themselves, and for the rest of the Allies.

Hedges stressed the need for England and Holland to 'appear to France to be uniform, and of one mind in the transaction of this great affair.' Reality was to prove otherwise. The dissolution of the Grand Alliance brought peace, just as peace and its prospect brought the end of alliances and the creation of new ones. One of the Under Secretaries, Erasmus Lewis, noted in December 1712. 'Marquis de Monteleon has made himself very agreeable here by the assurances he gives that the Crown of Spain begins to show its independency of that of France'. Utrecht was to be followed by a new British diplomatic alignment with former enemies.[74] The popularity of the peace represented a rejection of post Revolution foreign policy. One of the Under Secretaries, Richard Warre, wrote of the response in London,

The joy was suitable to so great a blessing, expressed universally in the City and suburbs, by such marks as might best declare it. The mob went from street to street, and broke the windows where the houses were not illuminated.[75]

The Tory ministry was criticised for the peace terms, but it was reasonable for the Earl of Strafford to claim that 'as for leaving France in the power they are it was actually impossible to have left them other ways, which I think by history, example etc may be proved next to demonstration'.[76] The prospect of a union of Austria and Spain in the person of the Habsburg Charles VI was the culmination of the problems Britain had encountered with her allies. It justified later Stuart caution about continental interventionalism and an active foreign policy and reflected the difficulties of adopting a planned and consistent approach to foreign policy in an international system made unstable and kaleidoscopic by the vagaries of dynastic luck. The Tory ministry of 1710–14 was to be attacked both by contemporaries and subsequently for failing to defend national and European interests, thus linking it up with the fate of James II. However, a good case can be advanced for suggesting that the attitude of each represented a reasonable response both to the unpredictability of international relations and to the problems of obtaining and maintaining domestic support for a difficult and expensive foreign policy. The cost of William's invasion was not only a civil war that brought much suffering to Scotland and Ireland, but also a foreign war that created considerable stresses within Britain and brought her into a dangerous international position. The Revolution divided and weakened Britain and her institutions,[77] far more than James had done, and precipitated them into a conflict that was 'necessary' only in light of William's views and because of the Revolution. The contemporary critique of interventionalism has never been adequately discussed and studied, but it reflected a real awareness of the costs, financial and otherwise, and dangers of the foreign policy of William and his successors. The shedding in part of the Williamite legacy in 1710–16 — the unilateral abandonment of the Grand Alliance, peace and subsequent alliance with France — suggests that the strains of this legacy were apparent to ministers who could not be accused fairly of being Jacobite, pro-Catholic and pro-French. George I and the Whig ministry did not resume hostilities with France in 1714–15 as was feared. Instead they consolidated the new relationship with France. In light of these developments, it could be suggested that James II's foreign policy and international attitude can be justified against many of the charges that have been flung at it.

NOTES

I would like to thank Eveline Cruickshanks for commenting on an earlier draft of this paper, and the British Academy and the Leverhulme Foundation for their support.

Unless otherwise stated all dates are new style. Old style dates are marked (os).

1. Gwynne to Lord Halifax, 20 Dec. 1703, BL, Egerton manuscripts (hereafter Eg.) 929 f.51.
2. J. M. Black, 'The Tory View of Eighteenth-Century British Foreign Policy', *Historical Journal* xxxi. (1988).
3. B. Neveu, 'Les derniers Stuarts et les Jacobites', *Livret de la IVe Section de l'Ecole pratique des Hautes Etudes I 1978–9 à 1980–1* (Paris, 1982), 157.
4. J. Jusserand, *A French Ambassador at the Court of Charles the Second* (London, 1892), 126; Courtin, French envoy in London, to Pomponne, French foreign minister, 1 Oct. 1676, Paris, AECP. Ang. 120 f.31. K. H. D. Haley, *An English Diplomat in the Low Countries. Sir William Temple and John de Witt 1665–1672* (Oxford, 1986), 313.
5. Ruvigny to Louis XIV, 3 Oct. 1667, AECP. Ang. 89 f.114.
6. G. E. Aylmer (ed.), *The Diary of William Lawrence* (Beaminster, 1961), 15.
7. M. F. Bond (ed.), *The Diaries and Papers of Sir Edward Dering second Baronet* (London, 1976), 64–5.

8. Haley, *William of Orange and the English Opposition 1672–4* (1953); Barrillon, French envoy, to Louis, 3 Mar. 1678, AECP. Ang. 128 f.24.

9. Ruvigny to Pomponne, 13 Ap. 1676, AECP. Ang. 118 ff.66–7.

10. Courtin to Louis, 4, 22 June 1676, AECP. Ang. 118 ff.154–5, 216.

11. Courtin to Pomponne, 27 July 1676, AECP. Ang. 119 ff. 69–70; Marquise Campana de Cavelli, *Les Derniers Stuarts à Saint-Germain-en-Laye* (2 vols., Paris, 1871) i, 196–7.

12. Barrillon to Louis, 3 Jan. 1678, AECP. Ang. 127 ff.20–4; Haley, 'The Anglo-Dutch Rapprochement of 1677', *EHR* lxxiii. (1958).

13. Louis to Barrillon, 2 May, Barrillon to Louis, 2 May 1678, AECP. Ang. 129 ff. 20, 30–1.

14. Barrillon to Louis, 2, 5 May 1678, AECP. Ang. 129 ff. 24, 42.

15. Barrillon to Louis, 3, 6, 10, 17 Sept. 1685, AECP. Ang. 156 ff. 25–6, 33–4, 37, 40, 58–9.

16. Barrillon to Louis, 10, 13, 20 Sept. 1685, AECP. Ang. 156 ff. 40–2, 46, 70.

17. Barrillon to Louis, 10 Sept. 1685, AECP. Ang. 156, f.39.

18. Barrillon to Louis, 17 Sept. 1685, 31 Jan. 1686, AECP. Ang. 156 ff.62–3, 158 ff.72–3.

19. J. Miller, *James II, a study in kingship* (Hove, 1978), 160–1; Barrillon to Louis XIV, 4, 11, 15 July 1686, AECP. Ang. 159 ff.17–18, 30, 44–5.

20. Barrillon to Louis, 6, 13 Jan. 1688, 5 Ap. 1687, 5 Ap. 1688, AECP. Ang. 161 ff. 15–16, 37–8, 165 f.219.

21. Bonrepaus to Marquis de Seignelay, 12 June 1687, Paris, Archives Nationales, Archives de la Marine, B¹ 757.

22. Barrillon to Louis, 7 July, 11 Aug., 20 Sept. 1687, AECP. Ang. 162 ff.21, 100, 169.

23. Barrillon to Louis, 25 Aug., 2 Sept. 1687, AECP. Ang. 162 ff.129, 141, 143.

24. Barrillon to Louis, 25 Aug., 2 Sept. 1687, 9 Feb. 1688, AECP. Ang. 162 ff.129, 141, 165 f.83.

25. Barrillon to Louis, 14, 31 July 1687, AECP. Ang. 162 ff.43, 79–80.

26. Barrillon to Louis, 19 Jan. 1688, AECP. Ang. 165 f.50.

27. G. Symcox, 'Louis XIV and the Outbreak of the Nine Years War', in R. Hatton (ed.), *Louis XIV and Europe* (London, 1976).

28. Barrillon to Louis, 9 Feb. 1688, AECP. Ang. 165 f.82.

29. Barrillon to Louis, 23 Feb., 26 Aug. 1688, AECP. Ang. 165 ff.116–17, 258–9.

30. Barrillon to Louis, 26 Feb., 1, 4, 11, 22 Mar. 1688, AECP. Ang. 165 ff.128–30, 133–8, 145–8, 158–9, 183–8.

31. Skelton to the Lord President, 24 March 1688, PRO 78/151 f.160.

32. Barrillon to Louis, 8, 12 Ap. 1688, AECP. Ang. 165, ff.224, 234–5; Louis XIV to Lusignan, envoy in Vienna, 2 June, Lusignan to Louis, 29 July 1688, AECP. Autriche 63 ff. 120, 202–3.

33. Louis to Lusignan, 28 June 1688, AECP. Autriche 63 f.140; Skelton to Lord President, 14 July 1688, PRO 78/151 f.193; Campana, *Derniers Stuarts* ii, 209.

34. Barrillon to Louis, 26, 29 July, 2, 5, 9, 19 Aug. 1688, AECP. Ang. 166 ff. 64–5, 74–5, 80, 87, 94–5, 113.

35. Barrillon to Louis, 26, 30 Aug. 1688, AECP. Ang. 166 ff. 130, 139–40; Avaux, French envoy in The Hague, to Gravel, French envoy in Berlin, 14 Sept., Avaux to Louis, 27 Sept., 4, 5, 7 Oct. 1688, AECP. Hollande 155 f.244, 156 ff.160–1, 208, 217–18, 220; Campana, *Derniers Stuarts* ii, 260, 264, 271, 278.

36. Gravel to Louis, 16 Oct. 1688, AECP. Prusse 32 f.60; Verjus, envoy at Regensburg, to Louis, 19 Oct. 1688, AECP. Allemagne 323 f.46; G. H. Jones, 'William III's Diplomatic Preparations for his Expedition to England', *Durham University Journal*, lxxiv. (1987).

37. R. Hatton, 'Louis XIV and his fellow monarchs', in J. C. Rule (ed.), *Louis XIV and the Craft of Kingship* (Columbus, Ohio, 1969), 155–95; Hatton, 'Louis XIV: Recent gains in historical knowledge', *Journal of Modern History*, xlv. (1973); Hatton, 'Louis XIV et l'Europe: Eléments d'une revision historiographique', *XVII Siècle* lxxiii. (1979); Black, 'Louis XIV's Foreign Policy Reassessed', *Seventeenth-Century French Studies* x (1988).

38. C. J. Ekberg, *The Failure of Louis XIV's Dutch War* (Chapel Hill, North Carolina, 1979).

39. R. Place, 'The Self-Deception of the Strong: France on the Eve of the War of the League of Augsburg', *French Historical Studies* vi. (1970).

40. Rebenac, envoy in Madrid, to Louis, 22 Oct. 1688, AECP. Espagne 75 f.120.

41. Villars to Louis, 20, 30 Oct. 1688, AECP. Bavière 41 ff.61, 86.

42. Cheverny, envoy in Copenhagen, to Louis, 9, 16 Nov. 1688, AECP. Danemark 34 ff.402, 409; Sir Gabriel Sylvius, envoy in Copenhagen, to Richard Tempest, 28 Dec. 1688, Add. 63780, f.187; Oakley, *William III and the Northern Crowns during the Nine Years' War* (New York, 1987) 43–4.

43. A. Lossky, *Louis XIV, William III and the Baltic Crisis of 1683* (Berkeley, 1954).

44. G. Pagès, *Le Grand Electeur et Louis XIV 1660–1688* (Paris, 1905).

45. Black, 'Anglo-Russian Relations after the Seven Years' War' *Scottish Slavonic Review* (1987); Black, 'Anglo-Portuguese Relations in the Eighteenth Century: A Reassessment', *British Historical Society of Portugal. Annual Report and Review* xiv. (1987).

46. *CJ* ix, 756.

47. Barrillon to Louis, 1, 11 Ap. 1678, AECP. Ang. 128.

48. Middleton to Sir Leoline Jenkins, Secretary of State for the Northern Department, 17, 24, 31 Aug., 7, 21 Sept., 7 Oct., 2, 16 Nov. 1680, 8, 22 Feb. 1681, PRO 80/16 ff.195, 211, 214, 218, 225, 236, 243, 269–70; G. H. Jones, *Charles Middleton* (Chicago, 1967) 53; Campana, *Derniers Stuarts* II, 160–1.

49. Jones, *Middleton*, 149; Campana, *Derniers Stuarts* ii, 260.

50. Louis to Villars, 2, 11 Nov. 1688, AECP. Bavière 41 f.76, 90; Louis to Rebenac, 3 Nov. 1688, AECP. Espagne 75 f.158.

51. Villars to Louis, 10, 17 Nov. 1688, AECP. Bavière 41 f.107, 120; Rebenac to Louis, 6 Nov. 1688, AECP. Espagne 75 f.177; Verjus to Louis, 7 Dec. 1688, AECP Allemagne 323 ff.183–5.

52. Lusignan to Louis, 25 Nov., 2 Dec. 1688, AECP. Autriche 63

ff.364–5, 368; Add. 63780, ff.293–4.

53. Carlingford to Middleton, 28 Nov., Wyche, envoy in Hamburg, to Preston, 16 Nov. 1688, Add 63780, ff.297–8, 244.

54. Rebenac to Louis, 7 Oct., 6 Nov. 1688, AECP. Espagne 75 ff.107, 177; Verjus to Louis, 9 Nov. 1688, AECP. Allemagne 323, f.103; C. Gerin, 'Le Pape Innocent XI et la révolution anglaise de 1688', *Revue des Questions Historiques* xx. (1876).

55. Avaux to Louis, 7, 8 Oct. 1688, AECP. Hollande 156 ff.221, 223, 236; Rebenac to Louis, 6 Nov. 1688, AECP. Espagne 75 ff.175–6.

56. J. Childs, *The Army, James II, and the Glorious Revolution* (Manchester, 1980) 168–98; Campana, *Derniers Stuarts* ii, 282.

57. J. L. Price, 'Restoration England and Europe', in J. R. Jones (ed.), *The Restored Monarchy 1660–1688* (London, 1979), 134–5.

58. Tallard to Louis, 4, 10 Sept. 1700, AECP. Ang. 188 ff.30, 57.

59. G. C. Gibbs, 'The Revolution in Foreign Policy', in G. Holmes (ed.), *Britain after the Glorious Revolution 1689–1714* (London, 1969), 60.

60. Verjus to Louis, 7 Dec. 1688, AECP. Allemagne 323 f.184; Memorandum by French envoy Frischmann, winter 1689–90, AECP. Saxe 14 f.104; Rebenac to Louis, 1, 16 Jan. 1689, AECP. Espagne 75 ff.298–9, 356; Holmes to Preston, 5, 6 Nov. 1688, Add 63780, ff.17, 26.

61. Louis to Verjus, 4 Nov. 1688, AECP. Allemagne 323 f.56.

62. M. A. Thomson, 'Louis XIV and William III, 1689–97', in R. Hatton and J. S. Bromley (eds), *William III and Louis XIV* (Liverpool, 1968), 24–48.

63. Oakley, *Northern Crowns* 316, 318, 330; Sir Paul Rycaut, envoy in Hamburg, to Paget, 6 Dec. 1690, 23 May, 26 Aug. 1691, Henry, Viscount Sydney, Secretary of State for the Northern Department, to Paget, 3 July 1691, Add. 61830 ff.9, 16, 24, 22; Paget to Earl of Nottingham, Secretary of State for the Southern Department, 2, 23 Nov, 1690, 25 Feb., 25 Mar., 7 Ap. 1691, Paget to Sydney, 25 Oct. 1691, 6 Feb. 1692, PRO 80/17 ff.108, 119, 172, 180, 185, 208, 235.

64. Stephens, *A Thanksgiving Sermon* (London, 1696) 15–16; *An Encomiastick and Congratulatory Poem. On the Glorious and Peaceable Return of His Sacred Majesty King William III Into England 1697* Bodl. Firth b 21 (39).

65. Paul Methuen, envoy in Lisbon, to Alexander Stanhope, envoy at The Hague, 21 June 1701, Maidstone, Kent Archives Office U1590 029/5.

66. Thomson, 'Louis XIV and the Origins of the War of the Spanish Succession' in Hatton and Bromley, *William III and Louis XIV* 140–161; W. Roosen, 'The Origins of the War of the Spanish Succession', in Black (ed.), *The Origins of War in Early Modern Europe* (Edinburgh, 1987) 151–75.

67. Chardin to Pitt, 30 Jan. (os) 1703, Add. 22,852 f.115; R. Doebner (ed.), *Briefe der königin Sophie Charlotte von Preussen und der kurfürstin Sophie von Hannover an hanoversche Diplomaten* (Leipzig, 1905) 49; A. J. Veenendaal (ed.), *De Briefwisseling van Anthonie Heinsius 1702–1720* iii (Hague, 1980) p.245; Extract of the Points explained to the English Ambassador in a Conference with the Marquis d'Alègre, 16 Sept. 1705, Add. 61,122 f.64; Earl of Manchester to Robert Harley, Secretary of State for the Northern Department, 25 Mar. 1707, Huntingdon, County RO, DDM36/8 p.3.

68. Letterbook of John Chetwynd, Secretary in Turin, 1 Feb. 1704, Stafford County RO, D 649/8/2; Stanhope to Harley, 5 Aug. 1704, PRO 84/227 f.11–12; Instructions for Earl of Peterborough and Admiral Shovell, 10 Sept. (os) 1705, Add. 61122 f.13; Chetwynd to Sir Charles Hedges, Secretary for the Southern Department, 10 Nov. 1706, Add. 61525 f.5.

69. Stepney to Halifax, 26 Sept. 1704, BL. Eg. 929 f.63.

70. G. Symcox, *Victor Amadeus II* (London, 1983), 108–9; Instructions for Chetwynd, 3 Aug. (os) 1706, Chetwynd to Hedges, 13 Nov. 1707, Add. 61525 f.2, 7.

71. Symcox, 'Britain and Victor Amadeus II: or, the use and abuse of allies', in S. Baxter (ed.), *England's Rise to Greatness, 1660–1763* (Berkeley, 1983) 163–5.

72. [Walpole], *A State of the Five and Thirty Millions mention'd in the Report of a Committee of the House of Commons* (1711); *British Mercury* 3 Jan. (os) 1711; *Flying Post* 8 Jan. (os) 1713.

73. Horatio Walpole, Secretary of Embassy at The Hague, to Stair, 8 Ap. 1710, Edinburgh, Scottish Record Office GD. 135/141/1.

74. Hedges to Marlborough, 21 Oct. (os) 1706; Add. 61122 f.137–8; Lewis to Lord Lexington, envoy in Spain, 27 Dec. (os) 1712, Add. 46546 f.5; D. McKay, 'Bolingbroke, Oxford and the defence of the Utrecht settlement in southern Europe', *EHR* lxxxvi. (1971); Cardinal de La Trémoille, French envoy in Rome, to Louis, 8 May, Louis to Trémoille, 28 May 1714, AECP. Rome 537 ff.47, 51.

75. Warre to Burch, Secretary to Lexington, 8 May (os) 1713, Add. 46546 f.62.

76. Strafford to Earl of Orrery, 29 May 1714, Bodl. Ms Eng. Lett. c.144 ff.300–1.

77. J. Childs, *The British army and William III, 1689–1702* (Manchester, 1987), 4–8.

9

PIERRE'S WHITE HAT:
THEATRE, JACOBITISM AND POPULAR PROTEST
IN LONDON, 1689–1760

Paul Monod

> The crowd, to restless motion still inclined,
> Are clouds that rack according to the wind.
> Driv'n by their chiefs they storms of hailstones pour;
> Then mourn, and soften to a silent shower.
>
> — Thomas Otway, *Venice Preserved*.[1]

Until recently, English historians never doubted that the Glorious Revolution was popular, or that King James II was not.[2] These views are no longer so certain. Tim Harris's research on the Exclusion Crisis of 1679–82 has shown that James, then Duke of York, enjoyed considerable support from the London crowds. Like the aristocracy and gentry, the common people of the capital were divided, primarily by religious beliefs, into two camps, the advocates of Exclusion and the defenders of hereditary right.[3] To be sure, Whigs and many Tories were apparently united at the Revolution, by their distrust of James II's Catholic policies; but over the next two decades, they were again separated by an increasingly bitter party conflict. By 1714, as Gary De Krey has argued, the Tories had emerged as the more popular of the two parties in London.[4] Nicholas Rogers has examined the extensive riots that broke out in London and the provinces after the Hanoverian Succession.[5] The discovery of a rash of Jacobite commemorations and widespread protests directed against Whigs and Dissenters suggested that the legacy of the Glorious Revolution had somehow gone awry, and that popular allegiance may have been drifting back towards the Stuarts.

The attention of historians has mostly focused on the political context of popular discontent in late Stuart and Hanoverian London. Yet unrest cannot be properly understood without exploring its cultural content, the system of behavioral or linguistic signs that informed the perceptions and actions of the crowds. Literary critics and social historians have proposed that popular political culture was strongly rooted in the forms and imagery of the Carnival, the central festive event in most European countries.[6] Although Carnival was only a vague memory in eighteenth-century England, it did retain considerable significance in the popular imagination, even in a fast-changing city like London.[7] In addition, an extraordinary variety of feast days, festivals and commemorative holidays, most of them religious in origin, still dominated the plebeian calendar in the eighteenth century, providing a cultural framework for popular politics in both town and country.[8] Many Jacobite disturbances took place on commemoration days such as May 29, the anniversary of Charles II's restoration, or June 10, the birthday of James Francis Edward Stuart, the Old Pretender.

Historians have argued, however, that the landowning and mercantile elites separated themselves from traditional culture in the seventeenth century.[9] In that case, one would not expect to find many links between the cultural assumptions of elite politics and those of the common people in eighteenth-century London. Yet the evidence of Jacobite disturbances points strongly in the opposite direction. They were aided and abetted by disaffected aristocrats, gentlemen and merchants. The words and symbols used by the crowds, moreover, were derived from a common store of Jacobite propaganda that was shared by all classes. The following discussion will argue that the process of cultural divergence in England was very slow, and was linked to political affiliations. Whigs were generally more hostile to popular customs than were Tories, and the separation of elite from popular culture could only be achieved after the Jacobites had been vanquished. In the first half of the eighteenth century, the distance between the so-called 'great' and 'little' traditions was small enough to be bridged.

An important arch in this cultural bridge was the theatre. Carnival was itself a theatre of the streets, and the term 'political theatre' can be applied to the rituals and symbolism of riots and demonstrations; but the theatre was more than just a metaphor for popular politics. The Elizabethan and Jacobean theatre, as Michael Bristol has pointed out, owed a great debt to Carnival; and even after the Restoration, the London stage did not entirely sever its filial ties to popular culture.[10] An awareness of the desires and aspirations of the public permeated the theatre world. London audiences of the late seventeenth and eighteenth centuries were once thought by theatre historians to have been predominantly aristocratic, but now they are seen as more socially diverse, drawing from the "middling" and lower classes as well as the elite. Audiences exercised a direct influence on what was presented by the playhouses; playwrights had to please them in order to survive.[11] The predilections of London audiences, moreover, tended to parallel the behaviour of crowds in the capital, making the theatre a factor in the dissemination of popular political culture. At the heart of this dialogue between the stage and politics lay the conviction that party divisions were essentially artificial or theatrical, and therefore undesirable in the real world. The elimination of faction was the happy ending of popular political theatre. 'Whatever storms of Fortune are decreed/ . . . truth and virtue shall at last succeed', concluded Nahum Tate's 1681 revision of *King Lear*, a favourite stage offering of the early 1700s, in which the King survives to hand over his crown to Cordelia and Edgar![12]

The concept of "theatre" will be applied broadly in this essay, to include street performances of all kinds, as well as the formal stage. It will be suggested that theatricality was an important element in Jacobite protest, and that this provided a cultural link between elite and plebeian politics. By no means should it be supposed that the political use of the theatre was an exclusively Jacobite trait, or that all Jacobite activity was in some way theatrical. Nevertheless, the adherents of the Stuarts had an important historical relationship with the theatre, which was always recognized, in spite of the ambivalent feelings of many Jacobites about the stage. This relationship stemmed from the Civil War period, and did not entirely fade away until the 1750s.

The political significance of the theatre after 1688 must be interpreted against the background of the struggles of the mid-seventeenth century. Political and religious commentary in plays had been forbidden by an Elizabethan proclamation of 1559, but in the troubled 1620s the theatre gradually became a forum for controversy.[13] Thomas Middleton's anti-Spanish satire, *A Game at Chesse*, was suppressed in 1624 by order of James I himself.[14] Martin Butler and Kevin Sharpe have shown that factionalism in Charles I's Privy Council encouraged a diversity of political approaches in the court theatres.[15] Butler emphasizes the survival of the popular playhouses of the 1630s and early 40s, like the Phoenix or the Salisbury Court; they specialized in comedies, such as those of Richard Brome, which criticized courtiers and wicked counsellors. The satirical "playlets" of 1641 went further in attacking Archbishop Laud himself.[16] To be sure, some of Laud's religious opponents among the 'hotter sort of Protestants', or puritans, were ferociously hostile to the theatre. Butler points out, however, that this was not an attitude common to all puritans, and he maintains that it was a desire to impose order, not an antipathy to the stage, that caused the Long Parliament in September 1642 to ban the performance of plays in England.[17]

Regardless of its motives, which may have been more ideological than Butler allows, this ban was one of the first moves in a wider campaign. David Underdown has documented the vigorous onslaught on the local level against the 'ungodly' and "superstitious" practices of the common people, including many forms of popular recreation, from church ales to maypole dancing.[18] Those who cherished the old traditions, as Underdown has shown, often supported the royalist cause in the Civil War; hence the significance of maypoles as a monarchist symbol.[19] Monarchy became associated with the "old England" of village sports, harvest festivals — and theatre, whether in the form of provincial Passion plays or the London playhouses. The distinctions among puritan attitudes towards the stage were obliterated in the eyes of their enemies; what remained was the caricature of the dour and repressive sectarian zealot. The memory of these years did not fade for more than a century, and was to animate later party conflicts.

Lord Protector Cromwell allowed plays to be performed in the mid-1650s, just as he began to accrue the trappings of quasi-monarchical power.[20] This may only have emphasized the perceived connection between theatre and kingship. With the Restoration, the rule of the "godly" came to an end, and the theatre flourished again — but only under tight control. As Pepys attests, Charles II loved the stage, and his public appearances, such as his entry into London in 1660 or his coronation, were carefully crafted theatrical performances. Gerard Reedy has shown that these royal spectacles were informed by concepts of a well-ordered and hierarchical universe.[21] The new king, however, kept his father's experiences in mind, and recognized that the stage, like the mob, was too unpredictable to be relied upon to serve royal purposes faithfully. Charles II did not trust the theatre, any more than he did the cheering crowds that welcomed him back to England in 1660. By granting only two patents to operate playhouses, he sought to discipline and regulate the protean energies of popular drama.[22]

His strategy almost collapsed during the Exclusion Crisis, when playwrights like Nathaniel Lee and Thomas Shadwell began to cater to virulently anti-Catholic audiences.[23] By 1681, however, belief in the Popish Plot was waning, and the harried Duke of York had managed to gain a popular following in London among those who disliked Dissenters more than they did Roman Catholics. Eventually, the Whigs were ousted from City government by the resurgent Tories.[24] James's triumph was celebrated in February 1682, by the performance of Thomas Otway's

Venice Preserved at the Duke of York's playhouse in Dorset Garden. The prologues and epilogues of Otway's play were masterpieces of legitimist propaganda, and were later to echo through Jacobite poetry:

> See, see, the injured prince, and bless his name,
> Think on the martyr from whose loins he came . . .
> Think what he'as borne, your quiet to restore,
> Repent your madness and rebel no more.[25]

Nevertheless, Otway, like his patron, remained wary of the "restless" crowd, which he pictured as driven "according to the wind". Even in the moment of Tory victory, the playwright declined to promote a populist message, preferring instead to attribute James's success to divine sanction. This was typical of the enduring High Church mistrust of the people.

In spite of its blatant Tory prologues, *Venice Preserved* was not originally designed for a partisan purpose, and it cannot easily be interpreted as a propaganda piece. True, the lecherous orator Antonio is a recognizable portrait of the Whig Earl of Shaftesbury, but the main 'heroic' character, Pierre, is a conspirator against the state, whose attempt to overthrow the Venetian Republic ends in his own death.[26] This illustrates a recurring aspect of the relationship between politics and the theatre. The political content of many plays depended more on the actors and the audience than on the intentions of the author. As will be seen, seemingly conservative works could become subversive, while some politically charged plays could change their meaning entirely when performed in a different context. The political significance of the theatre, in short, was mutable; it depended upon the circumstances of the performance and the assumptions of the audience. In this respect, as in others, it mirrored the proclivities of the crowds.

Thomas Otway died shortly after the Duke of York became King James II. If he had lived to the Revolution, Otway might have remained loyal to his old patron, as did the female Tory dramatist Aphra Behn.[27] Three years of James's pro-Catholic policies, however, alienated many of his staunchest High Church supporters. Yet remarkably, he retained his popularity with the London Tory mob until almost the end. When he returned to the capital after his first escape attempt in December 1688, the King was welcomed back by cheering crowds of Londoners.[28] Their enthusiasm was focused on the ruler, not on his policies. Some of the King's well-wishers may even have taken part in the violent sacking of Catholic chapels in the previous week. While they feared and hated

James's religion, they clung to the ideal of legitimate kingship, and to the sanctity of the king's person.

Sharing his brother's suspicion of the people, James refused to take hope from these demonstrations. He fled London again, this time for good, and most of his erstwhile supporters acquiesced, however reluctantly, in the accession of William and Mary to the throne. Lois Schwoerer has pointed out that the new regime was adept in mounting public spectacles, and disseminating propaganda that emphasized the Protestantism of the joint monarchs; through these methods, as much as through the errors of King James in Ireland and France, William and Mary extended their popularity to plebeian Tories as well as Whigs.[29] The joint rulers, however, had conflicting attitudes towards the idea of theatre. William, a strict Calvinist, disliked the stage, and encouraged the efforts of the societies for the reformation of manners to resurrect the old puritan crusade against 'ungodly' entertainments.[30] Mary, on the other hand, inherited her father's love for drama, but she was occasionally embarrassed by it. Soon after her accession, she ordered a performance of Dryden's anti-Catholic play *The Spanish Friar,* which deals with the seizure of a king's throne by his daughter; she was stared at by the audience whenever usurpation was mentioned.[31]

William's hostility, and Mary's occasional discomfort, did not alter the attachment to them of the formal playhouses. The Williamite tone of the stage was due to a number of causes. Centralized control was made easier by the fact that Drury Lane was the only theatre in London, until the rival Lincoln's Inn Fields company was founded, with William's blessing, in 1694.[32] Censorship by the Lord Chamberlain proved very effective. In 1692, for example, John Dryden's *Cleomenes,* a play about usurpation, was suppressed, and could only be staged after the offending passages were removed.[33] The need for censorship, however, may have diminished on account of the rise of a new generation of Whig playwrights, including Colley Cibber, John Vanbrugh and Nicholas Rowe, whose plays often proclaimed a strong Williamite bias. Above all, the tone of the theatre was attributable to the quiescence of its audiences, who welcomed the relative stability offered by the new rulers. The Jacobites were unable at first to raise a serious popular challenge to them. Nevertheless, they tried mightily, using all the techniques of the stage in order to raise public indignation against the 'usurpers'; and at one point, in the middle of William's reign, they almost succeeded.

King James's most active friends in London can be roughly divided into two groups, the High Churchmen and the Cavaliers.

These were not mutually exclusive factions, but they were often opposed to each other on key issues. The High Churchmen, many of them Nonjuring gentry and 'middling' folk, were men and women of stern moral probity, whose allegiance was based on conscience and adherence to legitimate hereditary right; they had no love for either the crowd or the theatre. Their views were typified by the Nonjuring divine Jeremy Collier, who produced in 1697 the most devastating critique of the immorality and impiety of the stage that had been seen in England since the Restoration.[34] The Cavaliers were mostly ex-officers of James's army, and they included a large number of Roman Catholics. Although they were usually small landowners, not impoverished adventurers, they had been drawn into a swashbuckling and reckless lifestyle, and shared a passionate loyalty to their exiled master.[35] They were creatures of the theatre, and they courted publicity on every occasion, especially by staging elaborate commemorations of Jacobite holidays in London taverns. It was no coincidence that their favourite haunts were near the playhouse in Drury Lane.[36]

In 1693–5, the Cavaliers began to sense an opportunity. The war against France was dragging on, and growing increasingly unpopular with a heavily taxed populace. In the summer of 1693, King James agreed to a radical "Whiggish" declaration, in which he pledged himself to defend the rights and liberties of Englishmen, to relieve the people of burdensome taxes, and to respect Parliament's wishes on religious matters.[37] In May, copies of the declaration were scattered throughout London, leading to the arrest of a Catholic bookseller, William Canning, and his assistant. On June 1, a printing press was seized in Westminster, along with copies of the declaration and some Jacobite songs, 'designed to be disperst among the weavers and other discontented persons, to animate them to rise in the holydayes'. The songs were to be distributed by ballad-singers, the most common street performers in the capital. The government responded by putting its troops in London on alert, and began arresting ballad-singers and printers. When Canning and his assistant were publicly pilloried at Charing Cross on July 20, however, they 'were favourably used by the mob', which must have increased official consternation.[38] The pillory was a kind of stage, and public punishment a form of theatre. The audience, by declaring its sympathy with the supposed villains of the piece, were subverting the intentions of the governmental authors.

The Jacobites were beginning to exploit street theatre, and in turn popular theatre was drifting towards Jacobitism. This was further evidenced by an incident at Bartholomew Fair in September, when a

G

Merry Andrew — the English equivalent of the Lord of Misrule — was arrested 'for telling the mobb news that our fleet was come into Torbay, being forced in by some French privateers, and other words reflecting on the conduct of great ministers of state.'[39] The Carnival culture of popular politics, represented by the Merry Andrew, was based on improvised oral communication; it was consciously contrasted here with the 'official', written culture of the Williamite 'public sheets' or newspapers. The setting, furthermore, reminds us of Jean-Christophe Agnew's creative comparison of the theatre and the marketplace.[40] Bartholomew Fair epitomized the older form of face-to-face, small-scale commerce, which contrasted with the big business of the Bank of England or the Exchange; in fact, the Merry Andrew of Bartholomew Fair was arrested and pilloried in 1696 for scandalous words insulting the Bank and the Exchange.[41] The Fair was unashamed of its own theatricality, unlike the self-important seriousness of the City. The Dissenters who took such a large role in the "financial revolution" were, after all, the descendants of Ben Jonson's Zeal-of-the-Land Busy, the "Banbury man" who had castigated the "puppet shows" of Bartholomew Fair.

The political crisis of 1693 passed with the replacement of William's Tory ministers by the Junto Whigs. Popular discontent continued, however, and in April 1695 severe riots took place in Holborn and Drury Lane. Angry crowds attacked the houses of army provost marshalls, releasing impressed soldiers who were to be sent to Flanders.[42] The Jacobite ex-officers may have been connected with these disturbances. On June 10 they met at the Dog Tavern in Drury Lane to celebrate the Prince of Wales's birthday, and attempted to raise a riot with drums, trumpets and a bonfire. The theatrical nature of this event was illustrated not only by the locale — a few feet from the Drury Lane theatre — but also by the presence of the actor Cardell Goodman, a former favourite of James II, and of the popular singing-men John Reading and William Pate, both of whom were members of the Lincoln's Inn Fields company.[43] By emphasizing these connections with the stage, the rioters were trying to tear down the separation between acting and reality, between players and spectators, in order to draw the London crowd into a seditious political drama. They were also commenting directly on Whig dominance over the official stage, by creating their own theatre of the streets.

The Jacobite riot was a failure; their performance was wrecked by the intervention of the trained bands and some Williamite butchers from Clare Market. As a result, they turned to a wider scheme involving a French invasion and a provincial uprising, to which a smaller group of conspirators engrafted in 1696 a plot to assassinate King William. The Cavalier obsession with the theatre influenced several aspects of the plan. When the Duke of Berwick, James II's illegitimate son, secretly visited England in February 1696, he attended a masked ball at Draper's Hall, where he reportedly whispered Jacobite tidings to the other guests.[44] Otway's *Venice Preserved* was reprinted in 1696, and may have been performed, probably in connection with the conspiracy; it had not been shown since 1688, on account of its Jacobite implications.[45] The Assassination Plot, however, was discovered at the last minute, and the principal conspirators were executed — a tragic finale not unlike that of Otway's play. Daniel Szechi has noted that some of the assassins broke with the traditional theatre of the scaffold by dying unrepentant, thus setting a precedent for later Jacobite rebels.[46] Perhaps they recalled Pierre's dying words in *Venice Preserved*: 'You say my conscience/ Must be mine accuser. I have searched that conscience,/ And find no records there of crimes that scare me.'[47]

The Jacobite Cavaliers of the 1690s achieved none of their main goals, but they did succeed in resuscitating much of the royalist political culture of the Civil War and Interregnum. They helped to turn the Jacobite cause away from aristocratic plotting and towards a more populist approach. The theatre was central to this change of direction, because it had a broad social appeal, and because its fortunes had been so closely associated with those of the Stuarts. No matter how much the Williamite regime tried to appropriate the stage as a popular political platform, a certain aura of Jacobitism lingered in the memory and imagination of the public.

The theatrical energy of the Jacobite Cavaliers had not been matched with a deep understanding of the popular mind. King James might make fine promises in his declarations, and the burdens of war might cause outbursts of protest, but only religious issues could truly ignite the people. In the years that followed the Assassination Plot, however, the High Church Jacobites gradually adopted a more friendly view of the mob, and a more benign stance towards the theatre. This transformation was inspired by the spread of Jacobite sentiment within the Tory party after years of Whig rule. It led to the rekindling of religious animosities and the reawakening of the London crowds.

By 1700, the question of the succession was again of great concern to Parliament, and some of the Tory leaders were making overtures to James II at St. Germain. The light comedian Scudamore of Lincoln's Inn Fields also paid him a visit.[48] The censors became particularly sensitive at this time to any hint of Jacobitism on the stage. Colley Cibber was amazed when the Master of the Revels struck out the whole first act of Shakespeare's *Richard III* from a performance in the winter of 1699–1700; the objection was that the murder of Henry VI 'would put people too much in mind of King James then living in France'.[49] In February 1700, with the Tories briefly in the ascendant both in Parliament and at court, *Venice Preserved* was produced at Drury Lane, for the first time since the Revolution; it was staged once more a year later.[50] At the end of 1701, Drury Lane presented *The Generous Conqueror,* a play which preached passive obedience and condemned the evils of usurpation. It was written by the Jacobite Bevill Higgons, with a prologue by his cousin George Granville, who as Baron Lansdowne was to become a noted Jacobite politician.[51] In a dedication to the Marquis of Normanby, Higgons defended his play against Whig critics, who 'hate the Innocent Child for the sake of the Father,' an obvious reference to James Francis Edward Stuart.[52]

Alarmed by the Jacobite tendencies of the Tories, William soon turned back to a Whig ministry, but his death in March 1702 once again altered the political situation. Queen Anne's preference for Tory advisers was reflected in the fact that *Venice Preserved* appeared at Drury Lane and at the Queen's own theatre eleven times between 1703 and 1707.[53] With a Stuart on the throne, the play had lost its treasonable connotations; indeed, English Jacobitism became largely dormant in the early years of Anne's reign. An important development, however, was taking place in the relationship between the High Church Jacobites and the Tory party. Nonjurors like Charles Leslie were emerging as the popular spokesmen for Toryism, mixing thinly veiled hints of hereditary right with virulent attacks on Dissenters.[54] The anti-populist stance of the Jacobite High Churchmen was at last giving way to a recognition of the power of public opinion; and in spite of Jeremy Collier, the Nonjuring polemicists began to borrow from the stage. Leslie's principal propaganda organ was a weekly paper that ran from 1704 until 1709, called *The Rehearsals.*[55] The obviously theatrical title was inspired by the still-popular Restoration comedy of the same name, written by Charles II's companion, George Villiers, Duke of Buckingham. It may also have referred to the "rehearsing" of Tory principles prior to a future performance, that is, a restoration.

The Whig-dominated government of 1708–10 feared such a prospect, and attempted to avert it. One indication of this may be found in the record of performances of *Venice Preserved,* which was presented only twice in these years.[56] A more significant sign of the government's anxiety was the prosecution of the Tory preacher Dr. Henry Sacheverell for a November 5 sermon that seemed to attack the Revolution.[57] At the height of the trial, on February 25, 1710, the Queen's theatre cancelled a performance of *Venice Preserved*, because circumstances had made it too controversial.[58] It was a propitious action. Four days later, riots broke out in London, and several Dissenting meeting-houses were demolished.[59] The social and religious tensions that had been building for two decades, exacerbated by the war and the policies of the Whig government, were finally released. The Jacobites were exultant; they sensed that popular hostility towards the Whigs would soon turn to their benefit.

A Tory administration swept into office in the wake of the riots. It had great difficulty in its dealings with the London stage, because most of the major dramatists remained Whigs; but it encouraged the nine performances of *Venice Preserved* that were offered between March 1710 and August 1714.[60] The Tories also sponsored the creation of a new theatre at Lincoln's Inn Fields in 1714. By the time it opened in December, however, Queen Anne was dead, King George had turned out the Tory ministers, and the London crowd was on the verge of a major outbreak of violence. The efforts of Charles Leslie and Henry Sacheverell were at last bearing fruit.

In his study of English drama in the late seventeenth century, Robert Hume has argued that the 'Court-oriented' Restoration tradition gave way around 1710 to the 'more bourgeois and Whiggish' Augustan style.[61] The London audiences, however, were not so quick to change their politics. The struggle between the Tory and Whig theatres reached its apogee after 1714, and the Whig victory was not complete until the mid-1720s. The interplay between the theatre and the London crowds in the years 1714–24 was more complex than at any time since the Exclusion Crisis. Building upon the connections that had developed over the previous two decades, the stage came to influence almost every aspect of popular Jacobitism, from songs and broadsides to riots and demonstrations. Jacobite theatricality was displayed by revellers on commemoration days, by state prisoners, and by condemned men on the scaffold. The Jacobite press, led by Nathaniel Mist's *Weekly Journal*, kept a large readership informed of the politics of the theatre and of the street. Although a second Stuart restoration never materialized, the spread of Jacobite sentiment seemed to herald a rebirth of popular culture, similar to that of 1660; and the theatre provided a framework for the whole scenario.

The rivalry between Drury Lane and Lincoln's Inn Fields in this period epitomized the political conflict that gripped the capital. While the Whig playhouse presented loyal Hanoverian propaganda in the form of plays like Colley Cibber's *The Nonjuror*, the Tory company flirted openly with Jacobitism.[62] In 1719, Lincoln's Inn Fields even dared to offer a new production of Shakespeare's *Richard II*; its theme of successful usurpation had made the play politically explosive, and had kept it off the stage since 1681.[63] At the end of 1722, in the midst of the Atterbury affair, John Ogden, a player at Lincoln's Inn Fields, was arrested for damning King George.[64] The Jacobite press, particularly Mist's *Weekly Journal*, championed the Tory playhouse. Mist was prosecuted in 1721 for printing a faintly disguised call for the Pretender's return, published to commemorate May 29, Charles II's restoration day.[65] Benjamin Griffin, an actor and playwright of Lincoln's Inn Fields, was taken up and examined in connection with this seditious libel, of which he may have been the author.[66]

The hint of treason, however, could even infiltrate the Whig bastion of Drury Lane, as Aline Mackenzie showed in an ingenious article. She traced the origins of a curious stage tradition associated with Otway's *Venice Preserved*, Pierre's white hat. John Mills and, later, James Quin, who held the role of Pierre at Drury Lane from 1707 until 1748, always wore a white hat when performing the part. The reason for sporting this peculiar headgear was eventually forgotten, but Mackenzie convincingly proposed that it was meant to be a mark of Jacobitism, white being the colour of the late Duke of York.[67] The actor John Bowman of Drury Lane, the last survivor of the old Dorset Garden company, proclaimed his Jacobite adherence in a more outrageous fashion during a special performance of Otway's *The Orphan*, given around 1717. Tickets for the event had been issued without charge, and no names of players were mentioned on them. Bowman appeared as Acasto, and began the evening with a line from Act Two of the play: 'It is the birthday of my Royal Master.' At this, according to a Whig who was present, the audience "recollected that it was the tenth of June, and half of us left the place, the rest with a redoubled applause called for the line again and again".[68] It is possible that the founding in 1718 of the High Church and Jacobite newspaper, Elizabeth Powell's *The Orphan Reviv'd: or, Powell's Weekly Journal*, was connected with this incident.[69]

Newspapers were not the only form of Jacobite propaganda to draw upon theatrical references. A large number of treasonable songs and ballads circulated in London in the decade after the accession of George I.[70] The playwright and poet Richard Savage, in fact, wrote a

number of Jacobite works in 1716.[71] Ballad-singing was the mainstay of
street theatre, and the formal stage provided a ready source of phrases
and images for Jacobite poetry. The lines of Otway's epilogue to *Venice
Preserved* that are quoted above, for example, inspired a Jacobite bard
in "A Prophetick Congratulatory Hymn", written about 1722: "See,
See, He comes of all Mankind the first,/ In sufferings, Pietie, &
Experience nurs'd. . ."[72] One Jacobite piece found in many surviving
collections is entitled "Cato's Ghost"; it refers directly to Addison's play
Cato, which was first produced in 1713. As Colley Cibber pointed out,
Cato was warmly greeted by both parties, although it was written by a
Whig.[73] The Jacobite version begins with a critique of Addison's play,
but goes on to urge Britons to imitate the ancient Roman by taking up
arms against the 'usurper':

> In such a Cause break thro' the thick array
> Of th'Usurpers Guard, and force your way.
> Some lucky band, more favour'd than the rest,
> May charge him home, and reach the Monster's Breast,
> Restore your King, and make your Country bless'd.[74]

Even assassination was a legitimate weapon against Hanoverian tyranny,
at least when it was couched in the rhetoric of the theatre.

Although few were willing to go so far in reality, many individuals
were accused of less serious crimes of sedition. They consequently
became caught up in the great theatre of the law, a long-running
English drama in which the majesty of justice commanded center-
stage.[75] The Old Bailey itself strongly resembled an open-air Italianate
theatre, a similarity that was not coincidental.[76] Criminal trials were
designed as theatre, and were meant to inspire awe. According to the
accepted script, the prisoner was supposed to acknowledge the crime,
and repent. The Jacobites, however, often chose to rewrite the play.
In 1718, one Robert Harrison was pilloried in the City for seditious
words against King George. The government hoped that he would be
abused by the crowd; but instead, an innkeeper's servant, along with
some friends, stopped several coaches in Aldgate, asking for money to
support the wretched Harrison. A joiner who refused to contribute was
insulted by the mob. Meanwhile, 'a vile lewd woman' named Catherine
Priest went among the 'vast Concourse of Mob . . . damning the Court
& the Jury who condemned the said Harrison'.[77]

Like the pillory or the scaffold, the government's prisons could
be turned into stages for the enactment of Jacobite dramas. A certain
James Sheppard, while imprisoned in the Gatehouse in 1718, allegedly
went about the place proclaiming Jacobite sentiments to anyone who

would listen, including the hope that George I would 'go to Hanover and How Turnips with his Horns upon his head'.[78] Sheppard also wore oak boughs on May 29, a reference to the Royal Oak in which Charles II hid after the battle of Worcester, and an open gesture of support for a Stuart restoration. Around the same time, a prisoner in the Marshalsea, who had been accused of riot and murder, was reported to the government for illuminating his windows on the Pretender's birthday.[79] An extraordinary account of Jacobite theatre and prison life was written by the overseer of Newgate in 1716. A large number of rebel captives of the '15 were incarcerated there, along with various other malcontents, and the overseer was filled with despair by the fraternizing which took place between the military guards and the prisoners. On May 28, King George's birthday, some of the soldiers on duty were heard singing the old Cavalier song, 'The King shall enjoy his own again'. The thanksgiving day for the victory over the rebels was satirized by several persons who came to the prison 'wearing Rhew and Thyme in their hatts & bosoms, in contempt of ye Day'; bricks were thrown at the guards from neighbouring buildings. On June 10, white roses appeared in the street opposite the prison, and were worn by visitors, while a journeyman printer who assaulted a guard was shot dead in Newgate Street.[80] The interaction between the audience outside and the actors within the prison illustrates clearly the breakdown of the elaborate theatre of the law.

The recurring London riots of 1715–16 made the whole City and its suburbs into a stage. The rioters were aware of the importance of putting on a show, and often resorted to spectacular displays in order to gain attention. The burning of effigies on commemoration days was a favourite tactic. On the anniversary of Queen Anne's accession in April 1715, for example, a crowd of Dr. Sacheverell's parishioners from St. Andrew's Holborn hung up a flag and the Queen's picture on the Snow Hill conduit, lit a bonfire and burned an effigy of King William.[81] On May 29, a Jacobite mob at the Exchange threatened to consign effigies of Luther and Calvin to the flames.[82] The government responded to such actions by organizing loyalist societies or Mug-houses to combat the Tory crowds.[83] The Pretender was burned in effigy by the 'Muggites' of the Roebuck tavern in Cheapside four times in 1714–15; on at least one occasion, the 'Jacks' tried unsuccessfully to rescue their King. The Roebuck loyalists also prevented a figure of William III from being sacrificed at Old Jewry on the late King's birthday in November 1715, and two weeks later they saved effigies of King William, King George and the Duke of Marlborough from immolation by the Jacobites.[84]

Effigy burning was a symbolic punishment that served to 'purify' the community in the same way as the witch-hunts or religious massacres of other ages.[85] Unlike these earlier customs, however, the destruction of effigies was a kind of symbolic or artificial violence, another reflection of the theatrical nature of politics. The formalization of party conflict since 1679 had actually lessened the level of partisan bloodshed; a society divided from top to bottom by political differences, and haunted by the bitter memory of civil war, was not willing to tear itself apart by sanctioning outright murder.[86] Instead, dissidence was channelled into ritual and theatre. Certainly, the threat of armed rebellion continued into the 1750s, but riots, commemorations and demonstrations became the ordinary forms of protest against the Hanoverian regime. In a similar fashion, gentry Jacobitism became centred on secret clubs and convivial societies. Here was another case in which elite politics and the politics of the streets followed the same development.

Nevertheless, effigy burning often led to real violence, and the battles between 'Jacks' and 'Muggites' culminated in the deaths of six men. On July 23, 1716, a Jacobite mob attacked Robert Read's Mug-house in Salisbury Court, off Fleet Street; the proprietor fired at them, and killed one of their leaders, a small-coals man named Daniel Vaughan.[87] The location of Read's Mug-house had strong theatrical connections. Salisbury Court was the site of one of the popular playhouses of the 1630s and early 40s; it had continued to operate secretly after the theatre ban of 1642, but had been demolished by order of the Rump Parliament in March 1649, shortly after the execution of Charles I. In 1670, the Duke of York's company of players moved to the Dorset Garden property, adjacent to Salisbury Court, and remained there until they merged with the King's company in 1682.[88] In short, the placing of a Mug-house in Salisbury Court was both a reminder of the Parliamentary campaign against theatres and a provocation to those who fondly remembered the Tory playhouse at Dorset Garden. The Whigs may not have intended the first of these effects, but they doubtless relished the second.

Seven rioters were tried for the Salisbury Court attack; all were found guilty, and five were hanged under the recently passed Riot Act.[89] One of them was Thomas Bean, a servant to the rebel prisoners in Newgate. At his funeral on September 23 at St. Bride's, a large number of mourners appeared sporting white favours and hoods. One week later, almost one thousand people gathered in Salisbury Court to commemorate Bean's death. Wearing white gloves and favours, with the women in sarcenet hoods, they paraded to St. Bride's and several other churches, planning afterwards to make a tour of the Mug-houses. They were finally stopped by the trained bands at Blackfriars, while trying to cross the river to St. George's Southwark; two men and three women were taken up and tried for riot. They were all young, and most of them were servants. The government was convinced that the rebel prisoners had incited them, but was unable to prove it conclusively.[90] In fact, Bean's mourners were following in a tradition of protest against unjust executions.[91] The white gloves, signifying innocence, were prominent features of such demonstrations, although in this case they also referred to the exiled Stuarts. The procession resembled a rogation day ceremony, and was doubtless meant to emphasize the contrast between the City churches, which marked the piety of Londoners, and the profane Mug-houses.

The commemoration of Bean's death illustrated the efforts of Jacobites to make the City into a stage for the enactment of a morality play whose central theme was the perversion of justice by usurped power. London was not the only place in England where this drama was acted out. Itinerant ballad-singers performed Jacobite doggerel verse for provincial audiences.[92] The theatre of civic ritual became politicized in many English towns. In Norwich, a town much troubled by Jacobite unrest, the Tory mayor celebrated the guild-day by decorating his doorway with portraits — Queen Anne and Sacheverell on one side, King William and Oliver Cromwell on the other. He also insisted upon marching through the cathedral close with his ceremonial sword whenever he pleased, in defiance of the town's charter.[93] The formal theatre, insofar as it existed in the provinces, became a battleground. In 1716, a new farce was staged by the Norwich Whigs at the King's Arms tavern. Entitled *The Earl of Mar Marr'd*, it was a satire on the leader of the recent rebellion in Scotland. When the Pretender's name was mentioned, however, the players and most of the audience clapped for it, at which some Whigs who were present drew their swords.[94] Jacobite actors did not always need a formal stage. Anthony Morgan, a shoemaker of Ellesmere in Shropshire, a county noted for Jacobite riots, celebrated King William's birthday in November 1715 by appearing in the market place late at night and proclaiming King James III; he called upon loyal souls to gather at 'the signe of the thing in my hand, which . . . was a Stick Staff or Clubb'.[95] Morgan was undoubtedly drunk, but even in his cups he had a fine sense of theatre.

Jacobitism waned after the failure of the Atterbury Plot in 1721–2. With its leaders in exile or in prison, the cause seemed without hope, and its popular support dwindled. In 1724 a member of the Lincoln's

Inn Fields company paid a last tribute to a decade of unrest generated by Jacobite politics, popular culture and the theatre. On August 1, the tenth anniversary of King George's accession, he rode through London in a turnip cart, wearing a mask, a crown and a pair of cuckold's horns on his head.[96] Faith in the imminence of a Stuart restoration was gone, but the Jacobite crowd could still laugh at its enemies.

In retrospect, the upsurge of popular Jacobitism after 1714 can be seen as the last great effort to preserve a traditional political culture which united the elite and the common people. The restoration of the Stuart monarch symbolized the revival of social harmony and old-fashioned customs — the same message that the Jacobite Cavaliers tried to convey in the 1690s. The fact that no restoration took place, and that Jacobite political culture was defeated, should not disguise the remarkable energy of popular discontent in the early years of Hanoverian rule. No political phenomenon of such vigour could easily be suppressed.

Jacobitism after 1724 was defeated but unwilling to surrender. It continued to exercise considerable influence on politics, especially in the City of London. In 1733, the capital was led in its opposition to the passage of Walpole's Excise Bill by the Jacobite Lord Mayor, John Barber.[97] A close friend of Nathaniel Mist, who was then living in exile, Barber was also the lover of the Tory Jacobite playwright Mary Delarivière Manley.[98] Her later plays were produced at Lincoln's Inn Fields, which shows the enduring ties between the Jacobites and the London stage. Manley's *The Court Legacy*, an anti-Walpolean satire of 1733, included a scene in which a ballad-singer cries out 'down with Excise and false Patriots', to the delight of 'Alderman Free-Port', ie. Barber.[99] Another dramatist of Jacobite leanings was Charles Molloy, who wrote several pieces for Lincoln's Inn Fields. In 1730, Mist recommended him to the Stuart court as a possible agent, and in 1737 he became the editor of a new journal, *Common Sense*, that was secretly funded by the Pretender.[100]

Jacobitism, however, was only one element in the opposition politics of this period. The so-called Country alliance that challenged Walpole in the years between 1727 and 1742 was composed of opposition Whigs and Hanoverian Tories as well as Jacobites, and it was careful not to adopt a position that could be interpreted as treasonable. Under the aegis of the Country alliance, the theatre became a serious threat to the Walpolean regime. Even Drury Lane was enlisted in the effort to unseat the Prime Minister. The passage of the infamous Licensing Act of 1737, which muzzled the opposition theatre, was not therefore a response to Jacobite or even Tory criticism; it clamped down upon a rhetoric of Country principles whose most famous spokesman was the dissident Whig playwright Henry Fielding.[101] Nevertheless, there was certainly a Jacobite element in this theatrical opposition. The Licensing Act, in fact, was ostensibly inspired by the production of an overtly seditious play, *The Golden Rump*.[102] The persistence of a Jacobite element among London audiences may also have been reflected in the renewed popularity of *Venice Preserved*. Otway's play was acted no fewer than eighty-nine times between 1729 and 1745, an average of five or six performances a year.[103] The sight of Quin as Pierre wearing his famous white hat may have rekindled an allegiance to the Stuarts in many flagging hearts — although, ironically, Quin himself held the principles of a republican.[104]

Walpole's fall in 1742 did not result in a change of ministry, and the disgruntled Tory leaders turned back to the Jacobite option.[105] The resurgence of Stuart loyalism may explain the political ambivalence of James Thomson's tragedy *Tancred and Sigismunda*, which was first acted in the spring of 1745; dedicated to Frederick, Prince of Wales, it deals with a lawful prince who claims his kingdom from a usurping tyrant. The play was reputedly designed to please both Hanoverian and Jacobite audiences.[106] Charles Edward Stuart's rebellion in Scotland, however, did not inspire a return to the theatrical turbulence of the early Hanoverian period. A rumour that the playhouses were to be closed on account of the rebellion proved false, although Thomson's play was not shown during the 1745–6 season, and *Venice Preserved* was performed only twice.[107] All of the theatres seemed anxious to proclaim their unwavering fidelity to the House of Hanover, by adding loyal prologues to their productions, and by reviving anti-Jacobite works like Cibber's *Nonjuror*.[108] The Licensing Act was partly responsible for this, but it also indicated the extent of Whig dominance within the theatre world.

The capital, as Nicholas Rogers has shown, saw little popular unrest during the rebellion.[109] Yet beneath the surface of Hanoverian loyalism may have lurked a strong undercurrent of Jacobite sentiment, which might still emerge in the theatre. For example, on May 2, 1746, shortly after news of the victory at Culloden arrived in the capital, Drury Lane offered a production of the anonymous comedy *The Merry Milkmaids of Islington*. A puff that appeared in the *General Advertiser* announced the performance:

I think it my Duty (lest among the Multitude of Diversions now

flourishing, some other might engross the attention of the Curious)
to inform the world, that the Farce which will be perform'd this
Evening at Drury Lane theatre, call'd *May Day, or the Merry
Milkmaids of Islington*, was written by the particular desire of King
Charles II. . .[110]

The play's affiliations with the Restoration, and with the popular
customs cherished by the adherents of the Stuarts, were particularly
suggestive at this juncture. The 'Multitude of Diversions' on show
elsewhere, moreover, included celebrations of Culloden at Sadler's
Wells and Goodman's Fields. To avoid the accusation of treasonable
intentions, however, Drury Lane staged a play by the Whig dramatist
Sir Robert Howard on the same night, and prefaced it with remarks
on the Duke of Cumberland's victory, spoken by Theophilus Cibber.
The common strategy of playing to both sides of the political arena was
nowhere better illustrated.

Memories of the strife of earlier decades lingered, and George II
could still be embarrassed by reminders of Jacobite criticism, as he was
by the performance of Edward Ravenscroft's 1681 comedy *The Royal
Cuckold* at Drury Lane on Lord Mayor's day in 1749.[111] The probably
intentional insult illustrates the devious politics of the theatre in the
late 1740s, when a large segment of the London audience continued
to retain Jacobite sympathies. Enduring disaffection to Hanover partly
inspired the activities of an important popular movement of the 1740s,
the Independent Electors of Westminster.[112] The meetings of the Independent Electors were highly theatrical. At their anniversary dinner
in March 1747, they allegedly drank to the King 'over the water',
toasted their refusal to illuminate their windows in commemoration
of Culloden, and threw out an interloper who was making notes.[113]
Two years later, after Charles Edward Stuart had been expelled from
France, the Independent Electors led the popular attack on a group of
French players who tried to set up a theatre in London.[114] Far more
disturbing to the government was the behaviour of Alexander Murray,
one of the leaders of the Independent Electors and a Jacobite agent,
who refused to kneel at the bar of the House of Commons in 1751
when summoned to defend himself against a charge of intimidating the
high bailiff of Westminster in a recent by-election. Murray was sent to
Newgate for four months; on his release, he was paraded through the
City by a huge crowd of supporters.[115] He later fled to the continent,
and became chief adviser to Prince Charles.

These antics kept alive the theatre of popular Jacobitism; but
they did little to alter the increasingly hopeless political situation of

the opposition in the late 1740s. Many Tories espoused Jacobitism more ardently as they saw their options narrow, but others pursued an alliance with the Hanoverian Prince of Wales. Although the party as a whole entered into an agreement with Prince Frederick in 1749, the Tories maintained their independence, as Linda Colley has shown, and were never under the Prince's control.[116] Tory Jacobites supported Frederick's initiatives, but did not sacrifice their own allegiances. This led to a peculiar collusion between the adherents of the Hanoverian and the Jacobite Princes of Wales, which was to find an expression in the theatre. *Venice Preserved*, that barometer of Jacobite fortunes, was performed sixty-six times between 1747 and 1753.[117] A more curious sidelight on the theatrical politics of the period, however, is provided by the renowned composer Thomas Arne.

Arne is best known today for his music to the English national anthem, 'God Save the King'. As Arne knew, this piece had originally been written for James II, and it had been adapted to Jacobite uses in the secret clubs of the 1720s.[118] Arne also composed 'Rule Britannia', which was written for Prince Frederick to accompany James Thomson and David Mallet's play *Alfred* in 1745. Mallet's politics, like those of many contemporary writers, were inconstant; *Eurydice*, a play which he wrote in 1731 on the instigation of Viscount Bolingbroke, had been attacked as Jacobite propaganda.[119] Thomas Arne was to enter into even stranger collaborations after the rebellion. His song 'The Highland Laddie', with words by the Scottish Jacobite Allan Ramsay, was the musical sensation of 1750. It was performed twice at Drury Lane in April, and by July was being 'sung at *Ranelagh* and all the other Gardens; often fondly *encored*, and sometimes ridiculously hiss'd.'[120] Although it was merely a bawdy ditty with no overtly treasonable content, 'The Highland Laddie' was obviously interpreted as a paean to Charles Edward Stuart.

Thomas Arne was a Roman Catholic, but he was probably not a Jacobite; like Thomson and Mallet, he simply appreciated the commercial possibilities of appealing to a Jacobite audience. Arne's involvement with Jacobitism was initially related to the efforts of his patron, the Prince of Wales, to cajole Stuart adherents into a broad opposition coalition. The composer continued, however, to follow a devious political path even after Frederick's death. In 1754, his opera *Eliza* was suppressed by the Lord Chamberlain at its premiere on May 29, a day cherished in every Jacobite heart.[121] A seemingly innocuous allegorical piece about the defeat of the Spanish Armada, *Eliza* opens with a mourning Britannia wondering when she will "find Repose,/ Beneath the Shade of her wide-spreading Oak".[122] As has been noted, the oak tree was a symbol for the Stuarts. The play continues with shepherds and shepherdesses disporting themselves in May-day gambols, emphasizing the link between monarchism and popular recreations. Britannia is comforted in her misery by a female character named 'Genius of England'. Five years earlier, the notorious Oxford Jacobite Dr. William King had delivered a speech at the opening of the Radcliffe Camera, in which he repeatedly intoned 'REDEAT ILLE MAGNUS GENIUS BRITANNIAE' — 'Restore that great genius of Britain'.[123] His listeners understood that the 'Genius' was Charles Edward Stuart; so did the Young Pretender himself, who issued a medal in 1752 with the slogan on it.[124] The government must have had little doubt that the 'Genius' of Arne's opera was not a politically innocent invention. They may also have objected to the work's implicit comparison of the warlike Elizabeth with the timid Pelham administration, which had negotiated the controversial Treaty of Aix-la-Chapelle in 1748. The popular play-houses of the 1630s had also used Elizabethan parallels to satirize the degeneracy of the present court.[125]

The libretto of *Eliza* was written by Richard Rolt. A former exciseman, Rolt had reportedly joined Prince Charles Edward's Jacobite army during its invasion of England. He luckily escaped transportation, and took to the stage.[126] In 1749, he wrote an elegy for the late Jacobite leader, Sir Watkin Williams Wynn, which was published in *Mitre and Crown*, a Jacobite periodical edited by George Osborne, a barrister of the Inner Temple.[127] Both Rolt and Osborne enjoyed the patronage of General James Edward Oglethorpe, the founder of Georgia. Son of a Jacobite Cavalier, Oglethorpe had served the Hanoverians until the '45, when he was dismissed from his command for dawdling in his pursuit of the rebels. In the early 1750s, he helped to fund George Osborne's *The True Briton*, a Jacobite magazine that strongly supported the Independent Electors. Oglethorpe stood unsuccessfully in the elections of 1754 as opposition candidate for Westminster.[128] *Eliza* was probably aimed at Osborne's readers and Oglethorpe's disappointed supporters, the Independent Electors of Westminster. Thus, Arne and Rolt's suppressed opera can be seen as a reflection of popular politics in the capital.

If these links are somewhat labyrinthine, they merely reflect the subterranean complexities of the last phases of Jacobite sentiment, when allegiance to the Stuarts was restricted to obscure gestures of defiance. After so many disappointments, and with Charles Edward sinking into alchoholic oblivion, Jacobitism had little hope left. At the same time, a new mentality was slowly developing in the upper levels of

English society. The political polarization of the seventeenth and early eighteenth centuries still prevailed, but it seemed to have led to a dead end. Jacobitism, Toryism, the Country alliance, even the coalition with Prince Frederick, had failed to overthrow Whig hegemony. By the early 1750s, the shattered remains of the opposition had almost no prospect of a final victory. The stage responded to the situation by gradually abandoning politics. The open warfare of 1714–24 and the veiled defiance of the 1730s were forgotten; dramatists increasingly sought to please everyone by eliminating partisan comments. The day was not far off when Whig and Tory principles would fade, and a largely unified elite could take its entertainment from genteel domestic comedies by Goldsmith or Sheridan that lacked political overtones.[129]

As this happened, however, elite and popular culture lost their common ground. Those who could not aspire to positions of power had no wish to compromise their old party divisions. The accession of George III transformed Parliamentary politics by crippling the Whigs and virtually eliminating the Tories, but their plebeian supporters were excluded from the new system, and soon developed a hostility to it. Jacobitism may have lasted longest within the sphere of popular culture, especially in the theatre of the streets. On June 10, 1763, the sentimental Jacobite James Boswell marked the birthday of James III by going to Chelsea, where he saw the famous equestrian Johnson (not the Doctor) ride while standing on two horses at full gallop; they 'moved about to the tune of *Shilinagarie*; for music, such as it is, makes always a part of John Bull's public amusement.'[130] *Shilinagarie* was a well-known Irish Jacobite song by Timothy O'Sullivan.

Five years later, the London crowds would be singing to a different hero, John Wilkes. In many ways, the Wilkites were the heirs of the Independent Electors, although they preferred not to advertise their links with earlier Jacobite protest. Unlike their predecessors, however, the followers of Wilkes could not count on the sympathy of an organized Parliamentary party. The radical program of the Wilkites epitomized the growing separation between the politics of the elite and those of the common people. Wilkes's supporters were aware of the power of ritual, ceremony and theatre; they enlisted in the promotion of their goals all the familiar features of 'John Bull's public amusement'.[131] Through them, the popular political culture that had been preserved by the Jacobites for fifty years was passed on to future radical movements. It would take some time for conservatives to respond effectively with a populist version of monarchism which bore a marked resemblance to the old Stuart myth of kingship.[132]

From Pythagoras to Shakespeare to J.–C. Agnew, writers have commented upon the ways in which the theatre both reflected and acted upon the world. It is not difficult to envision the stage as a metaphor for almost any public activity, and such comparisons can easily become inane. Moreover, the temptation to remove the imaginary line between theatre and reality is strong; after all, both are rooted in cultural concepts and linguistic assumptions. The idea that life is a form of creative play-acting is certainly charming. Nevertheless, past societies have always made distinctions between the purely fanciful culture of the theatre and the more restricted culture of everyday existence. Eighteenth-century English crowds did the same; they separated the theatre of popular politics from mundane realities, reserving it for commemoration days or other special occasions.

Theatre, in other words, was artificial, and was therefore kept apart from 'real' life. To mix the two was to invite disaster, because fantasy was self-centred and would destroy social harmony. Party politics was also seen as artificial, a product of selfish or mistaken motives, and an undesirable element in government. Factional divisions would ruin the tranquility of the state; hence, the ultimate aim of popular protest was the enforcement of unity, and the elimination of the personal corruption or religious errors on which faction was thought to rest. The theatre was not simply a metaphor for party politics. Both were part of the same artificial culture that had its place on the stage or in popular recreations, but not at the head of the polity. The London crowds, in other words, did not want to turn the state into a playhouse, or make Parliament into Bartholomew Fair. On the contrary, they sought to regenerate a House of Commons that was already viewed as a 'bear garden'. Popular political theatre constantly stressed the difference between the fixed values of justice and the anarchy of misrule. The images and rituals of Carnival, or of the stage, could be used to satirize or even correct political misconduct, but they were not substitutes for good governance.

These attitudes were shared by a large segment of the elite, in spite of the fact that the top of the social order might be threatened by plebeian discontent. Without sympathy from above, popular political theatre could not have established such strong links with the formal stage. From the Reformation onwards, however, part of the English elite had become adamantly opposed to what it saw as the superstitious impiety of popular culture. The puritans and later the Whigs attempted to construct a society that would be free from the interference of the 'ungodly' mob. Popular political culture sought refuge in royalism, and eventually in Jacobitism, because the Stuart kings were more responsive to traditional concepts of government than were their critics. Although the Whigs eventually won in the struggle for control of the state, popular political theatre endured, with the support of Tory landowners and merchants. The demise of the old Tory party in the 1750s ended the theatrical dialogue between elite and popular Jacobitism, but the culture of the crowd later found new defenders. Conservative populists upheld traditional customs and maintained the anti-Dissenting spirit that was expressed in 'Church and King' mobs, while radicals appropriated other elements of the Jacobite legacy. In the 1790s and again in the 1840s, *Venice Preserved* was viewed by the authorities as a seditious play — because it seemed to inspire Jacobins and Chartists.[133] Long after 1760, therefore, popular political theatre continued to challenge the government, sometimes through major actions like riots and demonstrations, sometimes through small individual gestures, like Pierre's white hat.

NOTES

I would like to thank Jan Albers, Eveline Cruickshanks and John Wilders for their comments on this essay.

1. Ed. by Malcolm Kelsall (Lincoln, Nebraska, 1969), 101: Prologue for April 21, 1682, lines 32–5.

2. For discussions of the subject, see Max Beloff, *Public Order and Popular Disturbances, 1660–1714* (London, 1938, 1963), 40–44, William Sachse, 'The Mob and the Revolution of 1688', *Journal of British Studies*, iv., 1 (1964), 23–40, and Lois G. Schwoerer, 'Propaganda in the Revolution of 1688–89', *American Historical Review*, 82, 4 (1977), 843–74.

3. Tim Harris, *London Crowds in the Reign of Charles II: Propaganda and Politics from the Restoration until the Exclusion Crisis* (Cambridge, 1987), chs. 6–7. Chapter 2 of Harris's book contains a fine discussion of the issue of popular culture.

4. G. S. De Krey, *A Fractured Society: The Politics of London in the First Age of Party, 1688–1715* (Oxford, 1985), chs. 2, 5–6.

5. Nicholas Rogers, 'Popular Protest in Early Hanoverian London', *Past and Present*, 79 (1978), 70–100; and his 'Riot and Popular Jacobitism in Early Hanoverian England', in Eveline Cruickshanks, ed., *Ideology and Conspiracy: Aspects of Jacobitism, 1689–1759* (Edinburgh, 1982), 70–88. Paul Monod, 'For the King to Enjoy His Own Again: Jacobite Political Culture in England, 1688–1788', unpublished Ph.D. thesis, Yale University, 1985, chs. 4–5.

6. See Mikhail Bakhtin, *Rabelais and His World*, tr. H. Iswolsky (Cambridge, Mass., 1968), ch. 3; Natalie Zemon Davis, *Society and Culture in Early Modern France* (Stanford, 1975), ch. 4; Emmanuel Le Roy Ladurie, *Carnival in Romans*,

tr. Mary Feeney (New York, 1979); Giovanna Ferrari, 'Public Anatomy and the Carnival: The Anatomy Theatre of Bologna', *P. & P.*, 117 (1987), 50–106.

7. See Peter Burke, 'Popular Culture in Seventeenth-Century London', in Barry Reay, ed., *Popular Culture in Seventeenth-Century England* (New York, 1985), pp. 35–9. For Carnival images in Jacobite poetry, see Monod, 'For the King to Enjoy His Own Again', ch. 2.

8. See Robert Malcolmson, *Popular Recreations in English Society, 1700–1850* (Cambridge, 1973), ch. 2, as well as the articles by Peter Burke, Jonathan Barry and Barry Reay in Reay, ed., *Popular Culture.*

9. See Peter Burke, *Popular Culture in Early Modern Europe* (New York, 1981), part 3; Robert Muchembled, *Popular Culture and Elite Culture in France, 1400–1750*, tr. Lydia Cochrane (Baton Rouge, La., 1985).

10. Michael Bristol, *Carnival and Theater: Plebeian Culture and the Structure of Authority in Renaissance England* (New York and London, 1985).

11. See John Loftis, Richard Southern, Marion Jones and A. H. Scouten, *The Revels History of Drama in English, vol. v: 1660–1800* (London, 1976), 13–25; Harry W. Pedicord, 'The Changing Audience', in Robert D. Hume, ed., *The London Theatre World, 1660–1800* (Carbondale, Ill., 1980), 236–52; Leo Hughes, *The Drama's Patrons: A Study of the Eighteenth-Century London Audience* (Austin, Texas, 1971).

12. Nahum Tate, *The History of King Lear*, ed. James Black (Lincoln, Nebraska, 1975), 95: V.vi, lines 158–9.

13. For Tudor censorship of the stage, see Glynne Wickham, *Early English Stages, 1300–1660* (3 vols. in 4 parts, London, 1959–81), ii, part 1, ch. 3 esp. pp. 75–6.

14. Jerzy Limon, *Dangerous Matter: English Drama and Politics in 1623/4* (Cambridge, 1986), ch. 4.

15. Martin Butler, *Theatre and Crisis, 1632–1642* (Cambridge, 1984); Kevin Sharpe, *Criticism and Compliment: The Politics of Literature in the England of Charles I* (Cambridge, 1987).

16. Butler, *Theatre and Crisis*, ch. 8.

17. *Ibid.*, ch. 4.

18. David Underdown, *Revel, Riot and Rebellion: Popular Politics and Culture in England, 1603–1660* (Oxford, 1985).

19. *Ibid.*, 177, 269, 274–5.

20. Leslie Hotson, *The Commonwealth and Restoration Stage* (Cambridge, Mass., 1928), ch. 3.

21. Gerard S. Reedy, S. J., 'Mystical Politics: The Imagery of Charles II's Coronation', in Paul J. Korshin, ed., *Studies in Change and Revolution: Aspects of English Intellectual History, 1640–1800* (Menston, Yorks., 1972), 19–42.

22. Loftis *et al.*, *Revels History*, v, 26–7.

23. See John Loftis, *The Politics of Drama in Augustan England* (Oxford, 1963), 15–17, 21.

24. Harris, *London Crowds*, ch. 6.

25. Otway, *Venice Preserved*, 102: Prologue for April 21, 1682, lines 17–18, 29–30.

26. For interpretations of the play, see Roswell Gray Ham, *Otway and Lee: Biography from a Baroque Age* (New Haven, Ct., 1931), ch. 16, and Aline

Mackenzie Taylor, *Next to Shakespeare: Otway's 'Venice Preserv'd' and 'The Orphan' and Their History on the London Stage* (Durham, N.C., 1950), ch. 2.

27. For Behn, see Angeline Goreau, *Reconstructing Aphra: A Social Biography of Aphra Behn* (New York, 1980).

28. Rev. J. S. Clarke, ed., *The Life of James the Second King of England, &c. Collected out of Memoirs writ of his own Hand* (2 vols., London, 1816), ii, 262; W. E. Buckley, ed., *Memoirs of Thomas, Earl of Ailesbury* (2 vols., Westminster, 1890), i, 214–15.

29. Lois G. Schwoerer, 'The Glorious Revolution as Spectacle: A New Perspective', in Stephen Baxter, ed., *England's Rise to Greatness* (Berkeley, 1983), 115–17, and her 'Propaganda in the Revolution of 1688–9', *passim*.

30. See Dudley W. R. Bahlman, *The Moral Revolution of 1688* (Hamden, Ct., 1957, 1968).

31. Loftis, *Politics of Drama*, 22, n. 2.

32. For the history of this enterprise, see Judith Milhous, *Thomas Betterton and the Management of Lincoln's Inn Fields, 1695–1708* (Carbondale, Ill., 1979).

33. Narcissus Luttrell, *A Brief Historical Relation of State Affairs from September 1678 to April 1714* (6 vols., Oxford, 1857), ii, 413, 422.

34. Jeremy Collier, *A Short View of the Immorality, and Profaneness of the English Stage, Together With the Sense of Antiquity upon this Argument* (London, 1698). The Nonjuror William Law took up the same theme three decades later in *The Absolute Unlawfulness of the Stage Entertainment Fully Demonstrated* (London, 1726), but by then, as will be seen, High Church opinion on the theatre issue had altered. See Sister Rose Anthony, S.C., *The Jeremy Collier Stage Controversy, 1698–1726* (New York, 1937, 1966).

35. See Jane Garrett, *The Triumphs of Providence: The Assassination Plot, 1696* (Cambridge, 1980), chs. 2–4, and Monod, 'For the King to Enjoy His Own Again', ch. 7.

36. See Luttrell, ii, 189, 353; iii, 207.

37. Paul Monod, 'Jacobitism and Country Principles in the Reign of William III', *Historical Journal*, xxx. (1987), 299.

38. Luttrell, iii, 104, 109, 111, 114, 117, 138, 140.

39. Luttrell, iii, 176. Not all those at the Fair agreed with these sentiments. A booth displaying a visual satire on the fleet was pulled down by the crowd; Bodl., Carte Ms. 233, f. 262.

40. Jean-Christophe Agnew, *Worlds Apart: The Market and the Theater in Anglo-American Thought, 1550–1750* (Cambridge, 1986), esp. chs. 1 and 3.

41. William Van Lennep, Emmett L. Avery, Arthur H. Scouten, George Winchester Stone, jr., and Charles Beecher Hogan, eds., *The London Stage, 1660–1800* (11 vols. in 5 parts, Carbondale, Ill., 1965–8), part 1, 464.

42. Luttrell, iii, 460–1.

43. Luttrell, iii, 483–4; Bodl. Carte Ms. 239, f. 146. For Goodman, see Garrett, 24–8; for Reading and Pate, see *The London Stage*, part 1, 440, and Milhous, 87, 133.

44. Garrett, 99, and illustration on inside cover.

45. *The London Stage*, pt. 1, 451; Taylor, *Next to Shakespeare*, 145.

46. Daniel Szechi, 'The Jacobite Theatre of Death', in Eveline Cruickshanks and Jeremy Black, eds., *The Jacobite Challenge* (Edinburgh, 1988), 57–73. For a general discussion of the theatre of the scaffold, see J. A. Sharpe, ' "Last Dying Speeches": Religion, Ideology and Public Executions in Seventeenth Century England', *P.&P.*, cvii. (1985), 144–67.

47. Otway, *Venice Preserved*, 91: Act V, scene iii, lines 12–14.

48. Monod, 'Jacobitism and Country Principles', 306–9; Duke of Manchester, *Court and Society from Elizabeth to Anne. Edited from the Papers at Kimbolton* (2 vols., London, 1864), ii, 106–7.

49. Colley Cibber, *An Apology for His Life* (Everyman edn., London, n.d.), 143. Cibber added that the Master 'strain'd hard for the parallel.'

50. *The London Stage*, part 1, 524, pt. 2, p. 7; Taylor, *Next to Shakespeare*, 145.

51. Loftis, *Politics of Drama*, 27, 30–1; *The London Stage*, pt. 2, p. 17. Higgons and his brothers were suspected of holding cabals at his Hampshire estate in 1698; see G. P. R. James, ed., *Letters Illustrative of the Reign of William III. From 1696 to 1708. Addressed to the Duke of Shrewsbury, by James Vernon, Esq. Secretary of State* (3 vols., London, 1841), ii, 178, 181–2, 184, 192. His brother Thomas became Secretary of State to James III in 1713; Daniel Szechi, *Jacobitism and Tory Politics, 1710–14* (Edinburgh, 1984), 7. For Granville, see Elizabeth Handasyde, *Granville the Polite* (London, 1938).

52. Bevill Higgons, *The Generous Conqueror; or, the Timely Discovery* (London, 1702), dedication. Normanby, who later became Duke of Buckingham, was another Jacobite sympathizer.

53. *The London Stage*, pt. 2, 48, 53, 79, 93, 110, 141, 146–7, 158.

54. See Monod, 'For the King to Enjoy His Own Again', ch. 1; Mark Goldie, 'Tory Political Thought, 1689–1714', unpublished Ph.D. dissertation, Cambridge University, 1977, chs. 6 and 11.

55. 'Philalethes' [Charles Leslie], *A View of the Times, their Principles and Practices: in the . . . Rehearsals* (reprinted in 6 vols., London, 1750).

56. *The London Stage*, pt. 2, 172, 188.

57. The best account of the affair is in Geoffrey Holmes, *The Trial of Doctor Sacheverell* (London, 1973). The manager of Drury Lane at this time was William Collier, a Tory lawyer and future M.P.; he lost money during the trial because Sacheverell was attracting larger audiences of "the better rank of people"! Cibber, *Apology*, 216–17.

58. *The London Stage*, pt. 2, 213.

59. Holmes, *Trial of Sacheverell*, 156–78, and his 'The Sacheverell Riots: The Crowd and the Church in Early Eighteenth Century London', *P. & P.*, lxxii. (1976), 55–85.

60. Loftis, *Politics of Drama*, 50–62; *The London Stage*, pt. 2, 220, 225, 240, 254, 256, 275, 302, 309, 317.

61. Robert D. Hume, *The Development of English Drama in the late Seventeenth Century* (Oxford, 1976), 487–94. Unfortunately, Hume does not define the term "bourgeois". It is far from evident that Augustan audiences were more middle class.

62. Loftis, *Politics of Drama*, ch. 4.

63. *The London Stage*, pt. 2, 559. For the political implications of the play, see

Ernst Kantorowicz, *The King's Two Bodies: A Study in Medieval Political Theory* (Princeton, 1957), ch. 2.

64. Loftis, *Politics of Drama*, 68.

65. *The Weekly Journal; or, Saturday's Post*, no. 130, May 27, 1721, 775; Abel Boyer, *The Political State of Great Britain* (40 vols., London, 1711–40), xxi., 619–27, 632–3.

66. Loftis, *Politics of Drama*, p. 68. Griffin's recent play, *Whig and Tory*, had transposed the story of Romeo and Juliet onto contemporary politics; *ibid.*, p. 71, n. 1.

67. Aline Mackenzie, 'A Note on Pierre's White Hat', *Notes and Queries*, cxcii. (1947), 90–3. The Whigs had hoped in 1715 that *Venice Preserved* could be presented as an anti-Jacobite play, but audiences refused to accept this interpretation; Taylor, *Next to Shakespeare*, 155–6.

68. Mackenzie, 'Pierre's White Hat', 92, quoting John Hill, *The Actor* (London, 1755), 170–1.

69. Copies of the paper, which ran from 1718–19, can be found in the Burney Collection in the British Library.

70. See Monod, 'For the King to Enjoy His Own Again', ch. 2; also Paul Chapman, 'Jacobite Political Argument in England, 1714–1766', unpublished Ph.D. thesis, Cambridge University, 1983.

71. They are printed in Clarence Tracy, ed., *The Poetical Works of Richard Savage* (Cambridge, 1962), 15–26.

72. PRO, State Papers 35/40/60, verse iii.

73. Cibber, *Apology*, 236; Loftis, *Politics of Drama*, 57–60.

74. Bodl. Rawl. Ms.D. 383, f.106; also Rev. Alexander Grosart, ed., *English Jacobite Ballads, Songs and Satires, etc. from Mss at Townley Hall, Lancashire* (Manchester, 1877), 101–4.

75. For theatre and the law, see Douglas Hay, 'Property, Authority and the Criminal Law', in Douglas Hay *et al.*, *Albion's Fatal Tree: Crime and Society in Eighteenth-Century England* (New York, 1975), 26–31.

76. Gerald Howson, *It Takes a Thief: The Life and Times of Jonathan Wild* (London, 1970, 1987), 27 and plates 2–3.

77. PRO, SP 35/12/93.

78. PRO, SP 35/12/56. This man was not the young James Shepheard, who was executed in March 1718 for threatening the life of King George. The career of the notorious burglar Jack Sheppard began in the 1720s, but it is possible that this was him. The turnip image was meant to convey the poverty and misery of Hanover, while the horns referred to George's cuckoldry.

79. PRO, SP 35/12/143.

80. Bodl. Rawl. Ms.D. 1133, *passim.*

81. Boyer, *Political State*, ix., 333–4; Peter Rae, *The History of the Rebellion, Rais'd against His Majesty King George I by the Friends of the Popish Pretender* (2nd edn., London, 1746), 135.

82. Rae, 141; PRO, SP 35/74/9.

83. For the Mug-houses, see Rogers, 'Popular Protest', and James Fitts, 'Newcastle's Mob', *Albion*, v. 1 (1973), 41–9.

84. John Timbs, *Clubs and Club Life in London* (London, 1872), 41–3; William

Matthews, ed., *The Diary of Dudley Ryder, 1715–1716* (London, 1939), 121, 138–9, 363.

85. For the purificatory significance of violence in Reformation France, see Davis, *Society and Culture*, ch. 6.

86. This point is suggested in J. H. Plumb, *The Growth of Political Stability in England, 1675–1725* (London, 1967), p. xviii.

87. Boyer, *Political State*, xii, 127–34, 211–27.

88. Hotson, 43, 229.

89. Boyer, *Political State*, xii., 227–31, 235–8, 428–40, 445, 551, 639–43. See also Bodl. folio theta 662, no. 31, a broadside entitled *The Case of the Five Rioters, That were Try'd and Condemn'd at the Sessions House in the Old Bailey, for the late Riot in Salisbury Court, London* (London, 1716).

90. Boyer, *Political State*, xii, 238–43, 440–44, 447–8.

91. See Peter Linebaugh, 'The Tyburn Riot against the Surgeons', in *Albion's Fatal Tree*, 65–117.

92. Investigations of wandering singing-men can be found in PRO, SP 35/22/57, 35/41/86, 35/42/135, 36/79, f. 19.

93. Add. 38,507, f.133. For civic rituals, see Peter Borsay, ' "All the town's a stage": urban ritual and ceremony, 1660–1800' in Peter CLark, ed., *The Transformation of English Provincial Towns* (London, 1984), 228–58. For popular politics in Norwich, see Kathleen Wilson, 'The Rejection of Deference: Urban Political Culture in England, 1715–1785', unpublished Ph.D. thesis, Yale University, 1985, ch. 5.

94. *Norwich Gazette*, June 21, 1716. I owe this reference to Kathleen Wilson.

95. PRO, Assizes 5/36, part 1, infos. nos. 13, 14, 15.

96. Loftis, *Politics of Drama*, 68.

97. Paul Langford, *The Excise Crisis: Society and Politics in the Age of Walpole* (Oxford, 1975), 55, 92. For a letter of March 1730, sent from Barber to the Pretender, see RA (Stuart) 134/145.

98. For Mist and Barber, see RA, (Stuart) 158/75, 169/44; for Mary Delarivière Manley, see her notice in *D.N.B.*, Myra Reynolds, *The Learned Lady in England, 1650–1760* (Gloucester, Mass., 1920, 1964), 208–11, and Fidelis Morgan, ed., *A Woman of No Character: An Autobiography of Mrs. Manley* (London, 1986).

99. [Mary Delarivière Manley], *The Court Legacy. A New Ballad Opera. As it is Acted At the Eutopean Palace* (London, 1733), 36.

100. RA, (Stuart) 137/68, 190/12, 199/108; G. H. Jones, 'The Jacobites, Charles Molloy, and Common Sense' *Review of English Studies*, n.s. iv, 13 (1953), 144–7.

101. Loftis, *Politics of Drama*, ch. 5–6.

102. The play, however, may never have existed; the government may have invented it in order to facilitate passage of the Act. See Pat Rogers, *Henry Fielding: A Biography* (New York, 1979), 94–5.

103. Calculated from Ben Ross Schneider, jr., ed., *Index to The London Stage, 1660–1800* (Carbondale, Ill., 1979), 629.

104. Taylor, *Next to Shakespeare*, 163–4.

105. See Eveline Cruickshanks, *Political Untouchables: The Tories and the '45* (London, 1979).

106. Loftis, 'Political and Social Thought', 274; John Doran, *London in the Jacobite Times* (2 vols., London, 1877), ii, 108–10; James Thomson, *Tancred and Sigismunda: A Tragedy* (London, 1745).

107. David M. Little and George M. Kahrl, eds., *The Letters of David Garrick* (3 vols., Cambridge, Mass., 1963), i, 69.

108. See *The London Stage*, pt. 3, 1179–1245, for the 1745–6 season.

109. Nicholas Rogers, 'Popular Disaffection in London During the Forty-Five', *London Journal*, i., 1 (1975), 5–27.

110. *The London Stage*, pt. 3, 1238–9.

111. *Letters of Garrick*, i, 136. The London Court of Aldermen was dominated at this time by a group of Tory merchants and bankers, most of whom harboured Jacobite sympathies. See Monod, 'For the King to Enjoy His Own Again', 467–70.

112. The best account of this body is Nicholas Rogers, 'Aristocratic Trade, Clientage and Independency: Popular Politics in Pre-Radical Westminster', *P. & P.*, lxi. (1973), 70–106. For its Jacobite connections, see Monod, 'For the King to Enjoy His Own Again', 306–11.

113. *The Gentleman's Magazine*, xvii, March 1747, p. 150. The intruder was a government agent who had in custody at his house a witness against the Jacobite Lord Lovat.

114. Rogers, 'Aristocratic Clientage', 100–1; *Letters of Garrick*, i, 136.

115. Rogers, 'Aristocratic Clientage', 77–8; *The True Briton*, ii, no. 1, June 26, 1751, 22; Cruickshanks, *Political Untouchables*, 109.

116. Linda Colley, *In Defiance of Oligarchy: The Tory Party, 1714–60* (Cambridge, 1982), 253–60.

117. *Index to the London Stage*, 629. It was shown no less than sixteen times in 1747 and again in 1853. David Garrick's portrayals of Pierre and Jaffier became famous in this period; Taylor, *Next to Shakespeare*, 165–84.

118. *The Gentleman's Magazine*, lxxxiv (1814), 42, 99, 323–4, 339, 430, 552; Albert Hartshorne, *Old English Glasses* (London and New York, 1897), 347; Joseph Bles, *Rare English Glasses of the XVII and XVIII Centuries* (London, 1924), 86.

119. Loftis, *Politics of Drama*, 108–9. The play dealt with a rightful king who had been overthrown by a cruel tyrant; [David Mallet], *Eurydice: A Tragedy* (London, 1731).

120. *The London Stage*, pt. 4, pp. 195–6; *The Gentleman's Magazine*, xx, July 1750, 325.

121. *The London Stage*, Pt. 4, 430.

122. Richard Rolt and Thomas Arne, *Eliza: A New Musical Entertainment* (London, 1754), 1.

123. David Greenwood, *William King, Tory and Jacobite* (Oxford, 1969), 192–233.

124. E. Hawkins, *Medallic Illustrations of the History of Great Britain and Ireland* (Illustrated edn., Lawrence, Mass., 1904, 1979), Plate CLXXV, no. 11.

125. Butler, *Theatre and Crisis*, 198–210.

126. See Rolt's biography in *DNB*. Rolt later wrote an even more blatantly Jacobite opera, *The Royal Shepherd* (London, [1764]), with music by George Rush.

It concerns the restoration of a lawful king to his crown, and was very popular in the 1760s; at least four editions were published.

127. *Mitre and Crown*, ii, no. 1 (Oct. 1749), 44, no. 2 (Nov. 1749), 94–5; *Letters of Garrick*, i, 133 n. 4. For George Osborne's journalism, see Monod, 'For the King to Enjoy His Own Again', 53–70, and Add. 28,236.

128. *HC 1715–1754*, ed Sedgwick. ii, 305–6; Add. 28,236, ff.29–30, 48–9, 61–2.

129. Taylor, *Next to Shakespeare*, 181, argues that Garrick gave up his roles in *Venice Preserved* in 1763 on account of the decline of Jacobitism. It should be noted, however, that Garrick was an ardent Whig.

130. Frederick A. Pottle, ed., *Boswell's London Journal, 1762–1763* (New York, 1950), 276–7.

131. See John Brewer, *Party Ideology and Popular Politics at the Accession of George III* (Cambridge, 1976), ch. 9.

132. See Linda Colley, 'The Apotheosis of George III: Loyalty, Royalty and the British Nation, 1760–1820', *P. & P.*, cii. (1984), 94–129.

133. Taylor, *Next to Shakespeare*, 144.

Index

Note: entries thus – [S] – indicate the Scottish peerage. [I] indicates the Irish peerage.